DANIEL *and the*
TWELVE PROPHETS
for
EVERYONE

OLD TESTAMENT FOR EVERYONE
John Goldingay

Genesis for Everyone, Part 1
Genesis for Everyone, Part 2
Exodus and Leviticus for Everyone
Numbers and Deuteronomy for Everyone
Joshua, Judges, and Ruth for Everyone
1 and 2 Samuel for Everyone
1 and 2 Kings for Everyone
1 and 2 Chronicles for Everyone
Ezra, Nehemiah, and Esther for Everyone
Job for Everyone
Psalms for Everyone, Part 1
Psalms for Everyone, Part 2
Proverbs, Ecclesiastes, and Song of Songs for Everyone
Isaiah for Everyone
Jeremiah for Everyone
Lamentations and Ezekiel for Everyone

DANIEL *and the* TWELVE PROPHETS *for* EVERYONE

JOHN GOLDINGAY

WESTMINSTER
JOHN KNOX PRESS
LOUISVILLE · KENTUCKY

© 2016 John Goldingay

First published in the United States of America in 2016
by Westminster John Knox Press
100 Witherspoon Street
Louisville, Kentucky

First published in Great Britain in 2016
by Society for Promoting Christian Knowledge
36 Causton Street
London SW1P 4ST

16 17 18 19 20 21 22 23 24 25—10 9 8 7 6 5 4 3 2 1

Unless otherwise indicated, Scripture quotations are the author's own translation.

Cover design by Lisa Buckley
Cover photo: Sunset in the clear waters of Swat © Shahid Ali Khan /
www.shutterstock.com

Library of Congress Cataloging-in-Publication Data

Names: Goldingay, John, author.
Title: Daniel and the twelve prophets for everyone / John Goldingay.
Description: Louisville, KY : Westminster John Knox Press, 2016. | Series:
  Old Testament for everyone
Identifiers: LCCN 2016025848 (print) | LCCN 2016026327 (ebook) | ISBN
  9780664233907 (pbk. : alk. paper) | ISBN 9781611647778 (ebk.)
Subjects: LCSH: Bible. Minor Prophets--Commentaries. | Bible.
  Daniel--Commentaries.
Classification: LCC BS1560 .G645 2016 (print) | LCC BS1560 (ebook) | DDC
  224/.077--dc23
LC record available at https://lccn.loc.gov/2016025848

Most Westminster John Knox Press books are available at special quantity
discounts when purchased in bulk by corporations, organizations, and special-
interest groups. For more information, please e-mail SpecialSales@wjkbooks.com.

CONTENTS

131767

CONTENTS

vi

ACKNOWLEDGMENTS

The translation at the beginning of each chapter (and in other biblical quotations) is my own. I have stuck closer to the Hebrew than modern translations often do when they are designed for reading in church so that you can see more precisely what the text says. Thus although I myself prefer to use gender-inclusive language, I have let the translation stay gendered if inclusivizing it would obscure whether the text was using singular or plural—in other words, the translation often uses "he" where in my own writing I would say "they" or "he or she." Sometimes I have added words to make the meaning clear, and I have put these words in square brackets. When the text uses the name of God, Yahweh, I have kept the name instead of replacing it with "the Lord" as translations usually do. And I've transliterated some other names in a way that's different from the way translations traditionally do, partly to make it easier to work out the pronunciation. At the end of the book is a glossary of some terms that recur in the text, such as geographical, historical, and theological expressions. In each chapter (though not in the introduction) these terms are highlighted in **bold** the first time they occur.

The stories that follow the translation often concern my friends or my family. While none are made up, they are sometimes heavily disguised in order to be fair to people. Sometimes I have disguised them so well that when I came to read the stories again, I was not sure at first whom I was describing. My first wife, Ann, appears in a number of them. A few months after I started writing the Old Testament for Everyone, she died after negotiating with multiple sclerosis for forty-three years. Our shared dealings with her illness and disability over these years contribute significantly to what I write in ways that you may be able to see but also in ways that are less obvious.

Then, two years or so before I started writing this particular volume, I fell in love with and married Kathleen Scott, and I'm grateful for my new life with her and for her insightful comments on the manuscript, which have been so careful and illuminating that she practically deserves to be credited as coauthor.

I'm also grateful to Tom Bennett for reading through the manuscript and pointing out things I needed to correct or clarify.

INTRODUCTION

As far as Jesus and the New Testament writers were concerned, the Jewish Scriptures that Christians call the "Old Testament" *were* the Scriptures. In saying that, I cut corners a bit, as the New Testament never gives us a list of these Scriptures, but the body of writings that the Jewish people accept is as near as we can get to identifying the collection that Jesus and the New Testament writers would have worked with. The church also came to accept some extra books such as Maccabees and Ecclesiasticus that were traditionally called the "Apocrypha," the books that were "hidden away"—a name that came to imply "spurious." They're now often known as the "Deuterocanonical Writings," which is more cumbersome but less pejorative; it simply indicates that these books have less authority than the Torah, the Prophets, and the Writings. The precise list of them varies among different churches. For the purposes of this series that seeks to expound the "Old Testament for Everyone," by the "Old Testament" we mean the Scriptures accepted by the Jewish community, though in the Jewish Bible they come in a different order, as the Torah, the Prophets, and the Writings.

They were not "old" in the sense of antiquated or out of date; I sometimes like to refer to them as the First Testament rather than the Old Testament to make that point. For Jesus and the New Testament writers, they were a living resource for understanding God, God's ways in the world, and God's ways with us. They were "useful for teaching, for reproof, for correction, and for training in righteousness, so that the person who belongs to God can be proficient, equipped for every good work" (2 Timothy 3:16–17). They were for everyone, in fact. So it's strange that Christians don't read them very much. My aim in these volumes is to help you do so.

My hesitation is that you may read me instead of the Scriptures. Don't fall into that trap. I like the fact that this series includes the biblical text. Don't skip over it. In the end, that's the bit that matters.

An Outline of the Old Testament

The Christian Old Testament puts the books in the Jewish Bible in a distinctive order:

Genesis to Kings: A story that runs from the creation of the world to the exile of Judahites to Babylon

Chronicles to Esther: A second version of this story, continuing it into the years after the exile

Job, Psalms, Proverbs, Ecclesiastes, Song of Songs: Some poetic books

Isaiah to Malachi: The teaching of some prophets

Here is an outline of the history that lies at the books' background. (I give no dates for events in Genesis, which involves too much guesswork.)

1200s	Moses, the exodus, Joshua
1100s	The "judges"
1000s	King Saul, King David
900s	King Solomon; the nation splits into two, Ephraim and Judah
800s	Elijah, Elisha
700s	Amos, Hosea, Isaiah, Micah; Assyria the superpower; the fall of Ephraim
600s	Jeremiah, King Josiah; Babylon the superpower
500s	Ezekiel; the fall of Judah; Persia the superpower; Judahites free to return home
400s	Ezra, Nehemiah

300s	Greece the superpower
200s	Syria and Egypt the regional powers pulling Judah one way or the other
100s	Judah's rebellion against Syrian power and gain of independence
000s	Rome the superpower

Daniel

The book of Daniel addresses the questions and pressures of Judahites in two situations. The questions and pressures are similar, but the situations are different. In 587 BC the Babylonians destroyed Jerusalem and transported its important people to Babylon. The first half of the book tells a series of stories about Judahites there, where they face the temptations and demands of living in this foreign land as immigrants looked down on by the superpower. The question is, can they remain faithful to their faith in this context? The stories tell of their being put under pressure by the foreign culture and its learning and expectations and of God's making it possible for them to keep faith, and indeed to show that their God could enable them to outperform the expertise that issued from Babylonian learning. One of God's acts is to give Daniel a revelation about how political events are to unfold over the next four regimes.

In 539 BC the Babylonians were defeated by Cyrus the Medo-Persian king, and in 333 BC the Persians were defeated by Alexander the Great. In the second century BC Jerusalem was under the control of one of his sub-empires, ruled by the Seleucids and centered in Syria. In 167 BC its king, Antiochus IV (Antiochus Epiphanes), banned the practice of Jewish faith in the temple and introduced his own religion there. So Jews faced questions and pressures that overlapped with the ones that had faced people such as Daniel in Babylon. The second half of the book takes up that earlier vision given to Daniel in Babylon, and relates a series of revelations spelling out its implications for people living in the crisis in Jerusalem in the time of Antiochus. The revelations concerned the history of the time from Babylonian supremacy to the time of Antiochus and promised that God would put down the oppressor. God did so, which is likely the reason the community took the book of Daniel into its Scriptures—it had been proved to be a message from God.

The Twelve Prophets

The twelve books that follow Daniel form a collection of a total length comparable to that of one of the long prophetic books, Isaiah, Jeremiah, and Ezekiel. For all we know, prophets such as Amos and Zephaniah delivered as many God-given prophecies as Isaiah or Jeremiah or Ezekiel, but the community apparently had reason for seeing a much smaller number of them as so important that they should be held onto for future generations.

The twelve fall roughly into three chronological groups. The first six mostly belong to the eighth century, the time of Isaiah ben Amoz. Hosea, Amos, and Jonah were all prophets in the northern kingdom, Ephraim (though the book of Jonah tells a story about his preaching to Nineveh in Assyria). Obadiah appears as an appendage to Amos because of its focus on Edom, where Amos ends. Micah was a prophet in Jerusalem (at the same time as Isaiah). Joel doesn't give any direct information on its date and it may appear among these first six in the conviction that it belongs here chronologically, and/or because its stress on Yahweh's Day and on Yahweh's capacity to relent of evil also appears in Amos and Jonah.

Whereas the period when Assyria is the superpower is the background to the eighth-century prophets, the next three, Nahum, Habakkuk, and Zephaniah, belong to the seventh century. By now Ephraim has ceased to exist. Assyria is in decline and Babylon is becoming the great power. These three prophets are thus contemporary with Jeremiah, and like him, they all work in Jerusalem. They live and work in the century before Judah will be overcome by a fate similar to the one that overcame Ephraim.

The last three books, Haggai, Zechariah, and Malachi, belong to another century or two later, to the period after the exile in Jerusalem, when they face a different set of issues there. Haggai and Zechariah preach in the context of the project to rebuild the temple in Jerusalem between 520 and 516, and urge on this project. Malachi preaches some decades later, when the temple has been rebuilt and is functioning, but there are yet other issues to confront.

DANIEL 1:1–21

On Drawing the Line

[1]In the third year of the reign of Jehoiaqim king of Judah, Nebuchadnezzar king of Babylon came to Jerusalem and blockaded it. [2]The Lord gave into his hand Jehoiaqim, king of Judah, and some of the accoutrements of God's house, and he brought them to the country of Shinar, to his god's house. He brought the accoutrements to his god's treasure house. [3]The king said to Ashpenaz, his chief of staff, to bring some of the Israelites, both some of royal descent and some of the important people [4](young men in whom there was no defect, of good appearance, skillful in all expertise, proficient in knowledge, insightful in knowledge, and in whom there was capacity to stand in attendance in the king's palace), and to teach them the learning and language of the Kaldeans. [5]The king assigned to them a daily allocation from the king's supplies and the wine he drank. [Ashpenaz was] to train them for three years, and some of them would stand in attendance before the king. [6]Among them were some Judahites, Daniel, Hananiah, Mishael, and Azariah, [7]but the chief of staff determined on names for them. He determined for Daniel "Belteshazzar," for Hananiah "Shadrach," for Mishael "Meshach," and for Azariah "Abed-nego."

[8]Daniel determined in his mind that he would not defile himself with the king's supplies and the wine he drank, and asked the head of staff that he might not defile himself. [9]God gave Daniel commitment and compassion before the head of staff, [10]but the head of staff said to Daniel, "I'm afraid of my lord the king, who assigned your food and drink: what if he sees your faces thinner than the [other] young men of your generation and you risk my head with the king?" [11]Daniel said to the guard whom the head of staff had assigned over Daniel, Hananiah, Mishael, and Azariah, [12]"Could you test your servants for ten days. They could give us some legumes to eat and water to drink, [13]and our appearance and the appearance of the young men who eat the king's supplies will be visible before you. Act with your servants in accordance with what

you see." [14]He listened to them regarding this matter, and tested them for ten days. [15]At the end of ten days their appearance looked better and they were heftier in body than all the young men who were eating the king's supplies. [16]So the guard would carry away their supplies and the wine they were to drink, and give them legumes.

[17]These young men, the four of them: God gave them knowledge and skill in all learning and expertise, while Daniel had insight into every vision and dreams. [18]At the end of the period that the king had said to bring them, the head of staff brought them before Nebuchadnezzar. [19]The king spoke with them, and from all of them there was not found anyone like Daniel, Hananiah, Mishael, and Azariah. So they stood in attendance before the king. [20]Every matter of insightful expertise that he asked of them, the king found them ten times superior to all the diviners and chanters that were in his entire realm. [21]Daniel was [there] until the first year of Cyrus the Persian.

Near where I live in the United States, there's a British store that I like to visit every few weeks. It has an aisle full of British teas, one full of British cookies (biscuits), one full of British candies (sweets), one full of British jams, one full of British cereals, and a refrigerator stocked with British bacon, pies, and cream. I'd like to claim that the fact that they do taste good is the reason why I buy most of these items, but of course part of the reason they taste good is that they remind me of home. On one occasion I got involved in a conversation with other British people in the store, including the owner, and then panicked at the checkout because I realized I didn't have any British money, which of course I didn't need; but entering the store had been like going through an Alice in Wonderland door straight into the U.K.

I'm in California voluntarily. I'm not in exile, like Daniel and his three friends. I love it here, and I want to die here. Yet I'll never be able to feel American. I'll always know I'm a resident alien, by choice (I haven't sought citizenship). Maybe subconsciously I want to preserve my Britishness. Daniel and his friends wanted to preserve their **Judahite** identity. They weren't obliged to avoid eating what the king ate; it was not inherently defiling. But food links with identity. It's odder that they accepted **Babylonian** names, even though the names make connections with Babylonian gods in the same way that the four young men's Hebrew names make connections with the God of **Israel**. (But significantly, as the names are reported, at least some of them make fun of the Babylonian gods. For instance, Abed-nebo would mean "servant of Nebo," but Abed-nego doesn't mean anything.) Maybe what's important is that you draw the line somewhere. You have to avoid the defiling effect of a culture that worships different gods. The Babylonians "determined" on names for the young men; but Daniel did some determining of his own in this connection.

It required God's support if it was to work. And it got that support. At the beginning of the story God "gives" Jerusalem to Nebuchadnezzar, but less oddly, later in the story God "gives" Daniel favor and "gives" all four men wisdom. They didn't attempt to evade education in Babylonian learning, the kind of learning that would fit them for jobs in the administration. Perhaps they were confident that their God could give them superior insight to that possessed by the **Kaldeans**. It would be quite an expectation, given the breadth and depth of Babylonian learning, in which the diviners and exorcists were experts. The fruits of God's doing so will emerge in the stories that follow. This first story introduces the various issues that will arise in the stories.

Its opening and its conclusion form a chronological bracket around them. At the beginning of Daniel's life, God does something strange in giving Jerusalem over to the Babylonian king. There's no allusion here to the way Judah had deserved this fate. Among its horrifying consequences were not merely the transportation of some people, but the appropriation of some of the objects used in worship in the temple (objects such as platters, chalices, knives, and other implements). These things that had been dedicated to **Yahweh** are deposited in a Babylonian god's temple. It would look as if the Babylonian god had defeated Yahweh, as the Babylonian king had defeated the king of Judah. But the chapter closes with a note that would have to refer to Daniel's old age—more than sixty years have gone by. Nebuchadnezzar has passed, and so have his four successors, and so has the Babylonian Empire itself, taken over by Cyrus the Persian. Daniel is still there, having outlasted the Babylonian Empire. Who'd have thought it?

DANIEL 2:1–24

Except the Gods, Whose Home Is Not with Humanity

[1]In the second year of Nebuchadnezzar's reign, Nebuchadnezzar had dreams. His spirit was agitated, but his sleep came over him. [2]The king said to summon the diviners, chanters, charmers, and Kaldeans to explain his dreams to the king. They came and stood in attendance before the king. [3]The king said to them, "I had a dream, and my spirit is agitated to know the dream." [4]The Kaldeans spoke to the king (in Aramaic): "Long live the king! Tell your servants the dream and we'll explain its meaning." [5]The king replied to the Kaldeans: "A firm decision has issued from me: If you don't make known to me the dream and its meaning, you'll be torn limb from limb and your houses turned into rubble. [6]But if you explain the dream and its meaning, you'll receive a reward and gift and great honor from me. Now. Explain to me the dream and its meaning." [7]They replied a second time, "May Your Majesty relate the dream to his servants, and we'll explain its meaning." [8]The king replied, "I know for sure that you're buying time, because you see that a firm decision has issued from me [9]that if you don't make the dream known to me, there's a specific decree for you. You've arranged with each other to tell me something

false and base, until the situation changes. Now. Tell me the dream, and I'll know that you can explain its meaning." [10]The Kaldeans replied to the king, "There's no one on earth who can explain the king's question. Thus no great king or ruler has asked a question like this of any diviner or chanter or Kaldean. [11]The question that the king is asking is so daunting that there's no one else who can explain it to the king except the gods, whose home is not with humanity." [12]At this, the king became furious, very angry, and he said to put to death all Babylon's experts.

[13]So the decree went out and the experts were to be killed, and they looked for Daniel and his companions to kill them. [14]Daniel responded with shrewdness and judgment to Arioch, the king's chief of police, who had gone out to kill Babylon's experts. [15]He replied to Arioch, "Royal marshal, why is there the severe decree from the king?" Arioch made the thing known to Daniel, [16]and Daniel went and asked of the king that he might give him a time, and he would explain the meaning to the king. [17]Then Daniel went home and made the thing known to his companions, Hananiah, Mishael, and Azariah, [18]for them to ask for compassion from the God of the heavens about this mystery, so that Daniel and his friends might not be put to death, with the rest of Babylon's experts.

[19]Then the mystery was revealed to Daniel in a vision by night. So Daniel worshiped the God of the heavens. [20]Daniel declared:

> The name of God be worshiped from age to age,
>   because expertise and might are his!
> [21] He changes times and eras,
>   removes kings and establishes kings.
> He gives expertise to the experts,
>   knowledge to the people who know insight.
> [22] He reveals things that are deep and hidden;
>   he knows what's in the dark, and light dwells
>   with him.
> [23] God of my ancestors, I confess and praise you,
>   because you've given me expertise and power.

> You've now made known to me what we asked
>> of you;
>> you've made known to us the king's question.

²⁴Thus Daniel went to Arioch, whom the king had appointed to do away with Babylon's experts. He came and said this to him: "Don't put Babylon's experts to death. Take me to the king and I'll explain the meaning to the king."

In our morning prayers today we happened to have Hannah's song of praise from 1 Samuel 2 when God enables her to have a baby against all the odds. The refrain in the Prayer Book version came from the story about Mary going to see her cousin Elizabeth (Luke 1), when both of them are also having babies against all the odds, and Elizabeth declares, "Blessed is she who has believed that the Lord would fulfill his promises to her." I had also been thinking about a friend who was rector of a thriving church and who was good at having big ideas and implementing them without worrying too much about the financial implications. He planned a mission, hired a famous name to speak, and booked a huge venue. Fewer people came than he expected, the event lost buckets of money, and he had to offer his resignation from his post.

Daniel has a big idea and doesn't think too much about the consequences. He has a crazy boss. Well, maybe his boss isn't so crazy. Like any national leader, Nebuchadnezzar has hundreds of expert advisers, here called diviners, chanters, charmers, and Kaldeans. There's no need to try to distinguish the terms too sharply; the story accumulates them to suggest how the experts would be impressive yet (in light of how things turn out) laughable. Nebuchadnezzar can't personally check all the databases that underlie their advice and can't be sure whether they're just making it all up. What do they really know? So he sets them a test. He's had a dream but gone back to sleep and forgotten it, as often happens. It's frustrating to be unable to recall a troublesome dream that might've been important.

Whereas Western thinking assumes that dreams simply reveal something about your subconscious (or what you ate for supper), traditional societies know that sometimes they tell you something about the external world—for instance, about an event that's going to happen. The **Babylonians** kept records of dreams and of events that followed them, for the advisers to use as resources for their work. But supposing it's all a confidence trick? The test has the potential to expose whether they really have any superior knowledge. It leads them to grant that the only thing they have is their dream books. They're experts, with technical resources, but they have no more supernatural insight than Nebuchadnezzar. They can't reach the gods and (they acknowledge wistfully) the gods don't reach down to them. Western culture places a touching, sad, ill-advised faith in expertise, and it's hard to acknowledge the parallel limitations of the bases on which we make huge decisions about political policy, social policy, economic policy—and war-making.

Daniel knows a God who does reach down to us and he knows how to reach up to this God, though the way he does so is risky. He acts amusingly like my rector friend rather than like Elizabeth (admittedly he may have thought he had nothing to lose if he was going to face execution with the Babylonian experts). He has no promise from God to claim, like Hannah, Mary, and Elizabeth, but he simply tells the king that he'll take his test, and then rushes home to tell his three friends that they'd better pray. Did they roll their eyes at the way he had the praying and the commitment in the wrong order?

Did God's eyes also roll? You can't assume that God will get you out of a mess when you make commitments first and pray second, but fortunately God may do so. God is certainly capable of it, being "the God of the heavens." That description doesn't mean God is remote, inaccessible, and uninvolved, as the experts thought. God is also "my ancestors' God," the God of Abraham, Isaac, and Jacob, the God who's been involved with Israel over the centuries. Being the God of the heavens means being able to reveal what's going to happen, because of being the God who makes things happen—as Daniel's thanksgiving prayer declares. Being the ancestors' God means being willing to reveal what's going to happen, maybe even when put on the spot by someone like Daniel who speaks first and thinks afterwards.

The reference to Aramaic indicates that here the book switches from being written in Hebrew. Aramaic became the international language of the Middle East. The change marks the fact that the experts wouldn't speak in Hebrew, but the book stays in Aramaic through chapter 7.

DANIEL 2:25–49

After Nebuchadnezzar, What?

[25]With haste Arioch took Daniel before the king and said to him, "I've found a man from the Judahite exiles who can make known the meaning to the king." [26]The king replied to Daniel (whose name was Belteshazzar), "Can you make known to me the dream that I saw, and its meaning?" [27]Daniel replied before the king, "The mystery about which the king asked—experts, chanters, diviners and exorcists can't explain it to the king. [28]But there is a God in the heavens revealing mysteries, and he has made known to King Nebuchadnezzar what will happen at the end of the time. Your dream, the visions in your head in bed, was this. [29]Your Majesty, in bed your thoughts came concerning what will happen after this, and the one who reveals mysteries made known to you what will happen. [30]And I—not because of expertise that there is in me above any other human being has this mystery been revealed to me, but in order that the meaning should be made known to the king, and you may know the thoughts in your mind.

[31]"Your Majesty, you were looking, and there—a large statue. This statue was big and its brightness extraordinary, standing in front of you, an awe-inspiring sight. [32]That statue: its head was of fine gold, its chest and arms of silver, its stomach and sides of bronze, [33]its legs of iron, its feet partly of iron and partly of pottery. [34]You watched as a stone broke off, not by hands, and hit the statue on its feet of iron and pottery, and shattered them. [35]All at once the iron, pottery, bronze, silver, and gold shattered. They became like chaff from a summer threshing floor. The wind carried them. No place was found for them. But the stone that hit the statue became a big crag and filled the entire earth.

[36]"That was the dream. We'll relate its meaning before the king. [37]You, Your Majesty, king of kings, to whom the God of the heavens gave royal power, sovereignty, power, and honor, [38]and gave into your hand, wherever they live, human beings, animals of the wild, and birds of the heavens, and made you rule over all of them—you're the head of gold. [39]In your place another regime will arise, inferior to you, and another, third regime, of bronze, which will rule over the entire earth. [40]The fourth regime will be strong as iron, because iron shatters and smashes anything. Like iron that crushes, it will shatter and crush all these. [41]In that you saw the feet and toes partly of clay pottery and partly of iron, it will be a split regime, but some of the toughness of iron will be in it. Insofar as you saw iron mixed with earthen pottery, [42]and the toes of the feet were partly iron and partly clay, to some extent the regime will be strong but in part it will be fragile. [43]In that you saw the iron mixed with earthen pottery, human beings will unite, but they won't stick with each other, as iron doesn't stick with pottery. [44]In the time of those kings, the God of the heavens will set up a regime that won't be destroyed through the ages; the regime won't pass to another people. It will shatter and terminate all these regimes, and it will stand through the ages, [45]insofar as you saw that a stone broke off from the crag, not by hands, and shattered the iron, bronze, pottery, silver, and gold.

"The great God has made known to the king what will happen after this. The dream is true. Its meaning is reliable."

⁴⁶King Nebuchadnezzar fell on his face and bowed prostrate before Daniel. He said to present an offering and fragrant oblations to him. ⁴⁷The king replied to Daniel, "Indeed your God is God of gods, Lord of kings, and Revealer of mysteries, that you can reveal this mystery." ⁴⁸The king elevated Daniel and gave him many great gifts. He would have made him ruler over the entire province of Babylon and chief officer over all the experts in Babylon, ⁴⁹but Daniel asked the king to appoint Shadrach, Meshach, and Abed-nego over the administration of the province of Babylon, with Daniel at the king's court.

It seemed odd that the media were discussing Barack Obama's "legacy" within moments of his inauguration for his second term as president. Will his legacy be finding a way through the illegal immigration dilemma? Will it be the health-care law? Will it be solving the fiscal crisis? Will it be gun control? Will it be getting the United States out of Afghanistan and leaving Afghanistan a stable and orderly country? Will it be reducing the gap between rich and poor? The questions are posed as questions about the future, but they're really questions about the present, about priorities for now, which is why it's not so odd that they became discussion topics straight after the inauguration.

Will President Obama lead the country in a way that makes it inclined to elect another Democrat? This question resonates with Nebuchadnezzar's dream. Apparently he really couldn't remember his dream, but when Daniel told him what it was, he recognized it. It's obviously bad news about his legacy. The phrase "the end of the time" is more literally "the end of the days," which in English can sound as if it denotes the end of history, but it isn't a technical term for the End. Nebuchadnezzar isn't asking that kind of question. The troubling question in his dream was, what's going to happen after him? He's the great king who reigned over the **Babylonian** Empire for forty years—for half its life. What's the future of this empire?

Given this basic clue to the dream's meaning, you don't need much insight to infer the significance of the metals in the statue. Louis XV of France is credited with the phrase "*Après moi le déluge*"—After me, the collapse of everything (the French Revolution came fifteen years after his death). Didn't he care very much? Nebuchadnezzar seems not to think that way. It's a shocking and troublesome revelation that a gradual decline will follow his reign, and eventually a collapse. But it's what happens to empires. Quite late on, it becomes apparent that they have feet of clay.

The vision doesn't say who or what is represented by the different metals. The second half of the book will refer to the Medo-Persian and Greek Empires, but this understanding needn't apply here. The metals might stand for the kings who'll follow Nebuchadnezzar (none of them anywhere near as significant) before the empire falls to Cyrus. But the point doesn't lie in exactly who the metals stand for, but in the inexorable decline and collapse. When an empire's at the height of its power, it's hard to believe it could ever fall. The vision declares that it can and will. It will provide no legacy for Nebuchadnezzar.

He's king now, by God's will. The rule of empires doesn't happen outside the control of the God of Israel. God gives empires their power and uses them to bring good, or more often to bring trouble to people who deserve it—as the Old Testament comments elsewhere about Babylon, Yahweh's agent in bringing trouble to Judah. Here, the statement reminds the king that he shouldn't think he's in power because of his own achievements, and reminds the Judahites for whom these stories are written that they shouldn't think he has a power that makes him independent of God. Their God is in control of him and thus of their destiny. One of the ways in which nations try to prop themselves up is by uniting with one another, but such unions have a habit of not sticking.

If the metals in the statue stand for Nebuchadnezzar and his Babylonian successors, one might infer that the stone falling from nowhere might be Cyrus, God's means of putting Babylon down. His empire will indeed last for way longer than the Babylonian Empire, but it will be just another human empire, and Daniel's talk of a regime that lasts forever and never gives way to another suggests that the vision has in mind something more radical. "The time of those kings" will turn out to cover more than the Babylonians; it covers the Persians, the Greeks, and the Romans, and the Turks and the British and the Americans. God did assert his kingship through Cyrus, the agent through whom the temple in Jerusalem was rebuilt and Judah gained a measure of independent life. God did later assert his kingship in Jesus. Other empires have continued, but they all have feet of clay.

DANIEL 3:1–30

But If Our God Does Not Rescue Us . . .

[1]King Nebuchadnezzar made a gold statue sixty cubits in height, six cubits in width. He set it up in the vale of Dura in the province of Babylon. [2]King Nebuchadnezzar sent to assemble the satraps, governors, and commissioners, the counselors, treasurers, judges, officers, and all the provincial officials, to come for the dedication of the statue that King Nebuchadnezzar had set up. [3]They assembled, the satraps, governors, and commissioners, the counselors, treasurers, judges, officers, and all the provincial officials, for the dedication of the statue that King Nebuchadnezzar had set up, and stood in front of the statue that Nebuchadnezzar had set up. [4]The herald proclaimed forcefully, "To you it is being declared, peoples, nations, and languages, [5]at the time when you hear the sound of the horn, pipe, cithara, trigon, psaltery, ensemble, and all types of music, you're to fall and bow down to the gold statue that King Nebuchadnezzar has set up. [6]Anyone who doesn't fall and bow down will at that moment be thrown inside a red-hot blazing furnace." [7]So at that time when all the peoples heard the sound of the horn, pipe, cithara, trigon, psaltery,

and all types of music, all the peoples, nations, and languages would bow down to the gold statue that King Nebuchadnezzar had set up.

[8]So at that time some Kaldeans came and denounced the Judahites. [9]They exclaimed to King Nebuchadnezzar: "Long live the king! [10]Your Majesty, you gave notice that anyone who hears the sound of the horn, pipe, cithara, trigon, psaltery, ensemble, and all types of music is to fall and bow down to the gold image, [11]and anyone who doesn't fall and bow down will be thrown inside a red-hot blazing furnace. [12]There are some Judahites whom you appointed over the business of the province of Babylon, Shadrach, Meshach, and Abed-nego. These men have not taken any notice of you, Your Majesty. They haven't revered your gods or bowed down to the gold image that you've set up."

[13]Nebuchadnezzar in rage and fury said to bring in Shadrach, Meshach, and Abed-nego, and these men were brought in before the king. [14]Nebuchadnezzar exclaimed to them: "Shadrach, Meshach, and Abed-nego, do you really not revere my gods and bow down to the gold statue that I've set up? [15]If you are indeed now ready, at the time when you hear the sound of the horn, pipe, cithara, trigon, psaltery, ensemble, and all types of music, to fall and bow down to the statue that I've made . . . But if you won't bow down, at that moment you'll be thrown inside a red-hot blazing furnace. And who is the god who could rescue you from my hand?" [16]Shadrach, Meshach, and Abed-nego replied to King Nebuchadnezzar, "We don't need to make any response to this. [17]If our God, whom we revere, exists, he's able to rescue us from the red-hot blazing furnace, and he'll rescue us from your hand. [18]But if he doesn't, be it known to you, Your Majesty, that we won't revere your gods or bow down to the gold statue that you've set up."

[19]Nebuchadnezzar filled with rage, and the expression on his face toward Shadrach, Meshach, and Abed-nego changed. He exclaimed that they should heat the furnace seven times higher than it was customary to heat it. [20]He said to the strongest men in his army to tie up Shadrach, Meshach, and

Abed-nego, to throw them into the red-hot blazing furnace.
[21]These men were tied up in their trousers, shirts, headwear,
and other clothes, and thrown into the red-hot blazing furnace.
[22]So because of the king's strict word, when the furnace was
heated excessively, the flames from the fire killed those men
who took up Shadrach, Meshach, and Abed-nego.

[23]These three men, Shadrach, Meshach, and Abed-nego,
fell into the red-hot blazing furnace, tied up. [24]King Nebuchadnezzar was startled and stood up in haste. He exclaimed to
his courtiers, "Wasn't it three men, bound, that we threw
inside the furnace?" They replied to the king, "Certainly, Your
Majesty." [25]He replied, "There, I see four men, free, walking
about inside the fire. There's no effect on them. The appearance of the fourth is like a divine being." [26]Nebuchadnezzar
went near the door of the red-hot blazing furnace. He
exclaimed, "Shadrach, Meshach, and Abed-nego, servants of
God on High, come out." Shadrach, Meshach, and Abed-nego
came out from inside the fire. [27]The satraps, governors, and
commissioners, and the king's courtiers, assembled. They
looked at these men, on whose bodies the fire had not had
power and the hair on whose head was not singed. Their
trousers were unaffected. The smell of the fire had not come
on them. [28]Nebuchadnezzar exclaimed, "The God of Shadrach,
Meshach, and Abed-nego be worshiped, who has sent his
aide and rescued his servants who entrusted themselves to
him. They defied the king's word and gave up their body so
they might not revere or bow down to any god but their God.
[29]Notice is given by me that any people, nation, or tongue that
says something remiss about the God of Shadrach, Meshach,
and Abed-nego will be torn limb from limb and his house
turned into rubble, because there's no other god who can rescue
like this." [30]The king promoted Shadrach, Meshach, and Abed-
nego in the province of Babylon.

Elie Wiesel wrote a play that was about a pogrom in Poland,
but was based on something he says he witnessed as a teenager
in Auschwitz. Three rabbis put God on trial for permitting the

massacre of his people. In due course they found God guilty. Then, after a long silence, one of them looked up and saw that it was getting dark, and said that it was time for evening prayers. So they broke off to say the prayers. I don't think they were just playing safe in case they were wrong about God. Wiesel has called his play a tragic farce.

The theme and the humor overlap with those of this story. There's no mention of Daniel himself, perhaps because the stories were of separate origin, though the previous story has implied an explanation—Daniel works in the palace, the other three in the provincial administration. It's a story of a deadly serious recurring experience of Jewish people living in a foreign context, where their differentness has often offended the people among whom they lived. Their unwillingness to live by other people's conventions and expectations raised questions about those conventions and expectations. It's one of the ways in which Jewish people have fulfilled their vocation to draw the rest of the world away from its usual assumptions about religion and life.

It's not quite clear what was the point about Nebuchadnezzar's statue, but whether it was an image of a god or of Nebuchadnezzar himself, the three men knew they couldn't bow down to it and thus imply that the other so-called gods or the foreign state were really important. The disdain shared by the story-teller is expressed in the way the story is told. The repeated lists of important officials and musical instruments make fun of the administration and of the important state occasion. The statue is a ridiculous size (a cubit is half a meter or half a yard). The king's rage at the young men who had so impressed him also makes him an object of fun, as does the fate of the burly bouncer-types. At the story's close, the king ricochets from one stupidity to another in making it a capital offense to disdain Yahweh. When you need to find a way to survive in a context where you're an unloved minority, it will help if you learn to laugh.

So the story is funny but deadly serious. The idea of dying because you stand by the truth about God and about the state was not just a theoretical idea for Jews. The seriousness of the humorous story takes a new turn with the three youths' declaration about God, which compares and contrasts with that of the three rabbis. When the youths say, "If he really exists," they don't imply any doubt about the question; they speak that way because it's the question at issue between them and the king. They themselves know that this God could rescue them from the red-hot blazing furnace (again the story is prevented from becoming too solemn by the gallows humor involved in the repetition of that phrase). Indeed, they're convinced that he's going to do so. But they're going to stay committed to this God whether or not he rescues them.

Did the story happen? I don't know. I'm inclined to assume that farces are more likely to be fictional than factual. Like the young men, I know that God can miraculously rescue people from their persecutors. God has many **aides** whom he can send to deliver people from red-hot furnaces of one kind and another. But I also know that he usually doesn't do so, and the story offers no promise that he'll do so for other people put in the position of these three youths. So it doesn't make a lot of difference whether it happened or not. It probably won't happen for us. The story constitutes an encouragement to live by the principle they enunciate to Nebuchadnezzar, or the principle embodied in the rabbis who find God guilty and then break off to say their prayers.

DANIEL 4:1–18

Say-so Time

¹King Nebuchadnezzar to all the peoples, nations, and languages that live in all the earth. May your **well-being** abound! ²It has seemed good to me to relate the signs and wonders that God on High has done with me. ³His signs—how great!

21

His wonders—how mighty! His kingship is a kingship that lasts forever, his rule continues generation after generation!

[4]I, Nebuchadnezzar, was thriving in my house, flourishing in my palace. [5]I had a dream and it disturbed me, and images while I was in bed; visions that came into my head alarmed me. [6]Notice was given by me to bring all Babylon's experts so they could make known the dream's meaning. [7]The diviners, chanters, Kaldeans, and exorcists came, and I told the dream before them, but they couldn't make its meaning known to me. [8]Finally there came before me Daniel, whose name is Belteshazzar in accordance with my God's name, and in whom is the spirit of the holy gods. I told the dream before him: [9]"Belteshazzar, chief of the diviners, I know that the spirit of the holy gods is in you and that no mystery defeats you. Tell me the visions in the dream that I had, and its meaning.

[10]The visions that came into my head: I looked, and there— a tree in the middle of the earth. Its height was great. [11]The tree grew and became mighty. Its height reached the heavens. It was visible to the end of the entire earth. [12]Its foliage was lovely, its fruit abundant, and there was food for everyone in it. Beneath it the animals of the wild sheltered. In its branches the birds of the heavens dwelt. From it all humanity fed. [13]I looked in the visions that came into my head in bed, and there—a lookout, a holy being, coming down from the heavens. [14]He called forcefully, 'Fell the tree, cut off its branches, strip off its foliage, scatter its fruit. The animals must flee from beneath it, the birds from its branches. [15]Yet leave its rooted stump in the earth. With a ring of iron and bronze, with the grass of the wild, with the dew of the heavens he is to be watered, and with the animals his share will be in the plants of the earth. [16]His mind is to be changed from that of a human being; the mind of an animal is to be given him. Seven periods are to pass over him. [17]The decision is by the decree of the lookouts, the intent is by the word of the holy ones, with the object that human beings may acknowledge that the One on High rules over human kingship. He can give it to whomever he wishes and set up over it the lowest of people.'

> [18]I, King Nebuchadnezzar, had this dream. You, Belteshazzar, tell me its meaning, since all my realm's experts cannot make its meaning known to me. But you can, because the spirit of the holy gods is in you."

I had an e-mail recently from someone who was at a camp (houseparty, in Brit-speak) with me when we were teenagers; her father was one of its leaders. In the evening meetings he ran "Say-so" times: the phrase comes from the opening lines of Psalm 107, "Let the redeemed of the Lord say so." The idea was that people should give their testimonies to times God had been involved in their lives in redeeming ways. It was great for the young people (and it's great for adults) to tell other people about how God had been doing things in their lives, and it's great for the people who listen to them, too.

Nebuchadnezzar is here "saying so." The chapter takes the form of his testimony (though it abandons that form for one paragraph near the end). When you're a teenager, it can be a bit laughable to follow the outline script for a testimony if it presupposes that you need to talk about the way God delivered you from a life of sin, but Nebuchadnezzar doesn't have that difficulty. Further, he's a perfect illustration of the way it's virtually impossible for someone in a position of power to avoid corruption. Because you're important, you get to think of yourself as important. The king of Babylon really matters. He makes a difference. He's key to his empire's survival and thriving. The symbolism of the tree, which stands for Nebuchadnezzar, makes the point. In light of the leader's importance, any country expects its people to respect the monarch or president. We may not respect the individual who holds that office; we are required to respect the office. When you're the office-holder, that distinction becomes harder to hold onto, and Nebuchadnezzar loses it. There's a sense in which it's quite proper to be proud of one's achievements as president or king; there's a right sort of pride and a wrong sort. Nebuchadnezzar loses the distinction.

It isn't always the case that leaders who get to think of themselves as important or who fail to be faithful pay the price for doing so, as it isn't always the case that people who pay the price for being faithful to God get rescued from martyrdom, but it sometimes happens. The dream warns Nebuchadnezzar about the possibility. The supernatural lookout is another of the **aides** from God's administration, like the one who appeared in the furnace. While he says that the judgment on Nebuchadnezzar is definite and inevitable, the implication of bringing such a warning is that it's inevitable unless people repent. The story of Jonah illustrates the point. Jonah told Nineveh that judgment was coming and gave no hint that there was a way out, but Jonah knew (and maybe its people knew) that if they repented, all bets were off. Here, too, part of the point about God sending the dream to Nebuchadnezzar is to get him to change, so that the warning in the dream need not come true.

You might not have thought that you needed to be a genius or a prophet to work out the dream's meaning, yet it's not so surprising that Nebuchadnezzar has a hard time seeing its implications. And maybe it's equally unsurprising that the other experts don't care for the idea of explaining it to the king.

DANIEL 4:19–37

Judgment and Change

[19]Daniel, whose name was Belteshazzar, was overcome at that very moment. His thoughts alarmed him. The king exclaimed, "Belteshazzar, the dream and its meaning shouldn't alarm you." Daniel exclaimed, "My lord, the dream should be for your enemy, its meaning for your foe. [20]The tree that you saw that grew and became mighty, its height reached the heavens and it was visible to the end of the entire earth, [21]its foliage was lovely, its fruit abundant, and there was food for everyone in

it, beneath it animals of the wild sheltered, in its branches the birds of the heavens dwelt: [22]you, Your Majesty, are the one who has grown and become mighty. Your stature has grown and reached the heavens, your rule to the end of the earth. [23]In that Your Majesty saw a lookout, a holy one, come down from the heavens and say, 'Fell the tree, destroy it, yet leave its rooted stump in the earth; with a ring of iron and bronze, with the grass of the wild, with the dew of the heavens he's to be watered, and with the animals his share will be, until seven periods pass over him': [24]this is the meaning, Your Majesty. It is the decision of the One on High that has befallen my lord the king. [25]They're going to lead you away from human beings, and your home will be with the animals of the wild. They'll feed you plants, like oxen, and water you with dew from the heavens. Seven periods will pass over you, until you acknowledge that the One on High rules over human kingship. He can give it to whomever he wishes. [26]But in that they said to leave the rooted stump of the tree: your kingship is going to arise for you from when you acknowledge that the heavens rule. [27]But, Your Majesty, may my counsel be pleasing to you. Break with your offenses by faithfulness, your waywardness by grace to the weak, in case there may be an extending of your thriving."

[28]It all befell King Nebuchadnezzar. [29]At the end of twelve months, he was walking on the royal palace in Babylon. [30]The king exclaimed, "This is great Babylon, which I myself built as a royal home by my sovereign might and for my majestic honor!" [31]The words still on the king's lips, a voice fell from the heavens: "To you they're saying, King Nebuchadnezzar: your kingship has passed from you. [32]They're going to lead you away from human beings and your home will be with the animals of the wild. They'll feed you plants, like oxen. Seven periods will pass over you, until you acknowledge that the One on High rules over human kingship and can give it to whomever he wishes." [33]At that moment the words were fulfilled upon Nebuchadnezzar. He was led away from human beings, he ate plants, like oxen, and his body was watered with the dew of the heavens, until his hair had grown long like an eagle and his nails like birds.

³⁴At the end of the time, I, Nebuchadnezzar, raised my eyes to the heavens. My sanity came back to me and I worshiped the One on High, praised and honored the One Who Lives Forever, whose rule is a rule that lasts forever, whose reign continues generation after generation. ³⁵All earth's inhabitants are counted as nothing. He acts in accordance with his wishes with the forces of the heavens and the inhabitants of the earth. There's no one who can restrain his hand or say to him, "What have you done?" ³⁶At that time, my sanity came back to me, and as for the honor of my kingship, my glory and splendor came back to me. My courtiers and important people sought audience with me. I was established over my realm, and exceeding power was added to me. ³⁷Now I, Nebuchadnezzar, praise, exalt, and honor the King of the Heavens, all whose deeds are true and his ways just, and who can put down people who walk in pride.

Some while ago, we had a speaker at a prayer day who talked about Paul's longing that people's love might abound. Paul doesn't make clear whether he means love for God or love for people; the speaker commented that if love is there, it will find expression toward whatever object presents itself. I thought of that comment again this week when I had students reading Psalm 116. The word order at the beginning is striking—not "I love the Lord because he listened to my voice" (as the translations have it), but "I love, because the Lord heard my voice." The psalm, too, invited the inference that this love that responds to God's love will find expression toward whatever object presents itself.

Conversely, Nebuchadnezzar has problems with his attitude to God and to other people. The New Testament calls Daniel a prophet, but the book of Daniel doesn't do so; he's a man of insight. Here, he does act like a prophet in confronting the king and exposing the problem in his attitude to people, which goes together with the problem in his attitude to God. It's the other form of corruption that leaders fall for. He doesn't tell

Nebuchadnezzar that he needs to give up his pride. He tells him, "Break with your offenses by **faithfulness**, your waywardness by grace to the weak." A leader's role in the Old Testament includes caring about weak people, and thus fulfilling a vocation to be faithful to them and to God. In practice leaders characteristically look after themselves and other strong people, which counts as waywardness. It contravenes God's standards for leaders. In effect, Daniel challenges Nebuchadnezzar to repent, though he doesn't use that word. He needs to repent, not in the sense of feeling sorry or saying he's sorry (though those reactions won't do any harm) but in the sense of changing the way he acts—specifically, how he exercises his leadership. Daniel then makes explicit that the judgment portrayed in the dream isn't inevitable.

If Nebuchadnezzar doesn't change, and God does act in judgment, it would seem likely to follow that Nebuchadnezzar will be disciplined until he has learned his lesson and has changed. The warning about judgment pointed in another direction. God had announced that it would be terrible and long-lasting, but not fatal or permanent. The deep roots of the tree will be left in the ground. The judgment will last "seven periods"—how long the expression "seven periods" implies isn't clear, but the sevenfold-ness means it's a "perfect" time. It's a judgment, not a discipline. It's designed to affirm publicly what's right and to condemn publicly what's wrong. In itself it's not a way of persuading Nebuchadnezzar to reform. It's designed to make clear that there's someone who rules the world, and it's not Nebuchadnezzar.

Yahweh doesn't seem to operate on the assumption that judgment changes people. Maybe it's unrealistic. When the **Judahites** were taken off into **exile**, Yahweh didn't wait until they had learned their lesson and then allow them to return. They were in the same state when they returned as when they went. Indeed, in Nebuchadnezzar's case, it's hard to see how he could have learned a lesson when he had apparently been

27

deprived of his regular human mental functioning. While punishment sometimes changes people, the Bible assumes that mercy and grace do a better job. Nebuchadnezzar is restored because God decides that enough is enough. He's put under judgment until he learns to acknowledge Yahweh. But it's the fact that Yahweh brings the judgment to an end that leads to his making that acknowledgment.

DANIEL 5:1–31

You've Been Weighed and Found Wanting

[1]King Belshazzar served a big dinner for his thousand important people, and in the presence of the thousand he was drinking wine. [2]Belshazzar said, when he tasted the wine, to bring the gold and silver vessels that Nebuchadnezzar his father had taken from the palace in Jerusalem so they could drink from them—the king, his important people, his queens, and his consorts. [3]The gold and silver vessels that had been taken from the palace in God's house in Jerusalem were brought in, and they drank from them—the king, his important people, his queens, and his consorts. [4]They drank wine and praised gods of gold and silver, bronze, iron, wood, and stone. [5]At that moment the fingers of a human hand appeared and wrote, over against the lamp stand, on the plaster of the wall of the king's palace. The king saw the palm of the hand that wrote. [6]The king—his face changed color. His thoughts alarmed him. His hip joints went loose and his knees knocked one against the other. [7]The king called forcefully to bring the chanters, Kaldeans, and exorcists. The king exclaimed to the experts of Babylon, "Anyone who can read this writing and tell me its meaning will wear the purple, and the gold chain on his neck, and will rule as Third in the realm."

[8]All the king's experts came, but they couldn't read the writing or make known its meaning to the king. [9]King Belshazzar became very alarmed, his face changed color further, and his important people were put in turmoil. [10]The queen—because

of the words of the king and his important people, she came into the drinking hall. The queen exclaimed, "Long live the king! Your thoughts shouldn't alarm you or your face change color. [11]There's a man in your realm in whom is the spirit of the holy gods. In your father's days, insight, ability, and expertise like the gods' expertise was found in him. King Nebuchadnezzar your father appointed him as chief of the diviners, chanters, Kaldeans, and exorcists—your father as king. [12]Since a remarkable spirit, knowledge, and ability—interpreting dreams, explaining puzzles, and resolving enigmas—was found in him, in Daniel whom the king named Belteshazzar, Daniel should now be called. He'll relate the meaning."

[13]Daniel was brought before the king. The king exclaimed to Daniel, "You're Daniel, one of the exiles from Judah that my father as king brought from Judah. [14]I've heard about you, that the spirit of the gods is in you, and insight, ability, and remarkable expertise is found in you. [15]The experts (the chanters) have now been brought before me so they might read this writing and make its meaning known to me, but they couldn't relate the words' meaning. [16]I myself have heard about you, that you can explain meanings and resolve enigmas. If you can now read the writing and make known its meaning to me, you'll wear the purple and the gold chain on your neck, and rule as Third in the realm."

[17]Daniel exclaimed before the king, "Your gifts can be for you; give your gifts to someone else. Nevertheless I'll read the writing for Your Majesty and make known the meaning to him. [18]You, Your Majesty—God on High gave kingship, greatness, majesty, and honor to Nebuchadnezzar, your father. [19]Because of the greatness given him, all peoples, nations, and languages trembled and feared before him. Whomever he wished, he killed, and whomever he wished, he kept alive. Whomever he wished, he elevated, and whomever he wished, he put down. [20]When his mind became elevated and his spirit arrogant, so that he became presumptuous, he was taken from his royal throne, and his honor was removed from him. [21]He was led away from human beings, and his mind was made like an animal, his dwelling with wild donkeys. They fed him grass

like oxen and his body was watered with the dew of the heavens, until he acknowledged that the God on High rules over human kingship and can set up over it whomever he wishes. [22]But you, his son, Belshazzar, have not humbled your mind because you knew all this [23]but have elevated yourself above the Lord of the Heavens. The vessels from his house have been brought before you, and you, your important people, your queens, and your consorts have drunk wine from them, and praised gods of silver and gold, bronze, iron, wood, and stone, that don't see, don't hear, and don't know. But the God who has your breath in his hand, and your entire way, you haven't glorified.

[24]"From his presence the palm of the hand was sent, and this writing inscribed. [25]This is the writing that was inscribed: Counted at a *mina*, a *shekel*, and two halves. [26]This is the words' meaning: 'A *mina*': God *counted out* the days of your kingship and handed it over. [27]'A *shekel*': you've been *weighed* on the scales and found deficient. [28]'A half': your kingship has been *broken in half* and given to Media and Persia." [29]Belshazzar commanded and they clothed Daniel with purple and with the gold chain on his neck and proclaimed concerning him that he would rule as Third in the realm. [30]That night Belshazzar the Kaldean king was killed, [31]and Darius the Mede acquired the kingship, as a man of sixty-two years.

The building where we live is showing its age and the entire plumbing system needs to be replaced. My wife, an architect by training, knows how important it is to take action soon, and she's anxious for the residents' association to agree to take action, but I tend to think, "Whatever." Our seminary president is retiring, and faculty and students are anxious about who'll take his place, but I tend to think, "Whatever." Indeed, revolutionary changes in higher education are also causing anxiety in the seminary, but I tend to think, "Whatever." On the other hand, I can get anxious about the future of the church where I'm priest in charge, and I need to take myself in hand over that anxiety.

Belshazzar looks like someone who needed to take more responsibility and resist the temptation to say, "Whatever." He was the last ruler before the **Medo-Persian** Empire took over the **Babylonian** Empire. Technically he was not king but a regent who ran affairs in Babylon after the last actual king, Nabonidus, left the capital a decade earlier, for reasons that are unclear. Belshazzar was also not literally the son of Nebuchadnezzar, though as Nebuchadnezzar's effective successor he could be described thus. The queen who plays a key role in the story is the queen mother, the wife of a previous king—often a politically influential person in a Middle Eastern court. The story may imply that she was Nebuchadnezzar's widow, who'd be in a position to give the advice that this queen gives.

Belshazzar was evidently having a good time as "king," along with his administration (and was ignoring the ordinary people whose needs he was supposed to make a priority). A state banquet led to action that will have seemed quite ordinary to the Babylonians. When an army wins a victory, it takes plunder; showing off the plunder on such occasions was a natural thing. But these vessels are no ordinary plunder. They came from the temple of the real God. (There's an irony that the word for *palace* and *temple* is the same word, so initially the idea was perhaps to use things from the royal palace in Jerusalem; only later does the story indicate that Belshazzar was using vessels from God's "palace".)

If the experts couldn't even read the writing on the wall (this story is where we get that saying), the reason may have been that the alphabet in some Middle Eastern languages uses only consonants (if I write on a whiteboard "th ct st n th mt," my students whose first language is English know it says "the cat sat on the mat," but other students have a harder time reading it). If the words had no context or didn't make a normal sentence, readers might well have made no sense of the bare consonants. But maybe they could tell that at one level the words sounded like a merchant's shout: "Counted at a *mina*, a *shekel*, and two halves" (*mina* and *shekel* are weights). It's Daniel's supernatural insight that enables him to see another way of reading the words (I point out to students that one could read those English consonants as "the coat set in the moat"). They declare God's judgment on Belshazzar. Daniel again speaks like a prophet in confronting the king with God's perspective on his reign.

As we noted in connection with Nebuchadnezzar's dream, the point about God's warnings isn't merely to declare what's bound to happen. It's to challenge people to change so they escape God's judgment. Belshazzar doesn't respond like the people of Nineveh, the superpower before the Babylonians, who received a similar message and repented. In effect, Belshazzar says "Whatever" in a situation where he needs to take responsibility. It's no coincidence that he loses his life that night. Is the implication that his own people slay him? What's the link with the transition from Babylonian rule to the rule of a Mede? Is there internal intrigue as the Persians advance toward Babylon? The story leaves those questions unanswered as it focuses on the portrayal of a king who pays the price for disdaining the true God and failing to respond to that God's warning, of the man who serves that God, and of the God who works out his will in political events.

DANIEL 6:1–28

On Standing Firm in Faith

[1]It seemed good to Darius to appoint over his realm 120 satraps who'd be spread through the realm, [2]and over them three supervisors, of whom Daniel was one, to whom these satraps would give report, and the king would not be troubled. [3]This man Daniel distinguished himself above the other supervisors and satraps because of the remarkable spirit in him, and the king was inclined to appoint him over the entire realm. [4]The

supervisors and satraps were seeking to find some fault on Daniel's part in the realm's affairs, but they couldn't find any fault or corruption because he was trustworthy; no negligence or corruption could be found against him. [5]Those men said, "We shall not find any fault in this Daniel unless we find it regarding his God's law."

[6]These supervisors and satraps mustered to see the king and said to him: "Long live King Darius! [7]All the supervisors of the realm, the governors, satraps, advisers, and commissioners have taken counsel about the setting up of a royal decree and the enforcing of an injunction that anyone who makes a petition of any god or human being for thirty days, except of you, Your Majesty, will be thrown into the lion pit. [8]Your Majesty, issue the injunction now and sign the document, so that it may definitely not be changed, as a law of Media and Persia, which won't pass away."

[9]So King Darius signed the document and the injunction. [10]When Daniel got to know that the document had been signed, he went to his house with its windows open on its top, facing Jerusalem, and three times a day he'd get down on his knees and pray and give thanks before his God, because he had been doing so before this. [11]Those men mustered and found Daniel petitioning and praying for grace before his God. [12]They approached the king and spoke before him about the royal injunction: "Didn't you sign an injunction that anyone who petitions any god or human being for thirty days except you, Your Majesty, will be thrown into the lion pit?" The king exclaimed, "The thing stands firm, as a law of Media and Persia, which won't pass away." [13]They exclaimed before the king, "Daniel, one of the exiles from Judah, has not taken notice of you, Your Majesty, or of the injunction that you signed. Three times a day he makes his petition." [14]When the king heard the thing, he was very displeased with himself, and regarding Daniel he applied his mind to delivering him. Until sundown he was working on rescuing him. [15]Those men mustered and said to the king, "Your Majesty, acknowledge that it is a law of Media and Persia that any injunction or decree that the king sets up cannot be changed." [16]The king

said they should bring Daniel and throw him into the lion pit. The king exclaimed to Daniel, "Your God whom you revere continually must deliver you." [17]A stone was brought and put on the mouth of the pit, and the king sealed it with his signet and with the signets of his important people, so that the intention regarding Daniel might not be changed.

[18]The king went off to his palace. He spent the night without food; nothing was brought before him. Sleep eluded him. [19]In the morning, the king got up at first light and went off in haste to the lion pit. [20]As he drew near to the pit, he cried in an anguished voice to Daniel. The king exclaimed, "Daniel, servant of the living God, your God whom you revere continually—could he deliver you from the lions?" [21]Daniel spoke with the king: "Long live the king! [22]God sent his aide to shut the lions' mouth. They haven't injured me, because before him innocence was found in me—and also before you, Your Majesty, I've done no injury." [23]The king was very glad about him, and said to bring Daniel up out of the pit. So Daniel was brought up out of the pit. No injury was found in him, because he had trusted in his God. [24]The king said to bring those men who had attacked Daniel and throw them into the lion pit, them, their children, and their wives. They hadn't reached the ground in the pit before the lions overpowered them and crushed all their bones.

[25]King Darius wrote to all peoples, nations, and tongues that live in the entire earth: "May your well-being abound! [26]From me notice is given that in every domain of my realm, people must tremble and fear before Daniel's God, because he's the living God and he stands forever. His reign is one that will experience no injury, his rule will continue to the end. [27]He delivers and rescues and does signs and wonders in the heavens and in the earth. He rescued Daniel from the hand of the lions."

[28]So this Daniel flourished during the reign of Darius and during the reign of Cyrus the Persian.

By a couple of years, I escaped conscription into "National Service," the requirement in Britain between 1945 and 1963 to serve in the military for two years when you turned eighteen. A friend of mine who is a bit older than me didn't escape. For these two years he shared sleeping quarters with twenty or more other young men, without any privacy, and he told me (a bit shamefacedly) how the only way he felt able to read the Bible and pray each day was to go and sit in the bathroom for longer than was strictly necessary.

Daniel could have prayed in privacy, but chose not to. As there's a link between the two stories about God issuing a warning to a **Babylonian** king, Daniel explaining it, and the warning coming true (Daniel 4–5), so there's a link between the stories on either side about **Judahites** having to defy the king, the king sentencing them to execution, and God miraculously rescuing them (we'll next find that there's a link between the visions on either side in chapters 2 and 7; each describes a sequence of four regimes and then the establishing of God's rule). The lion pit story also resembles the furnace story in being funny, larger than life, and designed to make fun of the Judahites' overlords. These facts suggest that it doesn't ask us to take it as a historical story, which fits with there being no references outside the Bible to "Darius the Mede" ruling Babylon. As with chapter 3, its being more like fiction than history doesn't detract from its point, because that point isn't that God always rescues people; it doesn't make this claim, and we know from experience that it's not so.

The story is realistic about the nature of politics. There's jealousy among the politicians and wheeling and dealing. Anyone who does well has to be wary of being stabbed in the back. A king or president or prime minister has to be wary of being manipulated by the people who are supposed to be his servants, but somehow the person who gets himself into that supreme position often isn't as bright as his subordinates, so he falls for manipulation. The ministers' edict looks stupid, but it's the only way to catch Daniel out. The higher ordinary people get, the more careful they have to be to avoid giving hostages to fortune. If there's anything shady in their life, people will uncover it. It's quite a compliment to Daniel that they couldn't find anything, except that he thought God was too important.

The nature of Daniel's action is the obverse of that of the three young men. The pressure there was to bow down to something other than God and thus do something that an **Israelite** couldn't do. The pressure here is not to bow down to the One to whom you must bow down and thus not do something that an Israelite must do. The Jerusalem temple was the place where **Yahweh** had undertaken to live and be there to hear Israel's prayers. Solomon's prayer at the temple dedication envisages Israelites even being taken off into **exile** and praying toward the country and the temple, and asks Yahweh to listen to such prayers. Daniel presupposes that Yahweh will do so.

Old Testament worship is designed to glorify God, and so it's offered in public. In a culture where worship is honored and respected, there's obviously a risk that you're doing it just for the sake of other people seeing you and not because you're serious. For Israelites in a foreign country, the danger is the opposite. The temptation is to hide. Daniel doesn't fall for the temptation. The "law" of Daniel's God doesn't exactly require him to pray in public, but he knows that he must continue to pray as he prayed before, if he isn't to fail to honor God properly and give the impression that he honors the king more than God. The **Torah** prescribes the offering of sacrifices twice a day, at dawn and dusk, and these sacrifices would be accompanied by prayer; most Israelites wouldn't be present for the sacrifices, but they could naturally make those times for prayer. Praying *three* times a day shows how Daniel is committed beyond anything you could call a legal requirement.

Another link with the story in chapter 3 is that questions are raised by the king's actions in the later scenes of the story, executing the entire leadership of the empire and their families, and making it a legal requirement to acknowledge Israel's God, as by his gullibility in the opening scenes. One implication is that it's unwise to rely on the king, whether he's for you or against you at a particular moment. If he's against you, the story's readers would know that not everyone who follows Daniel's example escapes the consequences, but it urges them to do so nevertheless, and it raises the possibility that God may honor their doing so.

DANIEL 7:1–28

The One Who Speaks Great Things Is Silenced

[1]In the first year of Belshazzar, king of Babylon, Daniel had a dream, visions that came into his head in bed. He wrote the dream down. The beginning of the account: [2]Daniel exclaimed, I looked in my vision during the night, and there—the four winds of the heavens stirring up the Great Sea, [3]and four huge animals coming up out of the sea, each different from the others. [4]The first was like a lion but it had an eagle's wings. I looked as its wings were plucked off and it was lifted up from the ground and set on its feet like a human being, and a human mind was given to it. [5]And there—another, second animal. It was like a bear, but it was lifted up on one side, with three ribs in its mouth, between its teeth. They said this to it: "Get up, eat lots of meat!" [6]After that, I looked, and there— another, like a leopard, but it had four bird's wings on its back. The animal had four heads, and authority was given it. [7]After that, I looked in my night visions and there—a fourth animal, fearsome, terrifying, and extremely powerful. It had huge iron teeth, devouring, crushing, and trampling what was left with its feet. It was different from all the animals that were before it. It had ten horns. [8]I looked at the horns, and there— another small horn came up among them, and three of the first horns were uprooted before it. And there—something like human eyes in this horn, and a mouth speaking great things. [9]I looked as

thrones were set in place
and someone advanced in years sat down.
His clothing was like white snow,
the hair of his head like lamb's wool.
His throne was flashes of flame,
his rings a blazing flame.
10 A river of flame was flowing,
coming out from before him.
A thousand thousands ministered to him,
a myriad myriads stood in attendance before him.
The court sat,
and books were opened.

[11]I looked from the sound of the great things that the horn was speaking. I looked as the animal was killed. Its body was destroyed and given to the burning fire. [12]The rest of the animals: their authority was taken away, but an extension of their lives was given to them for a set time. [13]I looked in my night visions, and there—

with the clouds in the heavens
someone like a human being came.
He reached the one advanced in years
and was presented before him.
14 To him was given authority, honor, and kingship;
all peoples, nations, and languages are to revere him.
His authority is an authority that lasts forever,
that won't pass away,
his kingship one that won't be destroyed.

[15]I (Daniel) was disturbed in my spirit within me at this. The visions that came into my head alarmed me. [16]I approached one of those standing in attendance and asked him the truth about all this. He told me and made known the meaning of the thing. [17]These huge animals, of which there were four: four kings will arise from the earth, [18]but the holy ones on high will acquire the kingship. They'll take hold of the kingship forever, forever and ever. [19]I wanted the truth about the fourth animal

which was different from all of them (extremely fearsome, its iron teeth, bronze claws), devouring, crushing, and trampling what was left with its feet, [20]and about the ten horns that were on its head, and the one that came up and three fell before it—and that horn had eyes and a mouth speaking great things, and its appearance was bigger than its companions. [21]I looked, and that horn made war with the holy ones and overcame them, [22]until the one advanced in years came and judgment was given for the holy ones on high, and the time arrived and the holy ones took hold of the kingship.

[23]He said this: "The fourth animal—there'll be a fourth regime in the earth that will be different from all the regimes. It will devour the entire earth, tread it down, and crush it. [24]The ten horns—from that regime ten kings will arise. After them another will arise. He'll be different from those before him. He'll bring low three kings. [25]He'll say things against the One on High and oppress the holy ones on high. He'll try to change times and a law. They'll be given into his hand for a period, periods, and half a period. [26]But the court will sit and his authority will be taken away, to be destroyed and wiped out permanently. [27]The kingship, authority, and greatness of the regimes under the entire heavens will be given to the people of the holy ones on high. Its kingship will be a kingship lasting forever. Every authority will revere and bow down to it."

[28]That is the end of the account. I Daniel—my thoughts were very alarming to me. My face changed color. I kept the thing in my mind.

A few months ago my wife and I went around the seven cities in western Turkey to whose churches John wrote in the book of Revelation. They're huge Roman cities that are mostly now simply ruins. There are modern cities on the sites of two or three, but in none of the seven is there much of a Christian presence. You wake up not to church bells but to the call of the minaret. John had warned most of these churches of their need to pull themselves together if they were not to meet such a fate, though he gave no such message to the church in

Philadelphia. Its remains are scattered about the modern city of Alasehir. The last Christians there were moved to Athens after the First World War in the course of a population exchange between Turkey and Greece.

In Daniel, the expression "the people of the holy ones on high" is a term to describe the "saints," the people of God. In cities such as Alasehir, the saints have ended up not counting for much. In the city of Jerusalem, to which Daniel's vision relates, it looked as if the saints were going the same way, but the vision promises that this dynamic will be reversed.

The location of the people on whom Daniel focuses has thus changed, though the pressure on them is similar. The vision backtracks into the time of Belshazzar and thus into the time of the **Babylonian** Empire. It covers the sequence of empires that unfold over four centuries, from the middle of the sixth to the middle of the second, beginning with Babylon and ending with **Greece**. The original Greek animal was Alexander the Great, who conquered the Middle East in the 330s but died in 323 when he was still only thirty-two. His empire broke up and much of it came under the rule of one or other of his generals.

In the 160s, **Judah** was under the control of one of these domains, based in Syria. The **Seleucid** king was now Antiochus IV, who called himself Epiphanes; the title suggested he was a manifestation of God. The Judahites were unlikely to appreciate this self-designation, which was perhaps the greatest of the great things that emerged from his mouth. Truly he spoke things against the God who is actually the One on High. Conversely, the Judahites didn't endear themselves to him by their political maneuverings—wheeling and dealing about who was to be high priest interwove with playing the Syrians to the north against the **Egyptians** to the south. The Judahites' seditiousness eventually led Antiochus to impose direct rule. He "made war with the holy ones and overcame them" and banned worship in accordance with the **Torah**.

The vision promises one of those moments when God intervenes. Whereas the account of the vision uses prose to describe the nasty animals symbolizing the four human empires, at its climax it moves to poetry to describe a scene in God's heavenly court. God is pictured as an august senior figure. Another human figure is presented to him and is given supreme **authority** in the place of the four empires. The Aramaic expression for "someone like a human being" is literally "one like a son of man"; in Aramaic or Hebrew, an expression such as "son of man" is a poetic way of saying "human being." Later Jewish thinking pictured this "human being" or "son of man" as an actual individual, which is part of the background to the use of the expression "Son of Man" in the Gospels. But the explanation of the vision makes clear that here the person like a human being stands for "the people of the holy ones on high." God has decided for this people and not for Antiochus's empire, symbolized by the small horn.

Antiochus stayed in control of Jerusalem for a little over three years, from 167 to 164, but then the Judahites rebelled. You wouldn't have bet on the Judahites, but they won. Antiochus's forces fled. Succeeding visions will give us more detail on these events.

For the first time in six centuries, Judah was free, and it stayed free until the Romans arrived a century later. You couldn't say that the Judahites ruled the whole world or that their freedom lasted forever. The vision's fulfillment worked in the way fulfillment in the Bible commonly does. The fulfillment doesn't give people everything—the ultimate fulfillment will involve the ultimate implementing of God's final purpose. It does give them something, and something big, something that is a first installment of that final fulfillment. It invites us to look at moments when things don't work out, as they didn't for the churches in Turkey, in light of such moments when they do work out.

41

DANIEL 8:1–27

God's Overview and the Man Who Goes Too Far

¹In the third year of the reign of King Belshazzar, a vision appeared to me (me, Daniel), after the one that appeared to me earlier. ²I looked in the vision (when I saw it, I was in Susa, the fortress city in Elam Province)—I looked in the vision and I was at the Ulay Gate. ³I raised my eyes and looked, and there—a ram standing in front of the gate. It had two horns. The horns were high, but the one was higher than the other. The high one came up later. ⁴I looked at the ram charging west and north and south. No animals could stand before it. There was no one could rescue from its hand. It acted according to its wishes and grew great. ⁵As I was seeking to understand it, there—a male goat coming from the west across the face of the entire earth, without touching the ground. The goat, a conspicuous horn between its eyes, ⁶came to the ram that possessed two horns, which I had seen standing in front of the gate, and ran at it in mighty fury. ⁷I looked at it reaching the ram. It raged at it, hit the ram, and broke its two horns. The ram didn't have the strength to stand before it. [The goat] threw it to the earth and trampled it. There was no one could rescue the ram from its power. ⁸The male goat grew very great, but just when it had become so strong, the big horn broke. Four conspicuous ones came up in its place, toward the four winds in the heavens. ⁹From one of them came up a small horn. It grew abundantly toward the south and toward the east and toward the fairest. ¹⁰It grew as far as the army of the heavens, and made some of the army, some of the stars, fall to earth, and it trampled them. ¹¹It grew as far as the army commander. By it the regular offering was removed and his sacred place and army were overthrown. ¹²It will be set over the regular offering in rebellion; it will throw truthfulness to the ground. It will act and succeed.

¹³I heard a holy one speaking, and a holy being said to the one who was speaking, "How long will the vision be—the regular offering and the desolating rebellion, the giving of both the sacred [place] and the army to trampling?" ¹⁴He said

to me, "For 2,300 evenings and mornings, but the sacred [place] will emerge in the right." [15]While I (Daniel) was looking at the vision and seeking some understanding, there—standing in front of me was a human-like person, [16]and I heard a human voice in the middle of Ulay. It called, "Gabriel, help this man understand the vision." [17]He came near where I was standing. When he came, I was overwhelmed and fell on my face. He said to me, "Understand, young man, that the vision relates to the time of the end." [18]When he spoke with me, I fell into a trance, on the face of the ground, but he touched me and stood me up where I had been standing. [19]He said, "Here am I; I'm going to make known to you what will happen at the conclusion of the wrath, because it relates to the time appointed for the end.

[20]"The ram that you saw possessing two horns is the kings of Media and Persia. [21]The buck (the he-goat) is the king of Greece. The big horn between its eyes—that is the first king. [22]The one that broke and four came up in its place: four regimes will arise from a nation, but not with its power. [23]At the conclusion of their reign, when the rebels reach full measure, a king will arise fierce of face and understanding enigmas. [24]His strength will be mighty, but without his [predecessor's] strength—but he'll perform astounding acts of devastation and succeed when he acts. He'll devastate the mighty, and a people of holy ones, [25]with his skill. He'll succeed in deceit with his power. With his mind he'll grow great. With ease he'll devastate many, and stand against the commander-in-chief. But without being touched he'll break.

[26]"The vision of evening and morning: what has been said is the truth. You, seal the vision, because it relates to many days."

[27]I (Daniel) fell ill for some days, but got up and performed the king's business. But I was overcome by the vision and there was no one could help me understand it.

I mentioned to my wife the discovery about Philadelphia in Turkey to which I referred in connection with Daniel 7, and we talked about the unlikelihood that the church there could claim to have walked through the open door that Revelation 2 said God had set in front of it, but then she reflected on the way the displacement of the Christians there likely contributed to the stability of Turkey over the past century—as the displacement of the Muslims in Greece likely contributed to the stability of Greece. In other words, their suffering bore fruit. They paid a price for their people. Sometimes God brings good out of bad, though this doesn't stop the bad being painful, or wrong, even years afterwards.

Something similar is true about the community in Jerusalem whose destiny this further vision describes. If we were not sure what were the events spoken of in the vision in chapter 7 (because it named no names), then this further vision removes any doubt. Once again Daniel functions not only as interpreter of a king's dreams and visions but as someone who receives dreams and visions that need interpreting for him by members of God's staff—here Gabriel appears for the first time in the Bible, as one of God's supernatural aides.

Once again the vision starts from the time when the Babylonians are in control of the Middle East, then moves on to the time of the Medes and Persians. Under King Cyrus, Persia had gained the upper hand over and had absorbed the former Median Empire, so the vision can think of the Medo-Persian Empire as resembling a ram with two horns of which the later one grew bigger than the earlier one. The goat is then the Greek Empire, with Alexander its spectacular horn that broke. The four horns that grew in its place suggest the carving up of Alexander's empire. The biggest part was controlled by Alexander's general Seleucus, covering vast territory to the north and east of Judah. One of its rulers is Antiochus IV Epiphanes, the small horn. The vision's particular concern is with the way the Seleucid Empire grew toward "the fairest"— that is, Judah itself.

The direct object of Antiochus's aggression is the worship offered in Jerusalem. The heart of that worship is the "regular offering" made at sunrise and sunset each day (two of the times when Daniel would pray). He banned that regular worship and replaced it with worship that suited the religion of his garrison, the kind of worship the rest of the empire offered. The vision pictures proper worship being suspended for 2,300 mornings and evenings—that is, 1,150 days, or rather more than three years, a similar time to the three and one half periods of the preceding vision, and about the time Antiochus's action lasted.

Antiochus's acts also have a costly effect on the people who exercise leadership in Jerusalem, which means the priests. But by attacking these and promoting himself as Epiphanes, God Manifest, Antiochus is also assailing the God who is worshiped there, the one whom these leaders serve. The heavenly army of which God is the commander-in-chief is the heavenly equivalent to the earthly "army" that serves in the temple and exercises leadership in the city (thus both the members of God's heavenly people and members of God's earthly people can be spoken of as "holy ones"). Antiochus's aggression means that some of this "army" lose their lives as a result of their faithfulness.

The vision has nothing to do with Daniel's own day. It relates to "the time appointed for the end." Old and New Testaments regularly speak of a great crisis or deliverance as "the end" or "the last days." It's as if the final judgment or the final implementation of God's purpose is happening. Indeed, it *is* happening, though each time it transpires that life goes on and history goes on. When Antiochus suspended proper worship in Jerusalem, it was as if the End had arrived. It was a period of wrath. The Old Testament sometimes uses that language to denote not that God is being wrathful, but that these are the kind of events that feel like the result of someone being wrathful. If Antiochus had been able to maintain that suspension of proper worship, it would have been the End. But Jerusalem's spectacular deliverance from Antiochus stopped this crisis being the End and turned it into an occasion that brought freedom.

It would be tempting for people in Jerusalem to think that history was out of God's control, as it can be for us who read Daniel. The vision assures them that it is not so. The Babylonians, the Medes, the Persians, the Greeks, the Seleucids: for a while they look so impressive. But God has an overview in relation to them. God is sometimes actively involved in their rise and fall, sometimes achieving things through them, sometimes simply letting them go their way, but always having that overview and prepared to step in when they go too far and need to be brought to heel.

DANIEL 9:1–27

The Seventy Sevens

[1]In the first year of Darius son of Ahasuerus, of Median birth, who was made king over the realm of the Kaldeans—[2]in the first year of his reign, I (Daniel) was seeking to understand in the scriptures the number of years that were (Yahweh's message to Jeremiah the prophet) to be fulfilled for Jerusalem's devastations, seventy years. [3]I set my face toward the Lord God, to make a plea and prayers for grace with fasting, sackcloth, and ash. [4]I pleaded with Yahweh my God and made confession: "Oh, Lord, great and awe-inspiring God, who keeps covenant and commitment to people who give themselves to him and keep his commands: [5]we committed offenses, we were wayward, we were faithless, we rebelled, we turned aside from your commands and your decisions. [6]We didn't listen to your servants the prophets who spoke in your name to our kings, our officials, and our ancestors, and to all the country's people. [7]To you, Lord, belongs the right; to us, shame of face this very day, Judah's people, Jerusalem's residents, and all Israel, near and far, in all the countries where you drove them because of their trespass that they committed against you. [8]Yahweh, to us belongs shame of face, to our kings, our officials,

and our ancestors, who offended against you. ⁹To the Lord our God belong compassion and acts of pardon, because we rebelled against him ¹⁰and didn't listen to the voice of Yahweh our God by walking according to his teachings that he set before us by the hand of his servants the prophets. ¹¹All Israel transgressed your teaching and turned aside so as not to listen to your voice. The curse and oath that was written in the teaching of Moses, God's servant, overwhelmed us. Because we offended against him, ¹²he confirmed his word that he spoke against us and against our leaders who led us, by bringing great evil upon us, which hasn't been done under the entire heavens as it has been done in Jerusalem. ¹³As it is written in Moses' Teaching, all this evil came upon us. We didn't supplicate Yahweh our God by turning from our waywardness and gaining insight through your truthfulness, ¹⁴so Yahweh kept this evil ready and brought it on us, because Yahweh our God was in the right in all his actions that he undertook, and we didn't listen to his voice.

¹⁵"But now, Lord our God, who took your people out of the country of Egypt with a strong hand and made yourself a name this very day, we committed offenses, we were faithless. ¹⁶Lord, in accordance with all your faithfulness, oh may your anger and wrath turn back from your city, Jerusalem, your sacred mountain, because through our offenses and our ancestors' wayward acts, Jerusalem and your people became an object of scorn to all the people around us. ¹⁷So now, listen, our God, to your servant's plea and his prayers for grace, and shine your face on your desolate sanctuary, for the Lord's sake. ¹⁸Bend your ear, my God, and listen, open your eyes and look at our desolations and at the city over which your name is called, because it's not on the basis of our faithful acts that we are making our prayers for grace fall before you, but on the basis of your abundant compassion. ¹⁹Lord, listen! Lord, pardon! Lord, pay attention and act, and don't delay, for your sake, my God, because your name is called over your city and over your people."

²⁰I was still speaking, pleading, confessing my offenses and the offenses of my people, Israel, and making my prayers for

grace fall before Yahweh my God concerning my God's sacred mountain—[21]I was still speaking with my plea when Gabriel, the person whom I saw in the vision I had before, tired and weary, approached me at the time of the evening offering. [22]He enabled me to understand and he spoke with me: "Daniel, I've now come out to give you insight in understanding. [23]At the beginning of your prayers for grace a message went out, and I myself have come to relate it, because you're highly regarded. So understand the message and gain understanding into the vision.

[24]"Seventy sevens have been assigned for your people and for your sacred city to bring the rebellion to an end, to do away with offenses, to wipe away waywardness, to bring lasting faithfulness, to seal vision and prophet, and to anoint a most sacred [place]. [25]You are to acknowledge and perceive: from the issuing of a word for restoring and building up Jerusalem to an anointed, a leader, there are seven sevens. For sixty-two sevens it will again be built up, square and moat. But in the pressure of the times, [26]after the sixty-two sevens, an anointed will be cut off, and will have neither the city nor the sacred [place]. A leader to come will devastate the people and its end will come by a flood. Until the end of battle, devastations are determined. [27]A covenant will prevail for many people for one seven. For half the seven he'll suspend sacrifice and offering. Upon a wing will be a great abomination, desolating, until a conclusion and something decreed overwhelms the desolator."

My wife Kathleen's investigations into her family history revealed not only that some of her sixteenth-century forebears were transported from Scotland for fomenting rebellion against the Crown but that one of her eighteenth-century ancestors was a slave-owner in the United States; she has seen images of the will in which he bequeaths each of his slaves to some new owner. Coming to the United States also made me as a Brit face up to my share in responsibility for Britain's involvement in the slave trade, at least in the sense that my ordinary British family had indirectly profited from the slave trade. We are not just private individuals. We are bound up in the web of life with our ancestors.

Daniel's prayer recognizes that reality. It starts from warnings in Jeremiah 25 and 29 that the **Judahites' exile** wasn't going to end quickly, as other prophets promised. It would last seventy years, long enough to mean that virtually no one listening to Jeremiah would still be alive. The point about the figure wasn't to designate a precise time (seventy, not sixty-nine or seventy-one) but to signify something like a lifetime. People needed to accept that they would not be alive when the exile ended.

This chapter presupposes that seventy years have passed, or more or less passed. Yet once again the focus of Daniel's message lies not with the situation of people in **Babylon** in his own time but with the situation of people in Jerusalem in the 160s BC. In a literal or geographical sense the exile is long over. People have been free to return to Jerusalem for centuries, and have been doing so. In another sense the situation is worse. The community has never been under greater pressure to abandon its commitment to **Yahweh** and to the teaching that Yahweh gave through Moses. So what's happened to that declaration that exile would last seventy years?

Daniel's prayer recognizes at length that in this connection the community in Daniel's day or in the 160s can only cast itself on God's mercy. Even if it can claim to be committed to Yahweh's way, it is one with a community that has not been faithful over the years. As it shares in the privileges of belonging to its community, it can't avoid sharing in the consequences of that faithlessness, of which Moses' Teaching in the **Torah** warned when it spoke of Yahweh's replacing blessing by calamity. Even someone such as Daniel who stands out for his faithfulness makes that assumption.

Alongside accepting a share in responsibility for what was wrong, the only hope lies in casting oneself on who God is.

Daniel appeals to God's compassion, to God's power to pardon, God's **faithfulness**, and God's own name. God is making himself look stupid by allowing Jerusalem to stay in its desolate state and his sanctuary in its defiled state, in Daniel's day or in the time of Antiochus. On that basis, even while acknowledging the community's faithlessness, the prayer can press God quite hard: "Pay attention, act, don't delay!"

The answer comes in a revelation that reworks Jeremiah's declaration. Yes, Jerusalem's affliction has lasted more like seventy sevens than seventy, but there's still a limit set to it by God, and that limit is about to be reached. There are various ways of understanding Gabriel's revelation; here is one possibility. The first seven sevens begin from the time when Jeremiah was prophesying about the destruction and restoration of Jerusalem in the 590s and 580s and go on to the end of the exile. The anointed will then be either King Cyrus (Isaiah 45 calls him Yahweh's anointed) or one of the Judahite leaders involved in the city's restoration, the Davidic governor Zerubbabel, or the high priest Joshua. The figures are again not designed to indicate exact numbers, though it was about forty-nine years from Jerusalem's fall to Babylon's fall and the beginning of Jerusalem's restoration. Then there were (roughly!) sixty-two sevens from that time to the crisis in Jerusalem in the 160s, a period during which Jerusalem was repopulated and rebuilt. But in the seventieth seven the city is in the midst of crisis and suffering. An anointed (that is, a high priest), Onias III, was deposed, and was killed in 171, which marks the beginning of this last seven. The faithful have lost power over the city and the temple. A false covenant made by other people has given them control in the city. Halfway through the final seven, in 167, regular temple worship is stopped and a pagan abomination is erected on the temple altar (which has wing-like top corners, usually referred to as its horns). God's promise is that the seventy sevens are thus more or less over. Disaster will overwhelm Antiochus; as it did. Jeremiah's prophetic vision (as reworked by Gabriel) will be fulfilled, and the sanctuary will be anointed—that is, cleansed and rededicated.

DANIEL 10:1–11:4

On Earth as It Is in the Heavens

[1]In the third year of Cyrus, king of Persia, a message revealed itself to Daniel who was called Belteshazzar. The message was true and [concerned] a great war. He understood the message; he had understanding through the vision.

[2]In those days I (Daniel) was mourning for a period of three weeks. [3]I ate no food held in high regard; meat and wine didn't come into my mouth. I didn't put on makeup at all until the completion of the period of three weeks. [4]Then on the twenty-fourth day of the first month I was on the bank of the Great River, the Tigris. [5]I raised my eyes and looked, and there—a man clothed in linen, his waist belted with pure gold, [6]his body like topaz, his face like the brightness of lightning, his eyes like fiery torches, his arms and feet like the gleam of polished bronze, and the sound of his words like the sound of thunder. [7]I (Daniel) alone saw this sight. The people who were with me didn't see the sight, yet a great terror fell on them and they fled into hiding. [8]So I remained alone. I looked at this great sight. No strength remained in me. My vigor turned to breakdown in me. I didn't retain any strength. [9]I heard the sound of his words, but when I heard the sound of his words, I fell into a trance onto my face, with my face to the ground. [10]But there—a hand touched me and shook me onto my knees and the palms of my hands. [11]He said to me, "Daniel, man held in high regard, understand the words that I'm going to speak to you. Stand up in your place, because I've now been sent to you." When he spoke this message with me, I stood up, trembling. [12]He said to me, "Don't be afraid, Daniel, because from the first day that you set your mind to understand and humble yourself before God, your words were heard. I've come because of your words. [13]The leader of the kingdom of Persia

was standing in front of me for twenty-one days, but there—Michael, one of the supreme leaders, came to help me. So I had remained there with the kings of Persia, [14]but I've come to enable you to understand what will happen to your people at the end of the time, because there's yet a vision for that time."

[15]While he spoke with me in accordance with these words, I put my face to the ground and kept silence. [16]But there—someone with the likeness of a human being touched my lips, and I opened my mouth and spoke to the one standing in front of me: "My lord, because of the sight my convulsions have overthrown me. No strength has remained in me. [17]How can this servant of my lord speak with this my lord when I—no strength now stays in me. No breath's left in me." [18]The one with a human appearance touched me again and encouraged me. [19]He said, "Don't be afraid, man held in high regard, things will be well for you. Courage, courage." When he had spoken with me I took courage and said, "My lord may speak, because you've encouraged me."

[20]He said, "Do you know why I've come to you? Now I shall return to do battle with the leader of Persia. When I go off, there—the leader of Greece is going to come. [21]Nevertheless, I shall relate to you what's inscribed in a truthful document. No one is strengthening me against these except Michael, your [people's] leader. [11:1]But I—in the first year of Darius the Mede, my place was to strengthen and fortify him. [2]Now I shall tell you some truth. There—three kings more are going to arise for Persia, and a fourth will possess great wealth, more than anyone. In accordance with the strength he gets through his wealth, he'll stir up everyone against the kingdom of Greece. [3]But a warrior king will arise, rule a great dominion, and act in accordance with his will. [4]But as soon as he arises, his kingdom will break and scatter to the four winds of the heavens, and not to his posterity nor in accordance with the dominion that he ruled, because his kingdom will uproot and belong to other people besides these."

At a Mardi Gras event last night in a local restaurant, the band's trumpet player asked whether anyone knew the significance of

"Fat Tuesday," the literal translation often used in the United States. Of the guests who claimed to know, I was the one who got called on to explain that the next day would be Ash Wednesday, when we begin six weeks of discipline as we prepare for Easter. So Fat Tuesday is the day for eating up rich food before the Lenten fast begins. Its everyday name in Britain is Pancake Day; it was the one day in the year when my mother would make pancakes. Its formal name is Shrove Tuesday, because people used to be shriven by confession and absolution to prepare for their Lenten discipline.

There are various degrees of fasting, and Daniel's was evidently somewhat like that tradition of being disciplined about what we eat. It's an outward sign of being serious about submitting ourselves to God. You don't eat huge meals when you're focusing on something important. In addition, Daniel doesn't pay lots of attention to making himself look good. He has another focus. He doesn't tell us why he's doing so, but perhaps we are to infer that the pattern of the previous chapter continues into chapters 10–12 (it's the longest section of the book, divided into three chapters for convenience). He's seeking further revelation from God to enable him and other people to understand what God is doing with **Judah**. Why does history unfold in the way it does? Why do centuries pass and Judah continues to be under the control of big empires—**Babylon, Medo-Persia, Greece, the Seleucids**?

The Bible offers various insights into this question; the fact Gabriel identifies is that events on earth reflect things happening behind the scenes in the heavens. Things are more complicated there than we might have thought. When we pray, "Your kingdom come on earth as in heaven," we probably assume that God's kingdom is a reality in heaven and we want that same reality to be reflected on earth, but maybe the prayer recognizes that there are things that need sorting out in heaven as well as on earth. Gabriel implies so.

He speaks in terms of there being "leaders" in the heavens who represent each of the earthly nations. They are beings often referred to as "angels," the equivalent of presidential **aides** who act as God's agents implementing God's intentions in the world. Conflicts can develop among a president's staff, and so it is with God's staff. Their job includes representing their individual nations' interests, and they can get into conflict in this connection.

Gabriel isn't the leader who represents Judah—that's Michael. Gabriel's job is to bring revelations to people. He'd been delayed because of opposition from the leader representing Persia. Maybe the leader representing Persia doesn't want it announced that Persia's days are numbered, or wants to harm Judah. The background to the delay offers an insight into one reason why prayers don't get answered immediately; it reminds us that it's wiser to persist in fasting and praying than to give up straightaway.

Eventually the aide with the revelation reaches Daniel. The revelation again concerns "the end of the time," which the chapters make clear again denotes the crisis in Jerusalem in the 160s. So the revelation begins by going over familiar ground, though supplying further detail. There'll be more kings of Persia, and the Persians will try to extend their empire westward into Greece. King Xerxes invaded Greece and was defeated at Salamis in 480. Eventually the Greeks under Alexander the Great overwhelmed the Persians, but after his early death the Greek Empire broke up.

DANIEL 11:5–35

Confused? Yes, You Should Be. That's the Point

⁵"The southern king will be powerful, but one of his officers will overpower him and rule a greater dominion than his dominion. ⁶At the end of some years people will make an alliance, and the southern king's daughter will come to the northern king to

effect an agreement. But she won't retain the vigor of her strength, nor will his strength stand. She'll be given up, she and her escorts and the one who fathered her and the one who gave her power. In time [7]one of the shoots from her roots will stand in [the southern king's] place. He'll come against the army and come into the stronghold of the northern king. He'll act against them and be powerful. [8]Also their gods with their images, with their accoutrements held in high regard, gold and silver, he'll take captive to Egypt. [The southern king] for some years will stand back from the northern king. [9][The northern king] will come against the realm of the southern king but will return to his own country. [10]His sons will wage war and gather a horde of many forces. It will come repeatedly, and flood and sweep through, and again wage war as far as his stronghold. [11]The southern king will rage and go out and do battle with him (with the northern king). He'll raise a large horde, but the horde will be given into [the northern king's] hand. [12]The horde will be carried off, but [the southern king's] mind will become superior; he'll make myriads fall, but he won't prevail. [13]The northern king will again raise a horde, greater than the first. At the end of a period of years he'll come repeatedly with a great force and much equipment. [14]In those times many will stand against the southern king. Wild men among your people will raise themselves, to confirm a vision, but they'll collapse. [15]The northern king will come, throw up a ramp, and capture a fortified city. The southern forces won't stand, even his company of picked soldiers. There'll be no strength to stand. [16]The one who comes against him will act as he pleases, and there'll be no one standing before him. He'll stand in the fairest country, destruction in his hand. [17]He'll set his mind to come into control of [the southern king's] entire realm, but will make an agreement with him and give him a wife, in order to destroy it. But it won't stand, it won't come about for him. [18]He'll set his face toward foreign shores and capture many, but a commander will stop his insolence for him so that he won't be able to turn back his insolence for him. [19]He'll turn his face back to the strongholds in his own country. But he'll collapse and fall and disappear. [20]There will stand in his place one who sends around an oppressor of royal splendor. But in a few days he'll break, not by anger or battle.

[21]"There will stand in his place someone despised, to whom they've not given royal honor. He'll come with ease and gain power over the realm by empty words. [22]Overwhelming forces will be overwhelmed before him and will break; so too a covenant ruler. [23]Through the making of alliances with him he'll exercise deceit. He'll arise and become strong with a small group, [24]with ease. He'll come against the richest of provinces and do what his father and forefathers didn't do. Plunder, spoil, and wealth he'll scatter among people. He'll devise plans against fortresses, until a certain time. [25]He'll assert his strength and will against the southern king with a large force. The southern king will wage war with a large and very powerful force, but he won't stand, because people will devise plans against him. [26]People who eat his provisions will break him. His force will be overwhelmed. Many will fall slain. [27]The two of them, the kings, their mind set on evil, at one table will speak lies, but it won't succeed, because an end will yet wait for the set time. [28][The northern king] will return to his country with great wealth and with his mind against a sacred covenant. So he'll act and return to his country. [29]At the set time he'll come against the south again, but it won't be like the first and the second time. [30]Ships from Kittim will come against him and he'll cower and turn back. He'll rage against a sacred covenant and act. He'll return and pay heed to the people who abandon a sacred covenant. [31]Forces of his will stand and desecrate the sanctuary, the fortress. They'll remove the regular offering and set up the desolating abomination. [32]People who act faithlessly toward a covenant he'll make into apostates by empty words, but a people that acknowledge their God will be strong and will act. [33]The discerning ones among the people will help the multitude to understand, but they'll fall by sword, by fire, by captivity, and by becoming prey, for a time. [34]When they fall, they'll receive a little help, but many will join them with empty words. [35]Some of the discerning will fall, to refine them, to purify, and to cleanse, until the time of the end, because it will yet wait for the set time."

Yesterday I listened to a psychology professor describing the United States as a nation living with unresolved trauma as a result of going through a series of wars: the Revolutionary War, the Civil War, the two World Wars, Korea, Vietnam, and now Iraq and Afghanistan. My gloss is that the further tragedy of this history is that it has not led us anywhere. The First World War in particular was supposed to be "the war to end all wars," and it was a war of unprecedented brutality and horror. How could it be repeated? Yet the description "the war to end all wars" seems ironic in light of the further wars of the twentieth century, and there seems no prospect of the trend changing. Are things even getting worse, in the sense that at least we know who supposedly "won" the First World War and why they fought? Yet perhaps we even wonder about that assumption, in light of the cost.

Daniel's vision speaks of several centuries of conflict that sees no one getting anywhere; indeed, the trend is downward. The vision is a lightly disguised, easily decoded account of events, focusing on the period of **Seleucid** and **Egyptian** control of **Judah** from Alexander (336) to Antiochus (164). The "northern king" is the Seleucid monarch of the day; the "southern king" is the Egyptian monarch of the day. The Seleucid kings were Seleucus I–IV and Antiochus I–IV; the Egyptian kings were all called Ptolemy (Ptolemy I–VI). One effect of calling each succession of monarchs by the same name (northern/southern king) is to underscore the unified and pointless nature of the story. If you lost the plot while reading this section, you're getting the point; there's no plot.

In the first paragraph the vision moves briskly through the first five Ptolemies, the first four Seleucuses, and the first three Antiochuses, who ruled from the 320s to 181 and 175 respectively. It focuses on the ongoing conflict between the two empires and on the place of marriage alliances in seeking to extend power one way or the other. The two empires lay either side of Judah, so that their rivalry reverberated in

Jerusalem. The references to "wild men among your people" and to a vision point to political conflicts in Jerusalem and to the conviction on some people's part that they were fulfilling God's purpose, while the reference to "the fairest country" indicates a specific incursion into Judah.

The second paragraph focuses on Antiochus IV (175–163), who was prominent in Daniel 7–9. The deposed covenant ruler is the high priest Onias III, whom Antiochus replaces with his own nominee. His acts against a sacred covenant are the actions those preceding visions have referred to, which involved manipulating potential collaborators in Jerusalem to get them to act in a more faithless way than maybe they ever envisaged, in erecting in the temple expressions of Antiochus's pagan means of worship. The action backfires. People have to make a choice. There are leaders in the community who succeed in encouraging a good number of people to stand firm and who are prepared to pay with their lives for doing so, which has the effect of refining the community and revealing whose commitment is serious.

Why does God give Daniel this detailed account of events to take place in three or four centuries' time? Comparable Middle Eastern writings give what look at first sight like prophecies but are mostly written after the event. For the most part they're historical accounts transcribed into predictions. There are two reasons why someone might write in that way. Speaking of past events as if they had been predicted is a vivid way of indicating that they were within God's control. And the historical section adds authority and reinforces the actual prediction that comes at the end—which in this case comprises 11:36–12:13. It's not merely that the pretend prediction gives authority to the actual prediction. One feature of the coded history is that much of the "code" comes from earlier Scripture, such as the books of Isaiah and Ezekiel. The vision thus shows it can make sense of the sequence of historical events by looking at them in light of Scripture.

We don't know whether the original audience would recognize the convention of writing history as if it were prophecy. Obviously the author knew the convention and knew what he was doing when he gave us a vision of this kind. How might he have gained the vision? My guess is that he was familiar with the preceding stories about Daniel in chapters 1–6, and in particular with the vision of four regimes in chapter 2, and made them the first part of his book. Wondering how God was involved in the history that lay nearer his own day, he longed to encourage people whose faith was under pressure. God used that earlier vision in chapter 2 to inspire him with the revelations in the second half of the book. His sense of being inspired by Daniel's story and Daniel's earlier vision, and his sense that he was simply working out the implications of Daniel's vision, would explain why he attached his own visions (chapters 7–12) to Daniel's story and Daniel's vision (chapters 1–6). While Western authors usually like to have their names on the jackets of their books, attitudes in traditional societies are different!

The fulfillment of the actual prediction in the latter part of these visions, of Antiochus's fall and Jerusalem's deliverance and restoration, would be a key reason why the community recognized that they did come from God and that God had been watching over that pointless sequence of events.

DANIEL 11:36–12:13

The People Who Helped Others to Be Faithful Will Shine Like Stars

[36]"So the king will do as he pleases. He'll exalt himself and magnify himself above every god, and against the God of gods he'll speak awful things. He'll succeed until wrath is complete, because what has been decreed has been done. [37]To his ancestors' gods he won't pay heed, nor to the one women hold in high regard. He won't pay heed to any god, because over everything

he'll magnify himself. [38]A stronghold god he'll honor in his place. A god whom his ancestors didn't acknowledge he'll honor with gold and silver, with precious stones and things held in high regard. [39]He'll deal with the securest of fortresses with the help of an alien god. To those whom he regards he'll give great honor. He'll let them rule over the multitude and divide up land as payment.

[40]"At the time of the end the southern king will wrestle with him, but the northern king will storm against him with chariotry, horsemen, and many ships. He'll come against countries, sweep into them and pass through, [41]and come against the fairest country. Many will fall, but these will escape from his hand: Edom, Moab, and the best of the Ammonites. [42]He'll lay his hand on other countries, and the country of Egypt won't find escape. [43]He'll rule the treasuries of gold and silver and all the things held in high regard in Egypt, with the Libyans and Sudanese at his heel. [44]But reports will alarm him from the east and north and he'll go out in great fury to destroy and annihilate many. [45]He'll pitch his royal tents between the seas and the fairest sacred mountain. But he'll come to his end. There'll be no helper for him.

[12:1]"At that time Michael will stand, the great leader who stands by those who belong to your people. There'll be a time of trouble such as hasn't happened since it became a nation until that time. But at that time your people will escape, everyone who is found written in the book, [2]and many sleeping in the country of dirt will wake up, some to lasting life, some to great shame, to lasting abhorrence. [3]The discerning people will be bright, like the sky's brightness, and the people who helped many to be faithful like stars, forever and ever. [4]You, Daniel, close up the words, seal the book, until the time of the end. Many will run to and fro so that knowledge may increase."

[5]I (Daniel) looked, and there—two others standing, one on the river bank this side, one on the river bank the other side. [6]Someone said to the man dressed in linen, who was above the waters of the river, "How long until the end of the awful events?" [7]I listened to the man dressed in linen who was above the waters of the river. He raised his right hand and his

left hand to the heavens and swore by the Ever-Living One, "For a set time, set times, and a half. When the shattering of the hand of the holy people ends, all these things will come to an end." [8]I did listen but I didn't understand. I asked, "My lord, what will be the final stage in these events?" [9]He said, "Go, Daniel, because the words are closed up and sealed until the time of the end. [10]Many will purify themselves, cleanse themselves, and refine themselves, but the faithless will act faithlessly. None of the faithless will understand, but the discerning will understand. [11]From the time when the regular offering is removed and a desolating abomination put in place will be 1,290 days. [12]The blessings of the one who waits and reaches 1,335 days! [13]You, go to the end and rest, so you may stand for your destiny at the end of the period."

It's the last of the Old Testament for Everyone volumes, and for the first time I wept as I was writing. I think I've more than once mentioned that I usually assume that nothing I write makes any difference to anyone, and readers therefore occasionally e-mail me to say it isn't the case (this isn't a hint to invite you to do so). In that connection I was moved to read the man in linen's comment about the people who helped others to be **faithful**. I'm not in the same league as the "discerning" who accepted a vocation to encourage people to stay faithful in the context of the crisis in Jerusalem to which these visions relate, but I appreciate the insight that all that is asked of a teacher is to offer people help in staying faithful. Whether they do so is then their business.

In the context of this crisis, there were people who didn't stay faithful and people who did. You had to decide which side you were on. In this last section of Daniel, after the summary of the vision so far in the first paragraph, the second paragraph marks the transition from history cast as talk of the future to actual talk of the future. In this second paragraph, the imagery and the language change. It doesn't come from turning past events into code, but nor does it come from the visionary's imagination. It comes more systematically from his reading of Scripture. The description of the way the crisis will reach a climax takes up imagery from passages in the Prophets such as Isaiah 10 and Ezekiel 38–39, and behind them from psalms such as 2, 46, 48, and 76. The climax of the crisis will constitute another embodiment of the End that the Prophets describe. Daniel's revelation compares with John's in the book of Revelation, which doesn't give us literal descriptions of things but takes up Old Testament imagery—including Daniel's!—in order to describe them.

The third paragraph makes further promises that reflect the Scriptures, though the content makes a new point. While the Old Testament elsewhere tells stories about individuals brought back to life, and about the nation brought back to life after it has "died" in **exile**, this is the only passage in the Old Testament promising that many people who've died will come back to life. As in those other stories and in the stories of Jesus bringing people back to life, it's resuscitation rather than resurrection. They're brought back to life with the same human nature, not a transformed one. More solemnly, like the New Testament the promise involves a bringing back to life that will issue in new life for some but a second death for others. The background is a sense that God can hardly leave unresolved a situation in which faithful people have been martyred and faithless people have gotten away with their unfaithfulness. The vision promises that things won't stay that way. The faithful will be vindicated and honored, the faithless exposed.

The timing envisaged by the revelation corresponds to that envisaged earlier—a time, two times, and half a time. You wouldn't be compelled to take this formula to denote three and a half years, but when the crisis did last that kind of time, you could hardly resist the temptation to see a link. The subsequent references to 1,290 days and 1,335 days confirm that inference. Perhaps those time references correspond to stages in the unfolding and resolution of the crisis. The books of Maccabees are our primary source for an account of the crisis, but they don't give us information about specific dates that enables us to interpret the figures.

As far as we know, people didn't come back from the dead after the city's deliverance from Antiochus. Yet evidently people were impressed enough by the correspondence in principle between the promise of deliverance and the event of deliverance that they recognized the vision as a divine revelation. The dynamic shared a characteristic that appears in the Prophets and the New Testament, where a coming great act of deliverance or judgment is described as the fulfillment of God's final and ultimate purpose. God's act doesn't bring the actual end of everything, but it does bring an installment of the end, an embodiment within history of God's ultimate purpose and a confirmation that this ultimate purpose will find fulfillment.

HOSEA 1:1–2:1

A Doomed Marriage

¹Yahweh's message that came to Hosea son of Be'eri in the days of Uzziah, Jotham, Ahaz, and Hezekiah, kings of Judah, and in the days of Jeroboam son of Joash king of Israel.
²The beginning of Yahweh's message through Hosea. Yahweh said to Hosea, "Go and get yourself an immoral woman and immoral children, because the country commits immorality away from Yahweh." ³So he went and got Gomer daughter of Diblaim, and she got pregnant and bore him a son. ⁴Yahweh said to him, "Call his name Jezreel, because in yet a little while I shall attend to Jezreel's bloodshed for Jehu's household. I shall make the regime of Israel's household cease. ⁵On that day I shall break Israel's bow in Jezreel Valley." ⁶She got pregnant again and bore a daughter. [Yahweh] said to him, "Call her name Not-compassioned, because I shall no more have compassion again on Israel's household or continue to carry

them. [7](But on Judah's household I shall have compassion and I shall deliver them through Yahweh their God—I shall not deliver them through bow, sword, and battle, through horses and riders.)" [8]She weaned Not-compassioned, got pregnant, and bore a son. [9][Yahweh] said, "Call his name Not-my-people, because you're not my people and I—I shall not be God to you."

[10]But the number of the Israelites will be like the sand in the sea that cannot be measured or counted. In the place where it is said to them "You're not my people" it will be said to them, "Children of the living God." [11]The Judahites and Israelites will assemble all together and set up one head for themselves. They'll go up from the country, because Jezreel's day will be great. [2:1]Say to your brothers, "My people," and to your sisters, "Compassioned."

When I was barely out of my teens I fell in love with another student; two or three years later she discovered that she had multiple sclerosis. We were unofficially engaged but she wasn't yet wearing a ring, so in theory I could have broken off the relationship, yet becoming unofficially engaged had meant we believed that God had brought us together. We were married for forty-three years, years of growing disability and loss (but also happiness) for Ann, years of growing stress and loss (but also happiness) for me. They were also years of making me more of a person who could minister to others.

There's no comparison with what God asked of Hosea, though there's a little bit of overlap between our experiences. God sometimes asks tough things of people, not least in connection with marriage (the same is true of Jeremiah and Ezekiel). The toughness applies to Gomer as well as Hosea, but we don't have her side of the story. Who knows what kind of experience had turned her into "an immoral woman"? Yet her being such a person made her someone God could use. Many translations describe her as a prostitute, but the word isn't as specific as that (though if she was a prostitute, the question about what drove her into prostitution would then arise). But the slang use of the word *whore* will sometimes convey the right impression of Hosea's language.

Hosea ministered in **Ephraim** in the last years before it fell to **Assyria**. His aim was to forestall that event. The opinion formers and decision makers in public life are the men, so it's the men he focuses on. Men can be both drawn by and condemning of a woman whose sexuality isn't under their control. So God tells these men that they themselves are whores. Ephraim was supposed to be "married" to **Yahweh**, but has been involved in a longtime affair with the **Master**, Baal.

Yahweh works with the fact that in this social context marriage is a patriarchal institution and the man is the master. That Hebrew word for *master*, *ba'al*, is also the Hebrew word for *husband*. The Old Testament itself rarely uses the word in this connection; usually "husband" and "wife" in English translations represent the ordinary Hebrew words for *man* and *woman* ("he's my man," "she's my woman")—the next section of the book will begin with an example. This usage points toward a more relational ideal of marriage, but it's the hierarchical model that provides a better model for understanding the relationship between God and us. Yahweh is the Master; we are subordinate to Yahweh.

In Ephraim it doesn't work that way. Ephraim looks to that other Master for its fertility and its blessing. The offspring of Hosea and Gomer underline the point by their names. A mother I know was incensed by Hosea calling his daughter "Not-compassioned"—what does that naming do to her as she grows up? Children may also pay a price for being part of a family that God is using; I was certainly fearful that our sons would pay a price for their mother's illness (but I also reassured Ann that this experience could be part of the making of them, as I believe happened). Yet we shouldn't misunderstand the way names in the Bible work. Many people are given odd names that don't look like the names people would use every day and would thus make the children the object of laughter at school. Maybe they were just used in some way at the child's naming ceremony.

Jezreel was Ephraim's capital for a while, so "Jezreel" can implicitly refer to Ephraim itself. It was the sight of a massacre involved in Jeroboam's great-grandfather's accession. Yahweh worked through this event (see 2 Kings 9–10), yet Yahweh also condemns it. But Jezreel will be restored. While Yahweh responds to Ephraim's breaking of its marriage commitment by speaking in terms of divorce ("you're not my people and I—I shall not be God to you"), he cannot maintain that stance and withhold compassion forever.

HOSEA 2:2–13

Like Mother, Like Sons and Daughters

2 Contend with your mother, contend,
    because she isn't my woman and I'm not her man.
She must put away her immorality from her face,
    her adultery from between her breasts.
3 Otherwise I shall strip her naked,
    and make her like the day she was born.
I shall make her like the wilderness,
    change her into dry land, let her die of thirst.
4 On her children I shall have no compassion,
    because they're immoral children.
5 Because their mother has been immoral;
    the one who conceived them has acted shamefully.
Because she has said, "I'll go after my lovers,
    the ones who give me my bread and my water,
    my wool and linen, my oil and my drink."

6 Therefore here am I,
    I'm going to hedge up your way with thorn bushes.
I shall build a wall for her,
    so she can't find her paths.

7   She'll pursue her lovers,
         but she won't catch them.
     She'll look for them but not find them,
         and she'll say, "I'll go and return,
     to my first man,
         because it was better for me then than now."
8   She—she has not acknowledged
         that I—I am the one who gave her
         the grain, new wine, and fresh oil.
     I produced an abundance of silver for her,
         and gold, which they used for the Master.
9   Therefore I shall take back my grain in its season
         and my new wine at its set time.
     I shall snatch away my wool and linen
         for covering her nakedness.
10   Now I shall uncover her grossness
         before her lovers' eyes.
     No one will rescue her from my hand,
11   and I shall make all her celebrating stop,
     her festival, her new moon, her Sabbath,
         every set event of hers.
12   I shall ruin her vine and fig tree,
         of which she said, "It's my pay,
         which my lovers gave me."
     I shall turn them into a forest;
         animals of the wild will consume them.
13   I shall attend to her for the Masters' days
         when she burns offerings for them.
     She decks herself with her ring and her jewelry,
         goes after her lovers,
         and she has disregarded me (Yahweh's declaration).

I had a conversation with a married woman about jealousy. She and her husband had married when they were in their thirties, so they both had had many friends of the opposite sex, but these were not sexual partners. After they married, her husband assumed he would keep up with his former female friends, but she didn't like this idea; she didn't expect to keep up with her former male friends. On the other hand, she did have a man who was a kind of spiritual director, though she didn't use that term—someone with whom she talked about her relationship with God. She wanted to continue seeing him, but she felt uneasy, as if her husband had a right to be jealous if she needed someone else other than him to be a conversation partner regarding matters of deep concern to her.

Jealousy is strange. It's one of the emotions like anger that we may think are inherently wrong, yet they are emotions God has. So the question is whether a given jealousy or anger is proper. For that matter, other emotions such as compassion and mercy, which we are inclined to see as inherently right, are also ambiguous. God sometimes withholds compassion and mercy, like a parent who knows there are times to say "That's it! Time out!"

It's a time of jealousy for **Yahweh** and a time-out moment for **Ephraim**, a much more serious relationship issue than the one I just described. Ephraim is guilty of immorality or adultery, the adultery that's involved when Ephraim as Yahweh's wife goes off with other gods. Hosea addresses the Ephraimites (the children) as if they are distinguishable from Ephraim itself (the mother), but really they aren't—they are being challenged to formulate an accusation against themselves and to imagine the penalty that threatens them. They themselves are "immoral children."

The calamity will take the form of drought and famine. It will be poetic justice. They think that the best way to ensure that their crops grow is to pray to the **Masters**. Actually that will be the best way to ensure that the crops fail. Why would they turn to the Masters? They knew that Yahweh had rescued them from servitude in **Egypt** and brought them into Canaan, but perhaps they were unsure that Yahweh could make crops grow. The local people had a theology that told them who made crops grow—it was the Masters. So **Israel** followed them, or maybe thought they could play safe by praying to Yahweh and also praying to the Masters. In reality, Yahweh points out, he was the one who gave Ephraim what it needed for its life. It's even turned the silver and gold he gave into material for making worship images.

While saying that his wife's going to pay a penalty, Yahweh also states the intention to stop her going off to the Masters. He doesn't indicate how he'd do so; the point of the declaration is that he has not surrendered her. She's going to have to come back. Indirectly, it's a piece of good news. It implies that the punishment needn't be exacted, though it's also a further warning that she can't mess around with him.

HOSEA 2:14–3:5

Trouble Valley Can Become Hope's Door

14 Therefore now—I'm going to charm her;
   I'll get her to go into the wilderness,
   and speak to her heart.
15 I'll give her vineyards from there,
   Trouble Valley as Hope's Door.
   She'll respond there as in her young days,
   as in the day she came up from the country of
      Egypt.
16 On that day (Yahweh's declaration) she'll call,
   "My Man";
   she'll no more call me "My Master."
17 I'll remove the Masters' names from your mouth;
   they'll be mentioned by their name no more.
18 (And I shall seal a covenant for them on that day
   with the creature of the wild,
   with the bird in the heavens,
   and with what moves on the ground.
   Bow and sword and battle I shall break from the
      country,
   and I'll enable them to lie down with assurance.)

19   I shall marry you to me forever,
      marry you to me with faithfulness and authority,
  with commitment and compassion,
20   marry you to me with truth.
  You'll acknowledge Yahweh,
21   and on that day I shall answer (Yahweh's declaration).
  I shall answer the heavens,
      and they'll answer the earth.
22   The earth will answer with grain, new wine and
        fresh oil,
     and these will answer with Jezreel.
23   I shall sow it for myself in the country
     and have compassion on Not-compassioned.
  I shall say to Not-my-people "My people"
     and it will say "My God"!

3:1 Yahweh said to me further, "Go, love a woman who is loved by a neighbor and who commits adultery—like Yahweh's love for the Israelites though they're turning toward other gods and loving raisin slabs." 2 So I acquired her for myself for fifteen silver [pieces], a barrel of barley, and a gallon of barley. 3 I said to her, "For a long time you're to live for me. You're not to commit immorality. You're not to belong to [another] man. So also will I be for you." 4 Because for a long time the Israelites are to live with no king, no official, no sacrifice, no pillar, no ephod or effigies. 5 Afterwards the Israelites will turn back and have recourse to Yahweh their God and David their king. They'll be in awe of Yahweh and of his goodness in the later days.

"Culturally we're too used to happy endings," a student said to me today. She was entitled to talk about such a subject, because she had lost two children to cancer. Further, her mother had been born in what is now North Korea; she has no prospect of even visiting there. Can we be faulted for wanting things to work out happily? When my wife and I watch a movie, we like there to be some realism but we like it to end happily. We don't care for unrealistic romanticism and we don't want people who seem unmatched to end up together. We'll sleep well if there's realism but also a happy ending.

The book of Hosea doesn't say whether the story of Hosea and Gomer has a happy ending, which is appropriate because Hosea's prophecy addresses a people faced by decisions that will determine which kind of ending its story has. In the context of Hosea's ministry, that people is **Ephraim**, but the prophecies also refer to **Judah**; Judah needs to learn from Ephraim's failure to respond to Hosea's message.

Hosea has been trying a stick; he now tries a carrot. He has tried threats; now he tries promises. Going into the wilderness means returning to the life where **Israel** wasn't directly tempted by the **Masters**, as happens in Canaan. While the story in the **Torah** shows that life in the wilderness put pressures on Israel's trust in **Yahweh**, the pressure meant trust in Yahweh, or despair more often than trust in Yahweh, or turn somewhere else. Israel went through Trouble Valley all right (see Joshua 7:24–26) but came out the other side. It can happen again.

Yahweh's declaration that they'll no longer call him "My Master" suggests another angle on the problem about their religious life. Sometimes, at least, people didn't see themselves as worshiping other gods. They worshiped Yahweh, but called him "My Master." Why was this habit objectionable? The problem was that this title was attached to Canaanite deities, and carried with it misleading understandings of God. In effect it meant people were worshiping a different god even if they saw themselves as worshiping Yahweh.

Putting the relationship right will mean Israel acknowledging Yahweh in the proper way. Such acknowledgment will involve **faithfulness** in the exercise of **authority**, commitment and compassion, and truth. Hosea doesn't specify whether these are aspects of the way God will relate to Israel, or aspects of the way Israel presently won't relate to God, or aspects of the way Israelites will relate to one another. Elsewhere Hosea indicates that he expects these qualities to characterize all three relationships, so perhaps he's content to imply the same expectation here.

The close of the promise leads appropriately into another scene from the relationship of Hosea and Gomer. Maybe it's Hosea's own account of the beginning of the relationship described in chapter 1, or maybe it indicates that Gomer had left Hosea or that he had thrown her out, so that he now takes steps to get her (back) and makes the payment needed because she's become a bondservant.

HOSEA 4:1–19

Knowing and Acknowledging

1   Listen to Yahweh's message, Israelites,
      because Yahweh has a contention
      with the country's inhabitants.
  Because there's no truthfulness or commitment,
      no acknowledging of God in the country.
2   Cursing, deceit, murder,
      robbery, and adultery have spread out;
      bloodshed follows on bloodshed.
3   Therefore the country withers;
      everyone who lives in it wastes away,
  with the animal in the wild and the bird in the
      heavens—
      even the fish in the sea are swept away.

4   Yet no one is to contend,
      no one is to reprove.
  Your people are the very ones contending with a
      priest,
5   and you'll fall by day.
  A prophet will also fall with you by night,
      and I shall destroy your mother.

6 My people are destroyed
    for lack of acknowledging [me].
  Because you've rejected acknowledging [me]
    I shall reject you from being a priest for me.
  You've disregarded your God's teaching;
    I shall disregard your children, too.
7 As they became many, so they offended against
        me;
    I shall exchange their honor for humiliation.
8 They feed on my people's offenses;
    they direct its appetite to their waywardness.
9 So it will be: as the people, so the priest;
    I shall attend to its ways for it.
  I shall bring back its deeds for it;
10   they've eaten but they're not full.
  They've been immoral but they don't spread out,
    because they've abandoned Yahweh
  to pay heed 11to immorality,
    as wine and new wine takes away sense.
12 My people consults its piece of wood;
    its stick informs it.
  Because an immoral spirit has led it astray;
    they've been immoral from under their God.
13 On the tops of the mountains they sacrifice,
    on the hills they burn offerings,
  under oak, poplar, and terebinth,
    because its shade is good.
  Therefore your daughters are immoral,
    your brides commit adultery.
14 I shall not attend to your daughters because
        they're immoral,
    or to your brides because they commit adultery.
  Because the men themselves consort with whores
    and sacrifice with sacred women,
    and a people that doesn't understand collapses.

15 If you're immoral, Israel,
    Judah must not become guilty.

> Don't come to Gilgal, don't go up to Beth-aven,
>   don't swear "As Yahweh lives!"
> ¹⁶ Because like a stubborn cow
>   Israel has been stubborn.
> Now Yahweh will graze them
>   like sheep on the range.
> ¹⁷ Ephraim is attached to images;
>   leave him to himself.
> ¹⁸ Their drink has gone as they've whored and whored,
>   loved and loved.
> Humiliation is its gift;
> ¹⁹   the wind has bound it up in its wings,
>   so that they'll be shamed because of their sacrifices.

In Britain and in the United States I've been stopped by the police and asked, "Sir, do you know what the speed limit was on that road?" In both places I knew it was sixty-five miles per hour and I was doing rather more (I've reformed now). In both contexts I amused myself by reflecting that if I ever had that experience in Israel, I'd be less sure how to answer the question, because the Hebrew word for *know* implies that you're recognizing something by the way you live, not merely that you're aware of some fact. I knew the speed limit but I was not acknowledging it.

The Prophets are fond of this word for *know* that carries over into *acknowledge*, and Hosea uses it three times in this section. First, there's no truthfulness or commitment in **Ephraim**: in other words, there's no acknowledging of God. We might think that he's continuing his attack on Ephraim's religious life, but he explains that this failure expresses itself in "cursing, deceit, murder, robbery, adultery and bloodshed." Cursing won't mean what we'd call profanity, but calling down disaster on other people. In this context, "adultery" will have its literal meaning. Hosea is castigating people for the most basic failure of covenant commitment: failing to pay attention to the Ten Commandments (praying to the **Masters** also breaches those basic, not very demanding expectations). It explains why things are going wrong with the community's life.

The second paragraph subverts that opening critique by declaring that responsibility for what's wrong in the community lies with the priesthood. When Hosea speaks of "a priest," he may mean the head priest (Amos 7 tells a story about a head priest in Ephraim) or may mean any priest. While the priests' role involved leading worship, they were like pastors; their role also involved teaching. If people behave as if they don't know what the **Torah** expects of them, it may mean the priests have been failing to fulfill their teaching role. It's easy for pastors or priests to focus on encouraging people and not say the hard things that need saying. The same applies to prophets, whom Hosea goes on to mention. Priests, prophets, and pastors are dependent on their people for their livelihood, so they're under pressure not to be too confrontational. There's a vicious collusion between the desires and the waywardness of both parties. The failure of priests and prophets will mean they lose their position, but it will also mean the community as a whole, their "mother," pays a terrible price. It will be a consequence of their failing to acknowledge **Yahweh**, and thus of the people's failing to do so.

Hosea subsequently reverts to the other sort of failure over acknowledging Yahweh: the metaphorical immorality and adultery, seeking help from other gods with their images. He derides them as mere lumps of wood. The worship at these sanctuaries may also have involved sex, as an acted prayer for fertility. Either way, Hosea says, "Don't just blame the women—especially the ones who are keen to conceive; blame the men, who also take part in worship with these pagan priestesses" (as he earlier said, "Don't just blame the people, blame the priests").

The last paragraph adds another snide comment along the lines of, "OK, Ephraim, indulge in your religious immorality, but don't let it infect **Judah**." Later prophets such as

Jeremiah will note that Judah itself needs to take this message to heart. Gilgal (near Jericho) and Beth-aven (a derogatory substitute name for Bethel) were near Ephraim's southern border with Judah.

HOSEA 5:1–6:3

When Moth and Rot Corrupt and Thieves Break In and Steal

1 Listen to this, priests;
    pay attention, Israelites!
Give ear, royal household,
    because authority belongs to you.
Because you've been a snare to Mizpah,
    you've spread a net over Tabor.
2 Rebels have made deep slaughter;
    I myself am the chastisement for them all.
3 I myself have acknowledged Ephraim;
    Israel has not eluded me.
Because you've now been immoral, Ephraim;
    Israel has become unclean.
4 Their deeds don't allow them
    to turn back to their God.
Because there's an immoral spirit within them,
    and they've not acknowledged Yahweh.
5 Israel's majesty will testify against it;
    so Israel and Ephraim will fall through their
        waywardness
    (Judah has fallen with them, too).
6 They may go out with their flocks and their cattle,
    to seek help from Yahweh.
But they won't find him—he has withdrawn from
        them;
7 they've been false to Yahweh.
Because they've given birth to alien children,
    the new moon will now devour them with their
        allocations.

76

8   Sound a horn in Gibeah, a trumpet in Ramah,
        raise a shout in Beth-aven; after you, Benjamin.
9   Ephraim will become a waste
        on the day of reproof.
    Against Israel's clans
        I have made known something certain.
10 Judah's officials have become veritable boundary movers;
        on them I shall pour out my fury like water.

11 Ephraim is defrauded, crushed by judgment,
        because he resolved and went after emptiness.
12 But I myself am like a moth to Ephraim,
        like rot to Judah's household;
13 Ephraim saw its sickness,
        Judah its sore.
    Ephraim went to Assyria,
        sent to the great king.
    But that man won't be able to heal you;
        he won't cure you of the sore.
14 Because I shall be like a lion to Ephraim,
        like a cougar to Judah's household.
    I, I myself, shall tear, and go;
        I shall carry, and there'll be no one to rescue.
15 I shall go, I shall return to my place,
        until they bear their guilt,
    and seek help from me;
        in their distress they'll seek me urgently.

6:1 "Come on, let's go back to Yahweh,
        because he's the one who tore, and he can heal us.
    He injured and he can bandage us;
2   he can bring us to life after two days.
    On the third day he can raise us up,
        so that we can live in his presence.
3   When we acknowledge, pursue acknowledging Yahweh,
        like dawn his coming out is sure.
    He'll come to us like rain,
        like spring rain that waters the earth."

While I was at class two evenings ago, my wife discovered that a stretch of the bottom of the wall underneath my desk had disintegrated. Rain had been getting into the base of the wall outside, and Californian walls aren't made of anything substantial such as brick, like British walls. They're made of wood covered in stucco, and if water gets in, they rot. The rain won't immediately come through to wet my feet as I work; in this sense it's not an immediate problem. But the problem needs urgent attention because it will spread. Eventually the entire wall will collapse.

In one of the Bible's more striking images, **Yahweh** declares that "I'm like rot to **Judah**'s household" (if I translated it "Judah's house," the analogy with our apartment would be even closer). "I'm like a moth to **Ephraim**." If the moths get at your clothes or your bedding, they soon become useless. If you see the slightest indication of rot, moth, or mold in your house, it's vital to deal with it straightaway. Otherwise things will simply fall apart.

If I were on my own, I mightn't have taken our rot very seriously, but Kathleen is an architect and knows what can follow from neglect. She knows we must take action. Hosea is in an architect's position in relation to **Israel**, but can't get it to take the problem seriously. It's as if he's blowing the horn to announce an enemy's approach, but they ignore it. There's a literal enemy to talk about. Ephraim is under pressure from **Assyria**, and the reference to Judah stealing land reflects the tension between Judah and Ephraim in this political context (see 2 Kings 15–16). But Ephraim has a more sinister enemy—Yahweh himself.

Once again Hosea addresses the whole people, and also the priests who teach them, but additionally the "royal household," the king and his administration. They're the people who have **authority** to support faithfulness and fairness in the community and to shield the vulnerable—but they're *being* a snare instead of protecting people from a snare. There's something mysterious about the community's unwillingness to face facts, as if we were to ignore our disintegrating wall. It's as if they're possessed by an immoral spirit, a spirit that insists on their persisting in their unfaithfulness to Yahweh. They won't let themselves turn back to Yahweh. They can take lots of animals to sacrifice, but in the absence of a change of life it won't put things right.

In the closing paragraph Hosea calls the community to the action that's required. The community needs to return to Yahweh, giving up seeking help and provision from other gods. It needs to acknowledge Yahweh. That verb makes the same point, but it adds to it, because acknowledgment means doing what Yahweh says about the nature of community life—about matters such as faithfulness and fairness and protecting the weak. It involves action; hence the reference to "pursuing" such acknowledgment. The good news is that Yahweh's having the capacity to overwhelm you like a lion, a warrior, a storm, or the sun's heat also means Yahweh has the capacity to heal and restore, and to do so quite quickly, within two or three days. Rain and sun can be destructive forces, but also life-giving ones.

HOSEA 6:4–7:16

June Gloom

4 What shall I do with you, Ephraim,
    what shall I do with you, Judah,
  when your commitment is like morning cloud,
    like dew going early?
5 Therefore I cut them down with my prophets,
    slew them with the words of my mouth;
    it's with judgments against you that light goes out.
6 Because I wanted commitment not sacrifice,
    acknowledgment of God more than whole offerings.
7 But they—as at Adam they transgressed the covenant;
    there they were false to me.

8 Gilead is a town of wrongdoers,
     trailed in blood.
9 The company of priests
     are like gangs waiting for someone.
   On the road to Shechem they commit murder,
     because they've made a plan.
10 In Israel's household I've seen something horrible:
     Israel's immorality is there.
   Israel has become unclean 11(Judah, too);
     he has appointed a harvest for you.

   When I restore my people's fortunes, 7:1as I heal
     Israel,
     Ephraim's waywardness reveals itself, Samaria's
       evil.
   Because people have practiced falsehood, a thief
     enters,
     a gang has made a dash in the street.
2 Their mind doesn't say,
     "I've kept in mind all their evil."
   Now their deeds have surrounded them;
     they've been in front of my face.
3 They make a king celebrate, with their evil,
     and officials, with their lies.
4 All of them are committing adultery,
     like an oven burning without a baker.
   He stops stirring
     from the kneading of the dough to its leavening.
5 On our king's birthday,
     officials got sick with the heat of wine.
   He extended his hand to mockers 6when they
       came near,
     their mind like an oven with intrigue.
   All night their baker slept,
     in the morning he's burning, like a flaming
       fire.
7 All of them burn as hot as an oven,
     they consume their rulers.

All their kings have fallen;
    there's no one among them calling to me.

8 Ephraim among the peoples, he wastes away.
    Ephraim has become a loaf not turned over.
9 Strangers have consumed his strength,
    and he has not acknowledged it.
Yes, gray hair has spread over him,
    and he has not acknowledged it.
10 Israel's majesty testifies against it,
    but they haven't turned back to Yahweh their
        God;
    they haven't sought help from him despite all
        this.
11 Ephraim has become like a simple pigeon, without
        sense;
    they've called on Egypt, they've gone to Assyria.
12 When they go,
    I shall spread my net over them.
Like a bird in the heavens, I shall bring them down;
    I shall chastise them
    in accordance with the report to their assembly.
13 Oh, those people, because they've strayed from me;
    destruction for them, because they've rebelled
        against me.
Whereas I'm the one who could redeem them,
    they themselves have spoken lies about me.
14 They haven't cried out to me in their heart,
    when they wail on their beds.
Over grain and new wine they quarrel;
    they turn against me.
15 I myself trained them, strengthened their arms,
    but they plan evil against me.
16 They turn back, not to the One on High;
    they've become like a false bow.
Their officials will fall by the sword
    because of the raging of their tongue
    (this is their jabbering in the country of Egypt).

Each year in our part of the world we experience "June gloom"; if it arrives earlier, it's "May gray." The sky's cloudy when we get up, and we can't be sure when or whether it will clear. At the beach, it may stay there all day, though where I live, thirty miles inland, it may disappear by lunchtime because the sun's evaporated it. If it stays, it won't produce the rain we need. It's simply a "marine layer," caused by the way the sea is still getting warm in early summer, whereas the land has already warmed up.

The problem with Israel's commitment and its acknowledging of God is that it resembles the marine layer and the morning dew, which is important to the crops during the rainless summer, but also disappears quickly. The chapter divisions in the Bible encourage us to read the first paragraph as Yahweh's response to the resolve expressed in the preceding section (6:1–3), and one can imagine that any resolve formulated by the people was short-lived. God has thus implemented judgment by means of the words of prophets; the sun coming out strong in summer is an expression of that judgment. It's easy for people to think that worship pleases God, but in these circumstances it does no such thing. Elsewhere in the section Hosea makes clear that he affirms the calling on God that is involved in worship, turning to God and then seeking God's help. But prayer and worship, and the sacrifice that gives outward expression to prayer and worship, are no use if they aren't accompanied by commitment and acknowledgment of God outside times of prayer and worship. (The references to Adam, on the Jordan, Gilead, and Shechem refer to incidents there that we don't otherwise know about.)

Given that shortcoming, Israel will experience a harvest in which it reaps what it has sown. The second paragraph underscores the point by noting that it's not as if Yahweh has refrained from acting in love and mercy. The trouble is that such acts only function as positive reinforcement, encouraging more wrongdoing rather than a recognition that Yahweh continues to note this wrongdoing.

The references to kings, officials, and intrigue point toward the political maneuvering that characterized Hosea's day, when there were at least two assassinations, and other regime changes. Yet a plotter never expects to be the next victim. The references to baking perhaps reflect the role of timing as one hatches a plot and has to discern the moment for implementation. Victims and plotters are all involved in adultery (that is, unfaithfulness to Yahweh); no one is calling on Yahweh.

The third paragraph notes once again that Israel is thus not only ignoring Yahweh but ignoring its own troubles. It's like a man who's become old and weak but hasn't faced the fact. Insofar as they acknowledge their difficulties, they think that the solution lies in the help of **Assyria** or **Egypt**, the big powers on either side. Reports to their assembly may commend such action, but it will simply provoke Yahweh to more judgment.

HOSEA 8:1–14

Leaders as Burdens

¹ Horn to your mouth,
  like an eagle over Yahweh's house!
Because they've transgressed my covenant,
  rebelled against my teaching.
² To me they cry out,
  "My God, as Israel we've acknowledged you!"
³ Israel has rejected what's good;
  an enemy pursues them.
⁴ They've made kings, but not through me;
  they've made officials, but I haven't acknowledged
    them.
With their silver and gold they've made images for
    themselves,
  so that [Israel] may be cut off.

⁵ He has rejected your bullock, Samaria;
    my anger burns against them.
How long will they be incapable of innocence?—
⁶   because [it was made] by Israel.
That thing—a metalworker made it;
    it's not a god.
Because it will be broken bits,
    Samaria's bullock.

⁷ Because they sow wind, they'll reap a tornado,
    a stalk that has no growth—it doesn't produce
      flour.
If perhaps it produces, strangers will swallow it;
⁸   Israel has been swallowed up.
They've now become among the nations
    like an object that no one wants.
⁹ Because they've gone up to Assyria;
    a wild donkey on its own, Ephraim has hired
      lovers.
¹⁰ Even when they hire among the nations,
    now I shall gather them.
They've writhed for a while
    because of the burden (king, officers).
¹¹ Because Ephraim has built many altars for
      committing offenses;
    for it, they've become altars for committing
      offenses.
¹² If I wrote for it many things in my teaching,
    they'd have been regarded as alien.
¹³ If they offer sacrifices to me as gifts, and eat flesh,
    Yahweh doesn't accept them.
Now he's mindful of their waywardness,
    and attends to their offenses;
    those people—they'll go back to Egypt.
¹⁴ Israel has disregarded its maker and built palaces
    and Judah has built many fortified cities.
I shall set fire to its cities;
    it will consume its fortresses.

I mentioned in connection with Daniel 5 that the president of my seminary is retiring and that the prospect of change causes anxiety among faculty and students. The seminary community is praying much about the transition, and not just because of that anxiety. It believes that God has a plan for such a transition, and it's important that we discover God's plan. I hold the heretical view that there's no basis for thinking that God has such a plan; God leaves decisions to us. Being a loving Father, God doesn't have plans for us, though God will have expectations about the principles needed by the person we appoint.

There's some overlap with the way **Yahweh** talks about **Ephraim** making kings but "not through me." There are several levels at which one might understand that evaluation. Monarchy in **Israel** began as an act of rebellion when Israel insisted on having human kings because it was dissatisfied with Yahweh as king. Subsequently, Yahweh designated David's line of kings; while some of Ephraim's kings were designated in Yahweh's name by prophets, the Ephraimite monarchy as an institution issued from a decision to leave the line that Yahweh had designated. Further, we've noted that Ephraim experienced several assassinations and coups; Yahweh hardly cares for that way of changing the government, as opposed to requiring the president or prime minister to depart after four or five years. Yahweh goes on to speak of refusing to recognize Ephraim's officials, which suggests that change involving assassinations and coups is uppermost in Hosea's mind. Even if Ephraim went through the motions of seeking Yahweh's will about its leadership, it then made its own decisions, as churches and seminaries do.

The evidence that it did so is the way the king and the government operated. They've led the people in transgressing the covenant's expectations (basically, the Ten Commandments) and in rebelling against Yahweh's teaching or **Torah**. King and officials are thus a burden the people have to carry, though they don't recognize these dynamics in their life. They have no more insight than their king and officials. If Yahweh increased the contents of his teaching (which ironically is exactly what Yahweh was doing over the centuries), they'd think its contents were weird.

Because people thus fail to acknowledge Yahweh (as they explicitly claim they do), Yahweh declines to acknowledge them. As Ephraim's leadership isn't from Yahweh but is chosen by Ephraim, so its worship is "from Israel," chosen by Israel. The people choose how to worship as they choose their leadership. They also make their own decisions about politics, entering into mutual commitments with Assyria—another breach of the covenant. Ephraim (*'eprayim*) is like an uncontrollable wild donkey (*pere'*), or like a whore paying for sex instead of being paid for it.

As well as having bad harvests, the Ephraimites will therefore have political experiences that are like bad harvests—their political plans will fail to produce the goods. Or they'll be "gathered" like wheat, which isn't a comfortable experience. To put it the worst way possible, they'll find themselves back in Egypt, needing a new exodus.

HOSEA 9:1–17

The Tender Trap

> ¹ Don't celebrate, Israel, with exultation like the peoples,
>> because you've gone whoring away from your God.
>> You've loved the payment
>> on every grain threshing-floor.
> ² Threshing floor and winepress won't feed them,
>> new wine will deceive her.
> ³ They won't live in Yahweh's country;
>> Ephraim will go back to Egypt,
>> in Assyria they'll eat unclean food.

4   They won't pour wine for Yahweh;
        their sacrifices won't be pleasing to him.
    Like mourners' bread to them,
        all who eat it will be unclean.
    Because it's bread for their own need;
        it won't come into Yahweh's house.
5   What will you do for the set day,
        for the day of Yahweh's festival?
6   Because there—they're going from destruction,
        Egypt will gather them, Memphis will bury them.
    Whereas high regard will attach to their silver,
        brier will dispossess them, bramble will be in
            their tents.
7   The days of visitation have come,
        the days of recompense have come,
        Israel must acknowledge it.
    The prophet is stupid,
        the person of the spirit is crazy,
    on account of the abundance of your waywardness,
        your abundant hostility.
8   A prophet, with my God,
        is a watchman over Ephraim.
    There's a hunter's snare over all his ways,
        animosity in its God's house.
9   They've gone deep in corruption, as in the days at
            Gibeah;
        he'll be mindful of their waywardness,
        he'll attend to their offenses.

10 I found Israel
        as like grapes in the wilderness.
    I saw your fathers
        as like the first fruit on a fig tree in its beginning.
    When those people came to the Master of Peor,
        they dedicated themselves to Shame,
        and became abominations like the thing they loved.
11 Ephraim—their splendor will fly off like a bird,
        away from birth, from the womb, from conception.

12 Even if they rear their children,
  I shall bereave them of people.
 Because—oh for them, indeed,
  when I turn away from them!
13 Ephraim—as I've seen with Tyre, planted in a meadow,
  so Ephraim will be taking out its children to the
  slayer.
14 Give them: Yahweh, what are you to give?—
  give them a miscarrying womb, dry breasts.
15 All their evil was at Gilgal,
  because there I repudiated them.
 Because of the evil of their deeds,
  I shall drive them from my house.
 I shall not add to my love for them;
  all their officials are rebellious.
16 Ephraim is struck, their root withers,
  they won't produce fruit.
 Even when they have children,
  I shall put to death the valuables from their
  womb.
17 My God will reject them
  because they haven't listened to him;
  they'll become wanderers among the nations.

Last night we listened to our favorite jazz/swing singer Steve Tyrell sing his romantic songs about falling in love. In the back of my mind as I listen is always the awareness that he lost the love of his life to cancer a few years ago, and then had a second marriage that lasted less than a year. He told a story about lyricist Sammy Cahn arriving at Frank Sinatra's home in Palm Springs to discuss a song for an upcoming movie. Sinatra came to the door looking the worse for wear and told Cahn, "I fall in love too easily. I fall in love too hard." Cahn said thank you, walked to the piano in another room, and in half an hour wrote the song that begins with those first words. "Love is the tender trap," Cahn later wrote and Sinatra later sang.

Falling in love is like being on a journey through the wilderness, where nothing very tasty grows, and suddenly coming across a grapevine. It's like experiencing that moment in spring when you've had nothing freshly succulent to eat, and the first fruit appears on a fig tree on the branches that grew the previous year. We shouldn't be too romantic about Yahweh's feelings for Israel, but those are the images Hosea uses. Or rather, we should be pretty romantic, because then we get the right impression of the contrast in what happened next. Yahweh thought Israel would be a delight to him and would delight in him, but actually, there in the wilderness before the Israelites got to the promised land, they had already turned away from Yahweh (you can read the story in Numbers 25). So the whoring that characterizes Ephraim's life is the continuation of whoring that goes way back. Turning to the Master aims to ensure the fertility of the family and of nature. It won't work.

There was a sanctuary at Gilgal, and it wouldn't be surprising if it was another sanctuary where people were turning to the Master rather than to Yahweh. It was also a place associated with Samuel's confirmation of Saul's position as king and with his dismissal of Saul as king (1 Samuel 11–13); here the context also refers to the rebelliousness of Ephraim's leadership. One way or another, Yahweh isn't going to keep showing the love he felt for Israel in the honeymoon period of their relationship. (Gibeah was Saul's home, though also the site of an earlier atrocity: see Judges 19–21; 1 Samuel 10–11.)

A festival like the one enjoyed at Master-of-Peor involved great rejoicing. The first paragraph begins by urging the Ephraimites not to think that they can join in such festivity; one can guess that Hosea made a point of preaching in the sanctuary courtyards on such an occasion. Such celebration is OK for people like the Moabites. They can only celebrate in light of what they know. If Israel joins in with them, it's going back on the way Yahweh has reached out to it. Here, too, Hosea refers to love, but to Israel's misdirected love. In seeking to ensure they'd have enough to eat by turning to the Master, Hosea again tells the people they're behaving like a whore. We can again imagine the reaction of the Israelite men. They think they're acting responsibly to ensure that their families do have food. A time will come (Hosea implies) when they'll wish they could offer sacrifices to Yahweh, but they won't be able to. They'll experience destruction in Ephraim and the plundering of their gold and silver, then they'll be taken off into exile in **Assyria** or in **Egypt**, where they'll die, leaving their land to grow wild. They'll have food there, all right, but they'll just have to treat it as ordinary food. They won't be able to come to celebrate a festival before Yahweh.

Prophets are Yahweh's servants in trying to forestall these events, but they meet only with attack and animosity when they speak in this way in the context of worship in the sanctuary courtyards. It's enough to drive a prophet crazy.

HOSEA 10:1–15

What You Sow You Can Expect to Reap

1 Israel is a wasting vine;
    its fruit resembles it.
  In accordance with the abundance of its fruit,
    it multiplied its altars.
  In accordance with the goodness of its country,
    they made good pillars.
2 Because their spirit was deceitful,
    now they bear their guilt;
  [Yahweh] will break down their altars,
    destroy their pillars.
3 Because they now say,
    "We have no King.
  Because we are not afraid of Yahweh;
    the King: what will he do to us?"

4   They've made statements with false oaths
        in sealing a covenant.
     Decision making has flourished like poisonous
            growth
        in the furrows of the field.
5   The resident of Samaria is in awe for the bullock
            of Beth-aven,
        when its people and its priestlings have
            mourned over it.
     They rejoice over its splendor,
        when it has gone away from it.
6   It, too, will be brought to Assyria,
        a gift to the great king.
     Ephraim will receive shame,
        Israel will be shamed by its plans.
7   Samaria—its king is coming to an end,
        like a twig on the surface of water.
8   The high places of Aven will be destroyed,
        Israel's offenses;
        thorn and thistle will grow on their altars.
     They'll say to the mountains, "Cover us,"
        to the hills, "Fall on us."

9   Since the days of Gibeah you have offended,
            Israel;
        there they stood.
     Will battle not overtake them in Gibeah because
            of wrongdoers?—
10   when I please, I shall discipline them.
     Peoples will be gathered against them,
        when they're disciplined for their double
            waywardness.
11   Whereas Ephraim was a trained bullock that
            loved threshing,
        and I—I passed over its fair neck,
     I shall drive Ephraim, Judah will plow,
        Jacob will harrow for itself.

¹² Sow for yourselves for faithfulness,
  reap in proportion to commitment,
  till the tillable ground for yourselves.
It's time for seeking help from Yahweh,
    until he comes,
  and showers faithfulness for you.
¹³ You have plowed faithlessness,
  you have reaped wrongdoing,
  you have eaten deceptive fruit.
Because you have relied on your way,
  on the abundance of your warriors.
¹⁴ A roar will arise against your people,
  and all your fortresses will be destroyed.
Like Shalman's destruction of Beth-arbel on
    a day of battle,
  when mother smashed on children.
¹⁵ Like this [Yahweh] is doing it to you, Bethel,
  because of your evil, your evil.
At dawn he's coming to an end,
  coming to an end—Israel's king.

We had dinner last night with two other couples who have children and grandchildren, and to their dismay these other couples discovered they had something heartbreaking in common. Both have grown-up daughters who were abused when they were young girls by people whom they thought they could trust. Both these daughters still live with the consequences of that abuse; it has issued in an unhappy harvest in their lives, and it still does so. You grieve for these women, you grieve for their mothers and fathers, and you grieve for the abusers who were probably the victims of painful experiences that issued in actions like this in their own lives. You wonder whether there's hope for the abusers, the victims, and the mothers and fathers.

To a community ruined by its turning from God in its religious life, its community life, and its political life, Hosea promises that God comes. It's never too late for a new start, not because of potential that lies in us, but because of potential that lies in God. God can shower **faithfulness** on us. It's an implausible image. If we were in the position of Hosea and of anyone who saw things his way, and grieved over how things were in **Ephraim**, it would be hard to keep such hope alive. But Hosea does so. Yet the realization of such hope does depend on a proper response from people. They need to turn to **Yahweh**, to seek help from him rather than from the resources they currently turn to. Only if they sow can they expect to reap.

Hosea begins the chapter by taking up a standard Old Testament image, of **Israel** as a vine. He could easily have reworked it in the manner of Isaiah 5 by describing it as a vine that has produced rotten grapes instead of edible ones. Instead he describes it as a vine that has wasted. It simply doesn't produce fruit. It had once flourished, but instead of making that flourishing a reason to rejoice in Yahweh, it has turned to those other gods.

Like Isaiah, Hosea puts words on the people's lips. They didn't actually say that Yahweh was not their King and that they weren't afraid of him acting like a King, but it was the implication of their attitude. Their government made agreements with other nations that had disastrous implications for its own people. They are deeply committed to their forms of worship (rather than to Yahweh), but these are doomed. The destruction when it comes will be so awful that people will ask to be overwhelmed by an earthquake rather than go through it.

The reference to Gibeah again recalls the stories in Judges 19–21 and 1 Samuel 10–11, which are grave for different reasons; perhaps these are the "double waywardness." Ephraim's once being a trained and thus responsive bullock contrasts with what it has become and with the harsh discipline Yahweh now has to impose on it. (We don't know any more about the destruction of a place called Beth-arbel by someone called Shalman.)

HOSEA 11:1–11

The Unfailing Nature of a Mother's Love

1 When Israel was a youth I loved him;
   from Egypt I called him my son.
2 When I called them, thus they went from me;
   they sacrifice to the Masters, burn offerings to
      images.
3 I myself taught Ephraim to walk, lifted them into
      my arms,
   but they didn't acknowledge that I healed them.
4 With human cords I led them,
   with loving ties.
   For them I was like people who lift a baby to the cheek,
      and I bent to him so that I might feed him.
5 No, they'll go back to the country of Egypt,
   Assyria will be their king,
      because they refused to come back.
6 A sword will whirl against its cities, consume its
      gate bars,
   devour them because of their plans.
7 My people are bent on turning from me;
   when they call to the One on High,
   he won't lift them up at all.
8 How can I give you up, Ephraim, hand you over,
      Israel,
   how can I make you like Admah, treat you like
      Zebo'im?
   My spirit turns around within me,
   my comfort warms all at once.
9 I shall not act on my angry burning;
   I shall not again destroy Ephraim.
   Because I am God and not a human being,
   the holy one in your midst,
   and I shall not come against the city.
10 They'll follow Yahweh—he'll roar like a lion;
   when he roars, children will come trembling from
      the west.

¹¹ They'll come trembling like a bird from Egypt,
  like a pigeon from the country of Assyria,
  I shall let them live in their homes (Yahweh's
    declaration).

Two months ago we took part in a Christmas party at a local juvenile hall (a youth detention center) with a couple we know whose son had been held there. The group we partied with comprised teenagers facing life imprisonment. My wife had a heartrending conversation with a boy of fourteen who was awaiting trial in connection with the killing of two other boys. "I daren't admit to my mother that I did it," he said. "But it's his mother," Kathleen said to me afterwards. "Mothers still embrace their sons even if they've done something terrible." It reminded me of a mother who was convinced that same-sex relationships were wrong and then experienced her son telling her that he was gay. How could she not continue to embrace him? He was her son.

Another mother speculated to me that this chapter in Hosea reveals Gomer's contribution to Hosea's message. Whereas Yahweh speaks elsewhere as a betrayed husband, here he speaks as a betrayed mother. And whereas a husband can divorce his wife, a mother can't divorce her children. No matter what they do, they remain her children. So Yahweh is torn between throwing the children out of the house and refusing to have anything else to do with them, and yielding to the instinct to comfort them the way a mother does. Perhaps it will need to be the comfort that a mother gives after severely chastising her children. We don't know much about Admah or Zebo'im except that they were near Sodom and Gomorrah and were devastated, like those cities (see Deuteronomy 29:22–23). How could Yahweh treat Ephraim as if it were an obscure place like those cities?

God cannot do so because he's the Holy One, not a human being. Our human instinct is to act in wrath when we have been deceived, let down, and betrayed. The boy I referred to knows about that human instinct. People often make God in their image and assume that God is the same. Does God's being the Holy One means God is austere and tough and certain to act in wrath? This expectation isn't exactly wrong, but Hosea turns such logic on its head. The holiness of Yahweh lies in his refraining from wrath against our faithlessness.

The last lines of the chapter promise another expression of Yahweh's comfort. Exile will come, but people will at last follow Yahweh, and Yahweh will bring them back to their country. Yahweh's roaring like a lion will make them tremble and thus submit to him, but the lion will be mainly concerned to roar against the overlords in the countries from which he's bringing them home.

HOSEA 11:12–13:11

Welcome and Confrontation

¹² Ephraim has surrounded me with lying,
    Israel's household with deceit,
but Judah still goes with God,
    keeps faith with the holy ones.
^{12:1} Ephraim feeds on the wind, pursues the easterly;
    continually it increases deception and
      destruction.
They seal a covenant with Assyria;
    oil is carried to Egypt.
² Yahweh will have a contention with Judah,
    and attend to Jacob in accordance with his ways;
    in accordance with his deeds he'll give back to
      him.
³ In the womb he grabbed his brother,
    and in his manhood he struggled with God.
⁴ He struggled with the aide and won,
    he wept and sought grace from him.
He would find him at Bethel, speak with him there,

96

⁵ Yahweh, God of Armies—Yahweh is his name.
⁶ So you yourself are to turn back to your God,
    to safeguard commitment in decision making,
    and wait for your God always.
⁷ A trader in whose hand are deceptive scales
    loves to swindle.
⁸ Ephraim has said, "Yes, I've become rich,
    I've acquired strength for myself.
All my gains won't acquire for me
    waywardness that amounts to offense."
⁹ I am Yahweh your God
    from the country of Egypt.
I shall make you live in your tents again,
    as in the days of your appointed festival.
¹⁰ I used to speak to the prophets
    and I—I gave many a vision;
    by means of the prophets I shall destroy.
¹¹ Did Gilead become wayward, yes, become
        emptiness,
    in Gilgal did they sacrifice bulls?
Their altars, too,
    are like stone heaps on the furrows of the
        field.
¹² Jacob fled to the open country of Aram;
    Israel served for a wife—for a wife he kept
        [sheep].
¹³ Through a prophet Yahweh brought Israel up
        from Egypt,
    and through a prophet he was kept.
¹⁴ Ephraim provoked with great bitterness;
    his Lord will leave his bloodshed on him,
    give back his reviling to him.
¹³:¹ When Ephraim spoke, there was trembling,
    when he lifted [his voice] in Israel,
    but through the Master he became guilty and
        died.
 ² Now they commit more and more offense,
    and they've made themselves an idol,

97

images from their silver in accordance with their
    insight,
  the work of craftsmen, all of it.
With regard to them they're saying, "Human
    sacrifices,"
  while they kiss bullocks.

3 Therefore they'll be like the morning cloud,
  like the dew that goes early,
like chaff that whirls from a threshing floor,
  like smoke from a window.

4 I am Yahweh your God
  from the country of Egypt.
You shall not acknowledge a god apart from me;
  there's no deliverer except me.

5 I acknowledged you in the wilderness,
  in a country of droughts.

6 When they grazed, they were full,
  when they were full, their attitude became
    superior;
  therefore they disregarded me.

7 I have become like a cougar to them,
  like a leopard I shall lurk by the road;

8 I shall attack them like a bereaved bear,
  rip open the casing of their heart.
I shall consume them like a lion,
  the animals of the wild will tear them apart:

9 it will mean your destruction, Israel,
  because in me is your help.

10 Where is your king, then,
  so that he may deliver you in all your cities,
and your leaders, of whom you said,
  "Give me a king and officials"?

11 I'd give you a king in my anger
  and take him in my wrath.

A friend of mine once gave a vivid description of a common
parental experience. Your eighteen-year-old son says he'll be

home at 11.30 and comes in at 3 a.m. How do you react? Ideally, you need two parents to be awake when that happens, so that one can say, "Where have you been?" and the other can say, "I'm so glad you're home." The first might be the father's question and the second the mother's expression of relief, but one shouldn't stereotype. My friend's problem was that his wife would be asleep, so he had to give both speeches. Much then depends on which of the responses gets articulated last and loudest.

It's tempting to read Yahweh's testimony in Hosea 11 as the book's climax, and perhaps it is, but it's not the end of the book. Yahweh is indeed like a mother who'll always embrace her son, but also like a husband who'll act in anger at being deceived and betrayed. Yahweh is the parent who has to give both speeches. In the book's closing chapters, Yahweh first gives the "I'm so glad you're home" speech (Hosea 11) but here gives the "Where have you been?" speech. Against the background of declaring a mother's love for Ephraim, he can also declare a husband's or father's willingness to be tough. This characteristic is already implicit in the closing verses of chapter 11, which presupposed that Yahweh would take Ephraim into exile.

Parents can easily fear that their child is hell-bent on self-destruction. It's Yahweh's fear. In Hosea's day Judah didn't turn to the Masters as Ephraim did, but it did turn to other nations for political and military help (which may underlie the swift move from affirmation of Judah to critique of Judah). Ephraim is in trouble in both connections. Waiting for God is a demanding expectation of a government; it looks like failure to take responsibility. In Ephraim's struggle with God it resembles its ancestor Jacob, not least in his deceptiveness (see Genesis 25–33). The line about the trader looks like a proverb, but it suggests that Ephraim's success (over which Ephraim goes on to express understandable satisfaction) is based on being good at deception—which is how business often works. The Hebrew word for *trader* is "Canaan" (the Canaanites were a trading people); that word's associations make the point more pungent. Ephraim is Canaanite in its business life as well as in its worship. But the allusions to Jacob's story also show how being Jacob-like doesn't mean you can't turn to God.

Alternatively, they'll find that the custom of living in bivouacs for the Sukkot festival in the fall, which reminds them of life in the wilderness, will become everyday reality again. Their unresponsiveness to their prophets will mean that the prophets' words of judgment will be fulfilled. The experience of the Gilead area across the Jordan needs to be a warning: its places of worship have already been turned into just heaps of stones. There's a sense in which Ephraim as a whole has already passed from life (and influence) to death, but soon that interim death will become destruction. Ephraim has blood on its hands and has the reviling of Yahweh and of Yahweh's servants on its conscience. Hosea includes reference to human sacrifice, a practice that shows how desperate a people can become (think of a mother being willing for her son to be a suicide bomber). They know that if the crops don't grow, they may die of hunger. One can even imagine someone being willing to be sacrificed for the sake of the family in this connection, perhaps also having a sense of there being nothing to lose if starvation is anyway to come. Yet the practice reflects a turning away from a true understanding of God.

HOSEA 13:12–14:9

Birth and Death

¹² Ephraim's waywardness is preserved,
    his offenses stored up.
¹³ When the pains of giving birth come to him,
    he'll be a child who isn't sensible.

Because at the time he won't present himself
    in the children's breach.
14 From Sheol's hand I could redeem them,
    from death I could restore them.
Where would be your scourges, death,
    where your destruction, Sheol?
Comfort will hide from my eyes,
15   because he's fruitful among the reeds.
An easterly will come, Yahweh's wind,
    coming up from the wilderness.
His fountain will dry up,
    his spring wither.
That will plunder the treasury,
    every object held in high regard.
16 Samaria is guilty,
    because it has rebelled against its God.
People will fall by the sword,
    their babies will be smashed,
    their pregnant women torn open.

14:1 Turn back, Israel, to Yahweh your God,
    because you have fallen through your
      waywardness.
2 Take words with you, and turn back to Yahweh;
    say to him, "Will you carry it all, the waywardness?
Receive something good:
    for bulls we'll render our lips.
3 Assyria isn't to deliver us,
    we won't ride on horses.
We will no more say 'our God'
    to the work of our hands,
    because in you the orphan will find compassion."
4 I shall heal their turning away, I shall love them
    with liberality,
    because my anger has turned away from me.
5 I shall become like dew to Israel; it will flourish like
    the lily,
    and strike roots like a Lebanon [cedar].

6 Its shoots will grow and its splendor will be like an
       olive tree,
     its fragrance like Lebanon.
7 People who sit in its shade will again raise grain,
       and flourish like the vine, its fame like Lebanon
       wine.
8 Ephraim, what shall I have to do with idols
       anymore?—
     I myself have responded and looked to him.
   I myself am like a verdant juniper;
     from me your fruit appears.

9 Who is sensible and understands these things,
     is discerning and acknowledges them?
   Because Yahweh's ways are straight, and the faithful
       walk in them,
     but rebels fall by them.

The last page of *The New Yorker* invites captions for an uncaptioned cartoon, and invites votes on people's caption suggestions for another cartoon. This week a cartoon pictures two people viewing the body of a man in an open coffin; the man still has an intravenous drip. The possible captions are, "He never could commit," or "We'll eventually miss him," or "He had great health insurance." Hardly anyone fancies the idea of dying, so it's good to joke about it. It's said that there was a notice on a hospital bulletin board reminding staff that the first ten minutes of someone's life are among the most dangerous; someone had written underneath, "The last ten minutes can be pretty tricky, too." Birth and death are opposites, yet they have much in common.

This section starts with juxtaposed talk about birth and death. **Ephraim** doesn't want to be born. Birth is painful and risky. But holding back from pain and commitment when the time comes will mean death. And the time has come. **Yahweh** doesn't have a three-strikes law (under which you get treated leniently regarding one or two offenses, but then more harshly), but he does have a thousand-strikes law. And Ephraim has a full crime sheet. To put it another way, Yahweh could rescue Ephraim from the death that threatens the nation, but it won't look to him for such healing. It insists on looking for such resources among the reeds (that is, in **Egypt**) rather than from Yahweh. Its policies will mean death in battle for the men and death in infancy for the little children and death of a horrifying kind in pregnancy for the women. We know from what we see and hear in the news that war works in this way. Nothing changes.

The affirmation that there'll be no comfort contrasts with the motherly declaration in chapter 11, but the second paragraph presupposes that this threat was not a final decision. It's always possible to turn. God's people always have a choice. If Ephraim has already fallen, this experience needs to make it turn, before something worse happens. It was a shot across the bow. Yahweh can always be urged to carry our waywardness instead of making us carry it, though the plea will work only if it's accompanied by the other necessary words, the words that indicate turning back from looking to **Assyria** or Egypt (with its horses) and seeking help from other gods.

In the event, there was no turning and no proving that Yahweh was able and willing to be Ephraim's source of renewal, in the way the second paragraph describes, though the book of Hosea itself doesn't describe how Hosea's warnings were fulfilled in Ephraim's destruction. Its effect is thus to leave us with the choice that was placed before Ephraim. So the closing verse asks, "Won't you see sense?" Don't be like the child that isn't sensible and won't come to birth.

JOEL 1:1–20

All You Can Do Is Pray

¹ Yahweh's message that came to Joel son of Pethuel.
² Listen to this, elders;

give ear, all you inhabitants of the country.
Has this happened in your days,
   or in your ancestors' days?
3 Tell your children about it, and your children, their
     children,
   and their children the next generation.
4 What was left from the cutter, the locust has eaten;
   what was left from the locust, the grub has
     eaten;
   what was left from the grub, the hopper has
     eaten.
5 Wake up, you drunks, and weep; wail, all you wine
     drinkers,
   about the new wine, because it has been cut
   off from your lips.
6 Because a nation has come up against my
     country,
   strong, and without number.
Its teeth are a lion's teeth,
   it has a lioness's fangs.
7 It has made my vine into a waste,
   my fig tree into a stump.
It has stripped its bark and thrown it away;
   its branches have turned white.
8 Wail like a girl girded in sackcloth
   because of her husband in his youth.
9 Offering and libation has been cut off from
     Yahweh's house;
   the priests, Yahweh's ministers, have mourned.
10 The countryside has been destroyed,
   the ground has mourned.
Because the grain has been destroyed,
   the new wine has withered, the fresh oil
     languishes.
11 Farmers, be ashamed; vinedressers, wail,
   over wheat, over barley,
   because the harvest of the countryside has
     perished.

12 The vine has withered, the fig tree languishes,
  pomegranate, palm, and apricot.
All the countryside's trees wither,
  because joy has withered from humankind.

13 Gird yourselves and lament, priests;
  wail, ministers of the altar.
Come, spend the night in sackcloth,
  ministers of my God.
Because offering and libation
  have been cut off from Yahweh's house.
14 Declare a sacred fast, summon an assembly,
  gather the elders, all the inhabitants of the
   country,
to the house of Yahweh your God,
  and cry out to Yahweh.
15 Ah for the day, because Yahweh's Day is near;
  it comes like destruction from the Destroyer.
16 Isn't food cut off in front of our eyes,
  joy and celebration from Yahweh's house?
17 Seeds have shriveled under their clods,
  storehouses are desolate, granaries are in ruins,
  because grain has withered.
18 How the animals have groaned,
  the herds of cattle have been befuddled,
because they have no pasture;
  even the flocks of sheep suffer punishment.
19 To you, Yahweh, I call,
  because fire has consumed the pastures in the
   wilderness,
Flame has burned all the trees in the countryside;
20   even the animals of the wild pant for you.
Because the streams of water dry up;
  fire has consumed the pastures in the wilderness.

Adam Mussa is a Darfuri from Sudan who lived in a refugee camp in Chad. After nearly ten years there, he decided he had to take his family back to Sudan; I don't know what happened to him subsequently. With the aid of equipment taken to the refugees from the United States, before he left he posted pictures of locusts around the camp. He commented that while the locust is a most devastating insect for crops, the refugee children have a different view of it. It's a source of free protein. His pictures showed hundreds of boys hunting for locusts. They hoped that the flock would remain there for a few days. The attitude to locusts in the Middle East as I write is different. Over the past three months enough of them have invaded Egypt from the south to consume ten million people's food supply for a year, and the insects have begun crossing into southern Israel.

The **Judahites** in Joel's day have everything to fear from locusts, and they've experienced the kind of invasion they'd dread. It's as if **Yahweh's Day**, the Day of the Lord, is arriving, the day that brings **Yahweh**'s ultimate judgment on the people. (The comparison with a girl who is mourning presupposes that she's a bride whose husband dies when they're about to get married.)

Sometimes things happen and people are helpless before them. A locust plague is such an experience. It's like a slow tsunami. It seems that people are avoiding facing the facts about what has happened. You can hardly blame them. Better just get drunk. Joel urges them to come before God to cry out to God. The term that's used is the one used for the **Israelites** crying out under their oppression in Egypt. That's how bad the situation is. Priests, elders, people should all assemble in a kind of protest. The bigger the protest, the more likely it is to be heard.

The day comes like destruction from the Destroyer. The Hebrew word for *Destroyer* is Shaddai. That name is commonly translated "Almighty," but it's similar to a word for *destruction*, and this passage indicates that Israelites could notice the similarity. It's a frightening fact that Yahweh can act as Destroyer. Yet the potential comfort is that the one who destroys can also be the one who has mercy. If Yahweh were not in charge, it might be hopeless to ask for restoration and relief. But Yahweh is in charge, and can therefore act in that way. All you can do is pray, but that's a huge "all." The locust epidemic means there won't be the wherewithal to offer Yahweh proper worship; Israelites knew that worship needed to be outward, concrete, and material, not merely inward and verbal. Paradoxically, that lack makes it all the more important to come to the temple to protest and pray.

JOEL 2:1–27

The Years the Locust Has Eaten

¹ Blow the horn in Zion,
    sound the alarm on my sacred mountain.
All the country's inhabitants are to tremble,
    because Yahweh's Day has come.
Because it's near, ²a day of darkness and gloom,
    a day of cloud and murk.
Like dawn spread over the mountains,
    there's a vast and mighty company.
Nothing like it has happened from of old,
    and it won't happen after it,
    through the years of generation after generation.
³ Before it fire has consumed,
    after it flame blazes.
Before it the country was like Eden Garden,
    after it like desolate wilderness—
    indeed, no survivors have been left to it.
⁴ Their appearance is like the appearance of horses;
    like steeds, so they gallop.
⁵ Like the sound of chariots,
    on the tops of the mountains they leap,
like the sound of a blazing fire consuming straw,
    like a mighty company drawn up for battle.

6 Before them, peoples shudder;
    all faces have collected a flush.
7 Like warriors they run,
    like fighters they climb a wall.
They go each of them on his ways,
    they don't deviate their paths.
8 They don't jostle one another;
    they go each man on his course.
When they hurtle through the weaponry,
    they don't break off.
9 They rush at the city,
    they run at the wall.
They climb on the houses,
    through the windows they go in like a
      robber.
10 Before it earth has quaked,
    heavens have shaken.
Sun and moon have gone dark,
    stars have gathered up their brightness.
11 Yahweh—he has given his voice
    before his forces.
Because his army is very vast,
    because it's mighty, performing his word.
Because Yahweh's Day is great,
    very awe-inspiring—who can endure it?

12 But even now (Yahweh's declaration),
    turn to me with your whole heart,
    with fasting, weeping, and lamenting.
13 Rip your hearts, not your clothes,
    and turn to Yahweh your God.
Because he's gracious and compassionate,
    long-tempered and vast in commitment,
    and relents of evil.
14 Who knows, he may turn and relent,
    and leave behind him a blessing,
    an offering and a libation for Yahweh your
      God?

¹⁵ Blow the horn in Zion,
   declare a sacred fast, summon an assembly.
¹⁶ Gather the people,
   sanctify the congregation.
Bring together the elders,
   gather the babies and those nursing at the breast;
the groom is to go out of his room,
   the bride out of her tent.
¹⁷ Between the foyer and the altar the priests,
   Yahweh's ministers,
are to weep, and say,
   "Spare your people, Yahweh.
Don't give your very own to reviling,
   as a byword against them among the nations.
Why should they say among the peoples,
   'Where is their God?'"

¹⁸ So Yahweh became passionate about his country,
   took pity on his people.
¹⁹ Yahweh responded to his people,
   "Here I am, I'm going to send grain to you,
new wine and fresh oil—
   you'll be full of it.
I shall not ever again give you over
   as an object of reviling among the nations.
²⁰ I shall drive the northerner far from you,
   thrust him into a dry and desolate country,
his face to the eastern sea,
   his rear to the western sea.
His smell will go up, his stench go up,
   because he has acted great.

²¹ Don't be afraid, earth, rejoice and celebrate,
   because Yahweh has acted great.
²² Don't be afraid, animals of the wild,
   because the wilderness pastures are green.
Because the tree has borne its fruit,
   fig tree and vine have given their riches.

23   People of Zion, celebrate,
        rejoice in Yahweh your God.
     Because he has given you
        the autumn rain in faithfulness.
     He has made rain come down for you,
        autumn rain and spring rain as before.
24   Threshing floors will be full of grain,
        presses will abound in new wine and fresh oil.
25   I shall repay you for the years
        that locust and grub have eaten,
     hopper and cutter,
        my great force that I sent off against you.
26   You'll eat and eat and be full,
        and praise the name of Yahweh your God,
     who acted wondrously with you;
        my people won't be ashamed forever.
27   You'll acknowledge that I'm in the midst of Israel.
        I am Yahweh your God,
     and there's no other,
        and my people won't be ashamed forever.

Maria Yellow Horse Brave Heart is a Native American professor of social work who realized that the issues people had to deal with in her community couldn't be understood in isolation from its experience of trauma over five centuries. It has undergone overwhelming physical, emotional, social, and spiritual distress and torment as a result of the arrival of European settlers and the events of subsequent centuries. The people who now belong to the community are not the ones who were alive during most of this distress, but trauma's impact on a people isn't confined to the generation that directly experiences it. It carries on having an effect over the generations.

Judah's history overlaps with this experience. It has been subject to repeated invasion by imperial powers, to its people's slaughter, and to its communities' destruction and displacement.

The book of Joel's reference to the **Greeks** in its last chapter implies that it's one of the later books in the Old Testament, and this present section also points to a time when Judah had indeed had plenty of that experience. One of my students has suggested to me that the book reflects the way trauma from the past can have a continuing effect on a people. Here, the trauma of the locust invasion brings back to life the trauma of invasion by a foreign army. Prophets were accustomed to describing that kind of event as the arrival of **Yahweh's Day**. Joel superimposes the description of an invading army on the description of an invading locust plague. A plague of insects might seem a trivial experience compared with an enemy invasion, but the implications of a locust invasion are in their own way as devastating as the implications of a military invasion. But when people reexperience trauma, even a trivial experience can trigger a reaction like the one caused by the original experience.

By portraying the locust invasion in this way, Joel heightens the impact of his message in the first chapter, and heightens the impact of his exhortation concerning the appropriate reaction. It needs to be more than the formal turning indicated by ripping one's clothes. It needs to involve fasting, weeping, and lamenting, and also the turning of the inward person. It needs to involve the whole person, inward and outward.

Joel further heightens the power of the appeal by pointing out some key aspects of who **Yahweh** is. Turning to him can be done in hope because Yahweh is "gracious and compassionate, long-tempered and vast in commitment." Joel picks up Yahweh's own self-description in Exodus 34, and thus reminds Judah about some basics of its knowledge of God. People could think that Yahweh was a God of wrath rather than a God of love, but it's not so. While Joel has assumed that Yahweh was in control of the locusts, he hasn't emphasized that fact—it's the horror of their action that he has stressed. He hasn't talked about the disaster as an act of judgment. But whatever its cause,

Yahweh's giving that revelation at Sinai involved relenting of trouble with which he threatened Israel, so Joel can raise the possibility of Yahweh again relenting of evil. They need to turn; Yahweh may also then turn—turn to them, turn from what he's doing at present. Like Moses, Joel thinks Yahweh may be compelled to do so by his own interests; he needs not to have the world asking, "Where is their God?" It's possible for Yahweh to turn from trouble to blessing. The blessing will have concrete content: the land will bear the wherewithal for people to make offerings and oblations, and thus resume worship of Yahweh.

Yahweh yields to the logic of the people's prayer and promises more than Joel explicitly bids people ask. Yahweh will repay them for the years the locust has eaten. Joel's account of this reaction follows straight on his message about turning to Yahweh, so it looks as if this message illustrates the fusing of an answer to prayer in words and the answer in deed. Joel can pass on to the people the good news that Yahweh has heard their prayer and has said "Yes" to it. That hearing means that the action is so certain to follow that it can be described as if it had also already happened. God's speaking guarantees God's acting. People can start celebrating as if the action itself has come.

JOEL 2:28–3:21

You Can't Control Who Receives God's Spirit

> [28] After that, I shall pour my breath on all flesh,
>   and your sons and daughters will prophesy.
> Your elderly will have dreams,
>   your youths will see visions.
> [29] I shall also pour my breath
>   on your male and female servants in those days.
>
> [30] I shall set portents in the heavens and the earth,
>   blood, fire, and columns of smoke.

31 The sun will turn to darkness, the moon to blood,
   before Yahweh's great and awe-inspiring day
      comes.
32 Anyone who calls in Yahweh's name will escape,
   because on Mount Zion and in Jerusalem
   there'll be an escape group, as Yahweh has said,
      among the survivors whom Yahweh is going
         to call.
3:1 Because there, in those days and at that time,
   when I restore the fortunes of Judah and
      Jerusalem,
2 I shall gather all the nations
   and bring them down to the valley of Yahweh-
      Has-Decided.
   I shall come to a decision with them there
      over my people, my own, Israel,
   whom they scattered among the nations,
      and they divided up my country.
3 For my people they cast lots,
   and they gave a boy for a whore,
      sold a girl for wine and drank it.
4 Now, what are you in relation to me, Tyre and Sidon,
      and all you regions of Philistia?
   Are you giving recompense to me?—if you're
      recompensing me,
   swiftly, speedily, I shall return your recompense
      on your head.
5 Because it was my silver and gold you took,
   the good things that I held in high regard you
      brought into your palaces.
6 Judahites and Jerusalemites you sold to the Greeks,
   so that you have sent them far away from their
      land.
7 Here am I, stirring them up from the place to where
      you sold them,
   and I shall return your recompense on your head.
8 I shall sell your sons and daughters
      into the hand of the Judahites.

113

And they'll sell them into captivity to a far-off
    nation
    (because Yahweh has spoken).

9 Proclaim this among the nations,
    declare a sacred battle.
Stir up warriors,
    all the fighters are to come near and go up!
10 Beat your hoes into swords, your pruning hooks
    into spears;
    the weakling is to say, "I'm a warrior!"
11 Hurry, come, all you nations around, assemble;
    "Make your warriors go down there, Yahweh!"
12 The nations are to stir themselves
    and go up to the valley of Yahweh-Has-
      Decided,
because there I shall sit to make decisions
    about all the nations around.
13 Ply the sickle, because the harvest has ripened,
    come, tread,
because the vat is full, the presses abound,
    because their evil is great.
14 Hordes, hordes, in Verdict Valley,
    because Yahweh's Day is near in Verdict Valley.
15 Sun and moon have gone dark,
    stars have gathered up their brightness;
16 Yahweh roars from Zion,
    gives voice from Jerusalem.
The heavens and the earth tremble,
    but Yahweh is a shelter for his people,
    a stronghold for the Israelites.
17 You'll acknowledge that I am Yahweh your God,
    who dwells on Zion, my sacred mountain.
Jerusalem will be sacred;
    strangers will no more pass through it.
18 On that day the mountains will drop sweet wine,
    the hills will run with milk,
    all Judah's channels will run with water.

> A fountain will go out of Yahweh's house
> > and water the Acacias Wash.
> ¹⁹ Egypt will become a desolation,
> > Edom will become a wilderness, a desolation,
> because of violence done to the Judahites,
> > in whose country they shed innocent blood.
> ²⁰ But Judah will dwell forever,
> > Jerusalem for generation after generation.
> ²¹ I shall treat as innocent their bloodshed
> > which I have not treated as innocent,
> > as Yahweh is dwelling on Zion.

I was a young curate (assistant rector in U.S.-speak) when the "charismatic renewal" happened in England. My rector was rather against it, and so was not too thrilled when my friend David, the other curate, "confessed" at our farewell event that he himself had had this kind of experience of the Holy Spirit coming upon him. Unbeknown to us, the same thing had happened to the rector's wife. The Holy Spirit was closing in on the rector. And yes, he had a similar experience in due course. You can't make this experience happen, because it's God's gift. Maybe you can stop it happening if you try hard; God may give up attempting to give the gift. It looks as if the rector didn't try hard enough.

Joel pictures God's spirit coming on sons and daughters and on male and female servants and on young people and old people. Maybe mothers and fathers aren't excluded, but the emphasis lies on people who don't count so much, by human reckoning. It fits with the way God takes and uses the younger brother rather than the older (people such as Jacob and David). You can't do anything about it if you're the father or mother or older brother—all you can do is smile and rejoice in what God does.

The Hebrew word for *spirit* is also the word for *breath* and *wind*. The translation "breath" reminds us that it is indeed out of our control; we can't decide when breath and thus life starts, nor when it ends. "Wind" has parallel implications; wind is powerful and we can't control it. Maybe Joel belongs to a period when there wasn't much vision and prophesying, like the time in the Church of England before the charismatic renewal happened. Joel promises that this lack won't continue forever. The New Testament sees Pentecost as a fulfillment of Joel's promise, but the church has often found itself back in the situation Joel presupposes, so it's good that his promise could be fulfilled more than once. The promise about **Yahweh**'s breath is the first of a series of separate promises and warnings that comprise the last section of Joel. The vague "after that," which opens the collection, suggests that there's no close link between these prophecies and the situation of the locust plague.

Alongside the promise of God's breath coming on people is the warning about judgment on the oppressive world of the nations, which is more worrying for those of us who belong to Western powers who are in the same position as the great nations of the time in which the prophets lived. Whereas Isaiah 2 describes the turning of swords into hoes, Joel envisages turning hoes into swords. It's a more realistic expectation, and it looks ironic. In effect, Yahweh is saying to the nations, "Make my day." Get yourself ready for battle because it's the last one you'll ever fight. You'll find yourselves in a scene where I shall make the decisions about your destiny, and I shall do so in light of the way you've behaved toward my people and my land and thus my purpose in the world. The repeated promise to a feeble people like **Israel** is that it will be protected when the great crisis comes.

The talk about portents in the heavens and a fountain issuing from Yahweh's house in Jerusalem shows that we are not to be too literal in interpreting the prophecies. Peter's Pentecost sermon in Acts 2 makes that assumption: the events on that Pentecost didn't literally correspond to Joel's picture, but Peter can still understand Pentecost as a fulfillment of it. So it's worth looking at things that happen in the world and asking whether we can see a particular blessing or judgment as another fulfillment of these promises and warnings.

Joel's final note reverses a threat that might seem to hang over Jerusalem. There has often been innocent blood shed by the city as well as in the city, and such blood cries out to heaven. As long as the city continues to be a place of violence, it must pay the price. But God's mercy means that on the basis of its repentance God can find another way of responding to that cry.

AMOS 1:1–2:5

Nations Held Responsible

[1]The words of Amos, who was among the sheep-breeders from Teqoa, which he saw concerning Israel in the days of Uzziah king of Judah and Jeroboam son of Joash king of Israel, two years before the earthquake. He said:

> 2 When Yahweh roars from Zion,
>   gives voice from Jerusalem,
>   the shepherds' pastures will mourn,
>   Carmel's head will wither.
> 3 Yahweh has said this:
>   For three rebellions by Damascus,
>   for four I shall not revoke it,
>   because of their threshing Gilead with iron sledges.
> 4 I shall send off fire against Hazael's house,
>   and it will consume Ben-hadad's fortresses.
> 5 I shall break Damascus's gate bar,
>   cut off inhabitants from Wickedness Valley,
>   the one who holds the scepter from Eden House,
>   and the people of Syria will go into exile to Qir,
>   Yahweh has said.
>
> 6 Yahweh has said this:
>   For three rebellions by Gaza,
>   for four I shall not revoke it,

because of their exiling an entire exile
community,
    handing them over to Edom.
7 I shall send off fire against Gaza's wall,
    and it will consume its fortresses.
8 I shall cut off inhabitants from Ashdod,
    the one who holds the scepter from Ashqelon.
I shall turn my hand against Eqron;
    the remains of the Philistines will perish,
    the Lord Yahweh has said.

9 Yahweh has said this:
For three rebellions by Tyre,
    for four I shall not revoke it,
because of their handing over an entire exile
community to Edom;
    they were not mindful of the brotherhood
covenant.
10 I shall send off fire against Tyre's wall,
    and it will consume its fortresses.
11 Yahweh has said this:
For three rebellions by Edom,
    for four I shall not revoke it,
because he pursued his brother with a sword,
    destroyed his compassion.
His anger tore ceaselessly,
    his wrath watched continually.
12 I shall send off fire against Teman,
    and it will consume Bosrah's fortresses.

13 Yahweh has said this:
For three rebellions by the Ammonites,
    for four I shall not revoke it,
because of their ripping open pregnant women
in Gilead,
    in order to enlarge their territory.
14 I shall set fire to Rabbah's wall
    and it will consume its fortresses,

with shouting on a day of battle,
with a hurricane on a stormy day.
15 Their king will go into exile,
he and his officials together, Yahweh has said.

2:1 Yahweh has said this:
For three rebellions by Moab,
for four I shall not revoke it,
because of his burning the bones of the king of
Edom to lime.
2 I shall send off fire against Moab,
and it will consume Qeriot's fortresses.
Moab will die amid an uproar,
amid shouting and the sound of a horn.
3 I shall cut off the ruler from within it,
and slay all its officials with him, Yahweh has said.

4 Yahweh has said this:
For three rebellions by Judah,
for four I shall not revoke it,
because of their rejecting Yahweh's teaching
and not keeping his laws.
Their lies led them astray,
after which their ancestors walked.
5 I shall send off fire against Judah,
and it will consume Jerusalem's fortresses.

This very morning I read a news item about Damascus. The Syrian president and government are involved in an ongoing battle with insurgent forces in which, at the time of writing, 70,000 people have died and hundreds of thousands been displaced and made homeless. Western sympathies are with the insurgents, but Western powers have been burned by their involvement in Iraq and Afghanistan and they're leery about getting involved. The news report presupposed that Western powers were under a moral obligation to take action, though it added the argument that chaos in Syria was not in the West's interests.

Amos would agree that there are ethical, political, and social obligations resting on both modern Damascus and the modern Western powers. He doesn't assume that anyone needs a special revelation from a prophet to know that certain things are right and certain things are wrong. The way God created human beings built into us a basic awareness of God, of the basic truths about God, and of right and wrong. We may be able to get those awarenesses to atrophy and die, but the awarenesses are natural; it's repudiating them that is unnatural.

God can therefore treat us as people who are responsible for knowing about right and wrong and responsible for failing to live by that knowledge, and God does so to Syria, Philistia, Tyre, **Edom**, Ammon, and Moab—in other words, each of the nations on **Israel**'s borders. Yet Amos is not addressing these peoples. He's talking *about* them, not *to* them. As far as we know, he never left Israel. Prophets regularly talk about the way God sees nations from all over the Middle Eastern world, but they talk about them in the course of communicating with Israel. God's way of looking at the nations is important to Israel.

Precisely how it is important varies. One can imagine Amos preaching in the courtyard of a sanctuary, declaring his judgment on the surrounding peoples ("three . . . four" is a kind of formula for "rebellion after rebellion," while "I shall not revoke it" means **Yahweh** won't revoke his verdict and sentence). And one can imagine that he'd raise a cheer among the Israelites, like a modern preacher declaring judgment on Iran or North Korea. Amos is a sheep-breeder from Teqoa, south of Jerusalem between Bethlehem and Hebron. He knows that Jerusalem is Yahweh's city; Yahweh's house is there. Yahweh thus roars like a lion from Jerusalem. The earthquake is mentioned because of the conviction that it brought a fulfillment of Amos's prophecies of calamity; we have independent evidence of at least one earthquake from Amos's time, in the archeological indications of an earthquake at Hazor in Galilee.

To judge from his book, Amos's main or entire ministry was exercised in **Ephraim**; he'll later tell us how he came to be there, even though he came from a little place in **Judah**. Given the ambivalent relationship between Ephraim and Judah, one can imagine the Ephraimite enthusiasm when Amos adds Judah to the list of peoples on whom God is bringing judgment. In connection with Judah, Amos doesn't simply speak in terms of what any people ought to know. Judah has the **Torah**, and Amos can critique Judah for its cavalier attitude to it and declare that it will be destroyed like the other peoples around. Of course if you were listening to Amos in Judah, or reading his messages in Judah in later times or hearing them read there, the impact on you would be less comforting.

AMOS 2:6–3:15

You, Too

6 Yahweh has said this:
   For three rebellions by Israel,
      for four I shall not revoke it,
   because of their selling a faithful person for silver,
      a needy person for a pair of sandals.
7 You who trample the head of poor people into the
         dirt of the ground,
      and twist the way of lowly people!
   An individual and his father go to a girl,
      so as to profane my sacred name.
8 On surrendered garments
      they lie down by every altar.
   In their God's house they drink
      the wine of people who have been defrauded.

9 And I'm the one who destroyed the Amorite before
         them,
      whose height was like the height of cedars,
      and who was as sturdy as oaks.

121

I destroyed his fruit above
and his roots below.
¹⁰ And I'm the one who brought you up
from the country of Egypt.
I enabled you to go through the wilderness for
forty years,
to take possession of the Amorite's country.
¹¹ I raised up prophets from your children,
nazirites from your young men.
Is this not indeed so, Israelites
(Yahweh's declaration)?
¹² And you made the nazirites drink wine
and commanded the prophets,
"You're not to prophesy."
¹³ There, I'm going to make a split beneath you
as a cart makes a split when full of its grain.
¹⁴ Flight will perish from the swift,
the mighty won't hold onto his strength.
The warrior won't save his life,
¹⁵ the one who wields the bow won't stand.
One swift on his feet won't save himself,
one riding a horse won't save his life.
¹⁶ The stoutest of heart among the warriors
will flee naked on that day (Yahweh's
declaration).

^{3:1} Listen to this message,
which Yahweh has spoken about you, Israelites.
About the entire family
that I brought up from Egypt:
² Only you did I acknowledge
from all earth's families.
Therefore I shall attend to you
for all your acts of waywardness.
³ Do two walk together
unless they've made an agreement?
⁴ Does a lion roar in the forest
and it has no prey?

Does a cougar give voice from its lair
    unless it has caught something?
5 Does a bird fall in a trap on the earth and there's no
      snare there,
    does a trap come up from the ground
    and it hasn't actually caught something?
6 If a horn sounds in a city,
    don't the people panic?
And if evil happens to a city,
    isn't it Yahweh who's done it?
7 Because the Lord Yahweh does nothing
    unless he has revealed his plan
    to his servants the prophets.
8 A lion has roared,
    who would not be afraid?
The Lord Yahweh has spoken,
    who would not prophesy?

9 Make it heard in Ashdod's fortresses,
    and in the fortresses in the country of Egypt.
Say, "Gather on Samaria's mountains,
    look at the great chaos within it,
    the oppressed in its midst."
10 They haven't acknowledged the doing of right
    (Yahweh's declaration)—
the people who store up violence
    and destruction in their fortresses.
11 Therefore, the Lord Yahweh has said this:
An adversary, and around the country,
    he'll pull down your strength from you—
    your fortresses will be plundered.
12 Yahweh has said this:
As a shepherd rescues from a lion's mouth
    two shank bones or the tip of an ear,
so the Israelites who live in Samaria will escape,
    with the leg of a bed or the damask of a couch.
13 Listen, and testify against Jacob's household
    (a declaration of the Lord Yahweh, God of Armies):

¹⁴ On the day I attend to Israel's rebellions for it,
   I shall attend to Bethel's altars.
The altar's horns will be cut off,
   and fall to the ground.
¹⁵ I shall strike the winter palace
   as well as the summer palace.
The ivory palaces will perish,
   the great houses will come to an end
   (Yahweh's declaration).

Yesterday at church a professor of preaching told me with some amusement that she had been called the previous evening by a former student who is now a pastor, who didn't know "what to do with" the set Gospel reading for the day, from Luke 13. (The pastor did acknowledge that Saturday evening is too late to be thinking about the sermon for the next day.) This Gospel reading reports a parable about a fig tree, which stands for the people of God. Jesus speaks of its owner saying that the fig tree can be chopped down next year if it doesn't produce fruit after one more year of manuring. The preacher didn't want to tell people that Jesus said that kind of thing.

Amos perhaps felt the same when he had a similar message to give (if the earthquake came two years later, perhaps Yahweh was less tough than Jesus promised to be). Like Jesus in his parables, Amos uses any means to try to get through his people's resistance. The congregation in the Ephraimites' sanctuary would cheer as Amos declared judgment on their neighbors; such a declaration on those self-righteous Judah-ites would raise an even louder cheer. Amos is serious in his declaration about the other nations, but his rabble-rousing is designed to set the Ephraimites up. The cheers will die as he continues, "For three rebellions by Israel, for four I shall not revoke it." The first words recorded in the book had previewed the point. When the lion roars from Jerusalem, it withers the

Carmel ridge in Ephraim. Yes, Ephraim was in the picture from the beginning.

Amos's critique relates first to the people who are doing OK in the community, who take advantage of people who are hit by bad times. The line about a man and his father going to a young girl also suggests the abuse of the vulnerable, though the issue there isn't quite clear. Amos moves on to the community's failure to respond to all that Yahweh had done for it. Instead, people told the prophets to shut up and persuaded the nazirites to lighten up instead of maintaining their provocative simple lifestyle. Israel was the nation Yahweh singled out—referring to the entire family would again challenge later Judahite readers to see themselves as included here.

The random-looking questions in the third paragraph constitute another attempt to get through to the people. All the questions relate in one way or another to the link between causes and effects. We assume things have explanations. There are reasons why things happen, and when things happen, there are appropriate responses. When trouble comes to Samaria, it won't be a random event. Yahweh will have caused it, and Yahweh has announced it beforehand. Amos speaks as if he's talking about every city, and in some sense God is the one who causes any calamity. But many calamities happen without God announcing them beforehand, and Amos's concern here isn't with a general point about God's sovereignty but with the particular deliberate actions Yahweh takes from time to time in Israel. Prophets announce these events beforehand so that people can respond—and thus give Yahweh reason to have a change of plan. And a prophet who receives such an announcement can hardly keep quiet about it (as people would prefer!).

Prophets sometimes talk about Yahweh's mercy in allowing something to **remain** after God's judgment. The only remains Amos refers to are the useless remains that will only provide the insurance company with evidence that someone once possessed this sheep or that bed.

AMOS 4:1–13

When Worship Is Offensive

¹ Listen to this message, you Bashan cows
    who are on Samaria's mountain,
you who defraud the poor,
    who crush the needy,
who say to their husbands,
    "Bring something so we can drink."
² The Lord Yahweh has sworn by his holiness:
    Now, days are coming upon you
when someone will carry you off with hooks—
    yes, the last of you with fish hooks.
³ Through the breaches you'll go out,
    each woman straight ahead,
and you'll be thrown out to Harmon
    (Yahweh's declaration).

⁴ Come to Bethel and rebel—
    to Gilgal, multiply the rebelling.
Bring your sacrifices every morning,
    your tithes every three days.
⁵ Burn your thank offering of leavened bread,
    proclaim voluntary offerings, make them heard,
because you love it, Israelites
    (the Lord Yahweh's declaration).
⁶ Even though I—I gave you
    emptiness of teeth in all your cities,
lack of food in all your places,
    but you didn't turn back to me (Yahweh's
      declaration).
⁷ Even though I—I withheld the rain from you
    when it was still three months to harvest.
I'd let it rain on one city
    but not let it rain on another city.
One plot would be rained on,
    and a plot on which it would not rain would
      wither.

8   Two or three cities would wander
        to another city to drink water, and not be full.
    But you didn't turn back to me
        (Yahweh's declaration).

9   I struck you with blight and mildew,
        multiplying it on your gardens and orchards,
    the locust would eat your fig trees and olives,
        but you didn't turn back to me (Yahweh's
            declaration).

10 I sent an epidemic among you
        in the manner of Egypt,
    slew your young men with the sword,
        with your captured horses,
    made the smell of your camps rise, even into your
            nostrils,
        —but you didn't turn back to me (Yahweh's
            declaration).

11 I overthrew some of you
        like the extraordinary overthrow of Sodom and
            Gomorrah,
    and you became like a burning stick pulled out
            of the fire,
        but you didn't turn back to me (Yahweh's
            declaration).

12 Therefore this is what I shall do to you Israel;
        because I shall do this to you,
        get ready to meet your God, Israel.

13 Because there is one who shapes mountains,
        creates the wind,
    tells human beings what his thinking is,
        makes dawn into darkness,
    treads on earth's high places—
        Yahweh, God of Armies, is his name."

In a class the other night we were looking at a passage in the Prophets where God says he isn't interested in the community's worship, because its members are worshiping only as an expression of their own self-indulgence. I commented that their attitude rather resembles the way we go to worship in the hope that we'll have a great time and come out feeling high. One of the students visibly blanched. He hadn't previously noticed how self-centered our worship can be.

When Amos invited people to come to Bethel or Gilgal, there's an irony about the invitation. Such cities were the locations of sanctuaries where the community would come and seek Yahweh's blessing at festivals. Amos again shows his rhetorical skill; here he speaks like a priest who is genuinely urging people to come and join in worship. In reality their worship makes their sin worse. The more they worship, the worse it becomes. No one offers sacrifices every day or tithes every three days; Amos is sarcastically encouraging people to be super-committed in their worship.

The problem is that Yahweh has been trying to get their attention and draw them to respond, but they've been ignoring his attempts. They come to worship, but there's no actual turning to God. When they came to worship after experiencing the calamities that Amos here describes, no doubt they prayed fervently for Yahweh to restore them and bless them, but the problem is that they haven't drawn the right conclusions from the troubles they've experienced. It's not always the case that drought, food shortage, epidemic, or defeat means that God is chastising a community for its rebellion, but on this occasion God was doing so, and the people don't consider the possibility. They're like the members of the Corinthian church that had experienced troubles and hadn't asked why (see 1 Corinthians 11). They need to think seriously about who is the God they're failing to take seriously.

Usually it's the men in the community that are the object of the Prophets' critique, because they hold formal authority in community life, but occasionally the Prophets turn to their wives. Bashan cows are well-fed, sleek animals (think Angus bulls). The women resemble them because they're in a position to enjoy the fruits of their husbands' dishonesty, and therefore to encourage it. When human beings swear oaths, they do so by something bigger than themselves. When Yahweh swears an oath, all he can do is swear by his own holiness. (We don't know where Harmon was.)

AMOS 5:1–27

When the Exercise of Authority Becomes Poisonous

1 Listen to this message, which I'm taking up,
   a lament over you, Israel's household:
2 She's fallen, she won't get up, Miss Israel;
   she's abandoned on her land—there's no one to
   help her up.
3 Because the Lord Yahweh has said this:
   The city that goes out as a thousand
   will have a hundred left.
   The one that goes out as a hundred
   will have ten left to Israel's household.
4 Because Yahweh has said this to Israel's household:
   "Seek from me, and live.
5 Don't seek from Bethel, don't go to Gilgal,
   don't cross over to Beersheba.
   Because Gilgal is to go into exile, into exile,
   and Bethel is to become nothing.
6 Seek from Yahweh and live,
   so he doesn't break out like fire on Joseph's
   household,
   and consume Bethel,
   and there's no one to quench it.

7 You who turn authority to poison
   and make faithfulness rest on the earth!
8 He's the one who makes Pleiades and Orion,
   turns deep darkness to dawn.

129

He darkens day into night,
    the one who summons the waters of the sea,
pours them out on the face of the earth—
    Yahweh is his name—
9 the one who flashes destruction on the strong,
    so that destruction comes on the fortress.
10 They repudiate the plaintiff in the gate,
    they detest the one who speaks the whole truth.
11 Therefore, because you tax the poor person,
    take a levy of grain from him:
you have built houses of square stone,
    but you won't live in them.
12 Because I have come to know your many acts of
      rebellion,
    your numerous offenses,
you adversaries of the faithful, takers of a bribe,
    who have turned aside the needy in the gate.
13 Therefore the sensible person keeps silent at such
    a time,
    because it's an evil time.
14 Seek good, not evil, so you may live;
    thus Yahweh, God of Armies,
    will be with you, as you've said.
15 Repudiate evil, give yourselves to good,
    establish judgment in the gate.
Perhaps Yahweh, God of Armies,
    will be gracious to what remains of Joseph."

16 Therefore Yahweh, God of Armies, the Lord,
    has said this:
In all the squares lamenting,
    in all the streets they'll say, "Oh, oh!"
They'll summon the farmhand to mourning,
    and for lamenting the people who know how
    to keen.
17 In all the orchards lamenting,
    when I pass through in your midst, Yahweh
    has said.

18 Hey, you who wish for Yahweh's Day,
    what good really is Yahweh's Day to you?—
  it will be darkness, not light.
19 As when someone flees from before a lion
    and a bear meets him,
  or he comes home, leans his hand on a wall,
    and a snake bites him.
20 Won't Yahweh's Day be darkness not light,
    gloom, with no brightness to it?
21 I have repudiated, rejected your festivals;
    I do not savor your assemblies;
22 If you offer me burnt offerings and your grain
        offerings,
    I shall not accept them;
    a fellowship offering of well-fed animals I shall
        not heed.
23 Take away from me the sound of your songs;
    I shall not listen to the sound of your harps.
24 The exercise of authority is to roll like water,
    faithfulness like a perennial stream.
25 Was it sacrifices and offerings that you presented
        to me
    in the wilderness for forty years, household of
        Israel?
26 You'll carry Sikkut your king and Kiyyun,
    your images, the star of your god,
    which you made for yourselves,
27 and I shall exile you beyond Damascus,
    Yahweh whose name is God of Armies has said.

I've just been listening to a man in his late forties from South Central Los Angeles telling his story. He has spent most of his life in prison because at the age of seventeen he helped two murderers escape from a murder scene, and would never reveal who they were—he knew that if he did so, terrible revenge would come on his own family. A Los Angeles priest got to know him and inspired him to find a new way of life within prison, and eventually to get parole. Before the murder, Vance had already been in a juvenile detention center, and we asked him what might have helped him at that stage, as a young teenager. His reply was, someone who'd have walked with him after he came out. But there was no such person, as few prisoners meet someone like that priest. We leave most inmates to the company of more experienced criminals and to be dragged down into more violence within prison.

It's possible thus to turn the exercise of **authority** to poison, in Amos's devastating phrase. Authority is designed to protect community and individual by providing a way of resolving conflicts. The elders gather at the city gate, and where there's a dispute, they can listen to the case and resolve it. It's a great theory that appears to have advantages over the Western system, but it's just as amenable to being perverted by our human selfishness.

At the beginning of this section, Amos tries another rhetorical maneuver, taking up the form of a mourning song over someone who's died. The audience wonders who's died, and realizes that the answer is, "You have." Amos is mourning the death of the community, which he wants people to see is imminent and inevitable unless they change. He again speaks like a priest in urging people to come to **Yahweh** to seek what they need. But they need genuinely to turn to Yahweh. Merely going to a sanctuary doesn't count—the sanctuaries are among the places that are going to die. Seeking Yahweh has to be expressed in seeking good. As usual there's a nice ambiguity about the use of the words *good* and evil. If the community seeks what's morally good, it will experience good in the form of blessing. If it seeks what's morally evil, it will experience evil in the form of trouble (but a thousandfold in the first case and only three- or fourfold in the second case, to judge from what God says elsewhere).

Amos's reference to **Yahweh's Day** is the first such reference in the Bible, but the idea is evidently a familiar one. "The Day of the Lord" is the day when Yahweh's purpose is fulfilled and people experience the fullness of Yahweh's blessing. That experience would naturally include the putting down of people who attack them—in Amos's day, **Ephraim** is under pressure from the **Assyrian** superpower to the northeast, and on Yahweh's Day the superpower will be put down. The repeated reference to festivals suggests that these would be occasions to look forward to the fulfillment of such hopes and pray for Yahweh to hasten the day.

Amos turns such ideas on their head. The nature of Ephraim's life means that the day when Yahweh's purpose is fulfilled and evil is put down must be one when Ephraim itself is put down, not one when it's blessed. They won't be rescued from the superpower; it will take them and their images far away into **exile**. They think worship is so important, but Amos reminds them that at the beginning of their story as Yahweh's people, when they were still on their way to settled life, they had no permanent sanctuary where the priests could make offerings and sing praise to Yahweh morning and evening. The relationship between Yahweh and the people can survive the absence of singing and offerings. It can't survive the absence of the **faithful** exercise of authority, which needs to roll.

AMOS 6:1–14

A Warning to Loungers

1 Hey, you people who are at ease on Zion,
     who are assured on Samaria's mountain,
   you notables of the first of the nations,
     to whom Israel's household come.
2 Pass over to Kalneh and look,
     go from there to Great Hamat,
     go down to Gat in Philistia.
   Are these better than your kingdoms,
     or their territory than your territory,

³ you who push away the evil day,
    and bring near the rule of violence,
⁴ you who lie on ivory beds,
    lounging on their couches,
  consuming lambs from the flock,
    bullocks from the midst of the stall,
⁵ making music to the sound of the harp like
      David,
    have composed for themselves on musical
      instruments,
⁶ drink from bowls of wine,
    anoint themselves with the finest oils,
    but haven't got sick at the breaking of Joseph?
⁷ Therefore now they'll go into exile at the head of
      the exiles,
    and the revelry of the loungers will stop.
⁸ The Lord Yahweh has sworn by himself
    (a declaration of Yahweh, God of Armies):
  I detest Jacob's majesty,
    I repudiate its fortresses.
  I shall deliver up the city and everything in it.
⁹ If ten people are left in one house, they'll die.
¹⁰ If someone's relative lifts him up
    (the person who burns spices for him)
  to take his bones out of the house,
    and says to whoever is in the inner parts of
      the house,
  "Is anyone still with you?" he'll say "No"
    and he'll say, "Hush, because we are not to
      mention Yahweh's name."
¹¹ Because there: Yahweh is going to command,
    and he'll smash the great house to pieces,
    the small house to bits.

¹² Do horses run on a crag,
    or does one plow it with oxen?
  Because you have turned government to venom,
    faithful fruit to poison,

¹³ you who celebrate at No-Thing,
>   who say "Wasn't it by our strength
>   that we took Qarnaim for ourselves?"
¹⁴ Because here am I, about to raise up against you,
>   Israel's household (a declaration of Yahweh,
>   God of Armies)—
> a nation, and they'll afflict you
>   from Lebo-hamat to the Arabah Wash.

In connection with Daniel, I mentioned that the building where we live is showing its age. Since I wrote that chapter, the situation has become more dramatic. In front of my feet a section of the wall has crumbled because of water intrusion from outside. It's a year since my wife spotted that rain could gain access through weakness in the wall's stucco, but nothing's been done about it. A friend of ours in an upper unit thought she didn't need to be concerned on her own account, but if we all continue to do nothing, the entire wall could collapse, and she'd find herself sitting on the patio of the unit below. Meanwhile, on a sunny afternoon her husband and I sometimes sit relaxing on loungers in the sun together.

So we'd fit well in Samaria, because the **Ephraimites** were doing the same thing (and the opening line makes clear that the **Judahites** were no better, as Jerusalem prophets such as Isaiah and Micah make clear). They were behaving as if everything was OK, enjoying a fine life. They included the notables to whom the community looked for leadership. They all had their head in the sand. It didn't take much intelligence to understand the writing on the wall (note the link with Daniel 5). **Assyria** had already conquered and/or taken control of places to the north and west. You hardly needed to be a prophet to see that Ephraim might be next. Such developments were inevitable not merely politically but morally. How could **Yahweh** not allow a similar fate to overcome Ephraim, given the state of its life? Amos again employs his rhetorical skill, this time in his over-the-top description of the fine life people are living in the capital, which contrasts with their lack of concern at the breaking of Joseph (another way of describing Ephraim—Ephraim was Joseph's son). They set the pace in enjoying life and they'll set the pace in the journey into exile.

The city's fall will mean total destruction. The note about not mentioning Yahweh's name may imply a recognition that Yahweh has acted in judgment and a desire that anyone who's survived the catastrophe may be able to continue hiding—not merely from the human forces but from God's further judgment.

In the third paragraph Amos invites people to imagine something incongruous, in order to note how incongruous are the actions of the people in power and the people's sense of achievement at trivial victories. Amos doesn't need to tweak the name of a place called Lo-debar much to make it mean "No thing." In contrast, the coming invasion will affect Ephraim from its northern border to its southern border. The Ephraimites resemble Nero fiddling while Rome burns.

AMOS 7:1–17

On Appearing before the Heavenly Parole Board

[1]The Lord Yahweh showed me this: there, he was forming a locust swarm at the beginning of the growth of the spring crop. There—the spring crop after the king's reaping. [2]When it had finished consuming the grass in the country, I said, "Lord Yahweh, do pardon, how can Jacob stand, because it's small!" [3]Yahweh relented about this. "It won't happen," Yahweh said.

[4]The Lord Yahweh showed me this: there, he was summoning contention by fire. It consumed the Great Deep and it was consuming the farmland. [5]I said, "Lord Yahweh, do spare, how can Jacob stand, because it's small!" [6]Yahweh relented about this. "It won't happen either," the Lord Yahweh said.

[7]He showed me this: there, the Lord was standing by a lead-weight wall, and in his hand was a lead weight. [8]Yahweh said to me, "What are you looking at, Amos?" I said, "A lead weight." The Lord said, "Here am I, I'm going to put a lead weight in the midst of my people Israel. I shall not again pass over it anymore. [9]Isaac's high places will be desolate, Israel's sanctuaries will be laid waste. I shall rise against Jeroboam's household with the sword."

[10]Amaziah, priest at Bethel, sent to Jeroboam, king of Israel, to say, "Amos has plotted against you within Israel's household. The country cannot put up with all his words. [11]Because Amos has said this: 'Jeroboam will die by the sword, Israel will go into exile, exile away from its soil.'" [12]But Amaziah said to Amos, "Seer, go, flee for your life to the country of Judah, eat bread there, prophesy there. [13]Don't prophesy again in Bethel anymore, because it's the king's sanctuary. It's the kingdom's house." [14]Amos answered Amaziah, "I wasn't a prophet and I wasn't a prophet's son. Rather I was a cattleman and a dresser of sycamore figs. [15]But Yahweh took me from following the flock, and Yahweh said to me, 'Go, prophesy to my people Israel.' [16]Now, listen to Yahweh's message. You're saying, 'You shall not prophesy against Israel. You shall not preach against Isaac's household.' [17]Therefore Yahweh has said this: 'Your wife will whore in the city. Your sons and daughters will fall by the sword. Your land will be apportioned by measuring line. You yourself will die on unclean soil. Israel will go into exile, exile away from its soil.'"

During his twenty-five years in prison, the man I mentioned in connection with Amos 5 appeared before several parole boards asking for parole, and was turned down. Although he was sentenced before the passing of a law that made it possible to commit people to life without the possibility of parole, he lived those years with the lifer's assumption that "When I die, they'll send me home." But the priest who got to know him and saw him change in prison eventually helped him make another request, and against all his expectations, it was granted.

It's possible to think about prayer the way such a person thinks about the parole board. You go through the motions of asking for something, but assume that God and his "parole board" decided long ago what was going to happen. Really your appeal's not going to make a difference. Is prayer designed to change us, not to change God? Of course God in himself doesn't change, but the Bible is clear that God can have a change of mind, particularly about bringing judgment. God's cabinet is indeed like a parole board operating on the old rules, when parole was possible for any prisoner. Indeed, it practically invites people to apply for parole. So God lets Amos see a frightening disaster that could come on the country in the form of a locust plague that could eat up the crops and leave it with no food. God's giving this revelation to Amos presupposes that a prophet is someone who stands between the cabinet and the people. He represents the cabinet to the people by telling them of the cabinet's expectations and decisions, and represents the people to the cabinet by making appeals on their behalf. He appeals; God relents.

The second vision pictures a devastating fire. In the third, a lead-weight wall is presumably a wall built with the aid of a lead weight attached to a cord to check that the wall is vertical. But Hebrew can use the word to mean a lead weight in the sense of a heavy burden. **Yahweh** intends to impose a weight of trouble on the people, including the slaughter of Jeroboam's kingly line.

Amos will shortly report a fourth vision, but the reference to Jeroboam prompts the addition here of an account of how Amos became a prophet. He had evidently delivered this warning at the sanctuary at Bethel. Like other prophets, he'd be preaching there in its courtyards, but he was delivering a quite different message from theirs. And he was delivering this message in a state sanctuary, a place like the National Cathedral or Westminster Abbey. While Bethel has a history going back to Jacob in Genesis, Bethel and Dan were the two sanctuaries in the far south and the far north of **Ephraim** that were set up by Jeroboam's namesake when he established Ephraim as a state. You can't deliver a message of this kind in a state sanctuary! Someone from **Judah** especially can't do that kind of thing! One has a bit of sympathy for Amaziah, who knows he has to report what's going on, but also tries to persuade Amos to get out of here (we don't know whether Amos did so). Amos has no sympathy for him. He believes that someone in Amaziah's position has to make a choice, not try to have it both ways. Amaziah will pay a terrible price for failing to respond to Amos's message. He and his family will be swallowed up in the coming catastrophe.

Amaziah treats Amos as if he's like any other prophet, who is like a preacher or pastor; being a prophet is his job. He's supported by the community for his work. So Amaziah urges Amos to return to his own country to earn his living. Prophecies of Yahweh's judgment on Ephraim will be more popular there! But Amos isn't that kind of prophet. Saying he was not the son of a prophet means he has not been to prophetic school; he isn't the disciple of another prophet. There's nothing wrong with being such a disciple; Elisha was Elijah's disciple and he himself had disciples. Amos is a different kind of prophet.

AMOS 8:1–14

How Many Times Can You Appear before the Parole Board?

[1]The Lord Yahweh showed me this: there, a basket of ripe fruit. [2]He said, "What are you looking at, Amos?" I said, "A basket of ripe fruit." Yahweh said to me, "The ripe time has come for my people Israel. I shall not again pass over it anymore. [3]The palace singers will wail on that day (a declaration of the Lord Yahweh): He has thrown down many a corpse in every place—hush!"

4   Listen to this, you who trample the needy person,
     who eliminate the lowly people in the country,
5 saying, "When will the new moon be over, so we
     can sell wheat,
    and the Sabbath, so we can lay out grain—
  making the measure small but the *shekel* big,
     falsifying the scales by deceit,
6 buying the poor people for silver,
     the needy person for a pair of sandals,
     and selling sweepings as grain?"
7 Yahweh has sworn by the Majesty of Jacob,
     If I ever disregard any of their doings . . .
8 For this, will the earth not shake,
     and everyone who lives in it mourn?
    Will it all not rise like the Nile,
     surge and sink like Egypt's Nile?
9 On that day (a declaration of the Lord Yahweh),
     I shall make the sun set at noon,
     make the earth dark during daylight.
10 I shall turn your festivals into mourning,
     all your songs into lamenting.
    I shall put sackcloth on all bodies,
     shornness on every head,
    I shall make it like the mourning for an only child,
     its end a truly bitter day.

11 There, days are coming (a declaration of the Lord
     Yahweh)
    when I shall send famine through the
     country—
  not famine of bread, not thirst for water,
     but rather of hearing Yahweh's words.
12 People will wander from sea to sea
     and roam from north to east,
  to seek Yahweh's message,
     but not find it.
13 On that day beautiful girls and young men
     will faint with thirst.

¹⁴ People who swear by the sin of Samaria
    and say, "As your god lives, Dan,"
and "As the way to Beersheba lives,"
    will fall and not rise again.

In due course the prisoner I referred to put in another application for parole because his priest friend badgered him to do so. He had no hope of its being granted, and it would have been easier to settle down and accept that he'd be in prison until he died. If he hadn't asked, his application wouldn't have been granted; but he did ask, and it was. Even then, he had a hard time believing that the parole board had said "Yes." When you're granted parole, apparently prisons put you in solitary confinement for a while because you may commit suicide or other prisoners may attack you.

In Amos's third vision **Yahweh** had said he wouldn't pass over **Ephraim** again, and Amos didn't put in another application for mercy, as that prisoner did not for some while. This dynamic recurs in his fourth vision, which completes the sequence after the digression describing Amaziah's reaction to his message and relating how Amos came to be a prophet. There are times when prayers get answered and times when they don't. And the sequence within the four visions (two where Amos prays and gets an answer, and two where he doesn't) might seem to imply that there are times to pray and times not to pray.

Yet maybe the visions declaring that Yahweh will never again pass over the people are designed as another way to get through their thick skulls, to make them change and seek God's restoration. While the point about Amos's prayers is to get God to have a change of mind and relent about acting in judgment, the point about reporting the prayers to people, so that they end up in Amos's book, is to change the people. The report of the first two visions seeks to get them to see that it's possible for God to relent. The report of the third and fourth

141

is to get them to see that you can't assume that this possibility will be open forever. If a child asks a parent for something and the parent has reason to say "No," this refusal may not stop the child asking again, and sometimes the parent may then have reason to have a change of mind; and the relationship of children to parents is a scriptural model for prayer.

The main part of this chapter further nuances the wrongs in Ephraim that demand Yahweh's judgment. Yahweh has already made clear that he doesn't care for the people's coming to worship. He also doesn't care for the way they have itching feet during worship because they want to resume business, especially because the business they want to resume is based on dishonesty.

The final paragraph adds a new twist to the nature of God's judgment. Amos has referred already to the way the Ephraimites in effect told prophets not to prophesy. OK, then, says God, I'll send no more prophets. You can want to hear a message from God but be unable to get one. Once again this is a threat designed to be self-frustrating: if only they'll start listening to Yahweh's message! Then the threat need never be implemented. But people are so committed to their loyalty to the "sin" of Samaria (that is, the alien god that the Samarians worship) that they won't do so. The reference to pilgrimage to Beersheba completes a pairing of the sanctuaries at the northern and southern extremes of Israel as a whole ("from Dan to Beersheba").

AMOS 9:1–15

You Can't Get Away from God

1 I saw the Lord standing by the altar. He said,
Strike the capitals so the thresholds shake;
    break them off onto the head of all of them.
The last of them I shall slay with the sword;
    not one of them will flee as a fugitive,
    no escapee will escape.

2 If they dig into Sheol,
   from there my hand will get them.
If they go up into the heavens,
   I shall bring them down.
3 If they hide on the top of Carmel,
   from there I shall search them out and get them.
If they conceal themselves from before my eyes
   at the bottom of the sea,
from there I shall command the serpent
   and it will bite them.
4 If they go into captivity before their enemies,
   from there I shall command the sword and it will
      slay them.
I shall set my eye on them for evil,
   not for good.

5 The Lord Yahweh Armies—
   he touches the earth and it melts,
and all the people who live in it mourn,
   and all of it rises like the Nile,
   sinks like Egypt's Nile.
6 He built his lofts in the heavens
   and founded his structure on the earth,
the one who summons the sea's waters
   and pours them over the face of the earth—
   Yahweh is his name.

7 Aren't you like the Sudanese to me, Israelites
   (Yahweh's declaration)?
Didn't I bring Israel up from the country of
      Egypt—
   and the Philistines from Caphtor, and Syria from
      Qir?
8 There: the Lord Yahweh's eyes are on the offending
      kingdom;
   I destroy it from on the face of the earth.
Except that I shall not totally destroy Jacob's household
   (Yahweh's declaration).

⁹ Because here I am, I'm going to command,
 and shake Israel's household among all the
  nations,
As someone shakes in a sieve,
 and no pebble falls to the earth.
¹⁰ All the offenders in my people will die by the sword,
 the people who say, "The evil won't reach or
  meet us."

¹¹ On that day, I shall raise David's fallen bivouac
 and repair its breaches,
I shall raise its ruins
 and build it as in days of old,
¹² so they'll enter into possession of what remains
  of Edom,
 and all the nations that were called by my name
 (a declaration of Yahweh, who is going to do this).
¹³ There, days are coming (Yahweh's declaration):
 the plowman will meet the reaper,
 the treader of grapes the one trailing the seed.
The mountains will drop sweet wine,
 all the hills will flow.
¹⁴ I shall restore the fortunes of my people Israel;
 they'll build up ruined cities and live [there].
They'll plant vineyards and drink their wine,
 they'll make gardens and eat their fruits.
¹⁵ I shall plant them on their soil and they won't
  uproot again
 from on their soil, which I have given them,
 Yahweh your God has said.

More than once I have been involved in a day of prayer when the theme passage of Scripture has been Psalm 139, which speaks of God being able to reach us wherever we are and knowing all about us. These themes can be an encouragement on such occasions, though it's noticeable that people then usually stop the reading of the psalm before the darker part at the end, which speaks of God slaying the wicked, and makes one wonder whether God knowing all about us and being able to reach us wherever we are is necessarily good news.

Amos uses the same phrases as the psalm in his final attempt to scare the **Ephraimites** into turning from the destructive path they're walking. Imagine you could dig into **Sheol** (the place where dead people are) or climb into the heavens, climb to the top of Mount Carmel (not the highest mountain in Ephraim, but a spectacular one because of the way it soars from the ocean and the plain on either side of it) or dive to the bottom of the sea. You couldn't get away from God's judgment. Amos has one more vision to share, and in this last vision there's no more talk of even the possibility of God passing over the people. In this vision, Amos sees the sanctuary thrown down.

How can **Yahweh** act in that way to his own people? The tough answer is that if you don't behave like God's people, you can't expect to be treated like God's people. God brought the **Israelites** from **Egypt**, but also brought the Philistines from across the Mediterranean and the Syrians from somewhere in the opposite direction (we don't know exactly what locations "Caphtor" and Qir refer to). It's quite a claim about God's sovereignty in the lives of peoples that are more Israel's foes than its friends, and it's quite a put-down for Ephraim itself. Whatever is the kingdom that does wrong, it may find itself in trouble, and being Israel may not make you an exception.

Or maybe it will make you an exception. The Philistines disappeared; Israel didn't. In Israel's case, Yahweh commits himself to a judgment that involves separating the wheat from the chaff. He has made a commitment to Israel and he can't get out of it, but it's still the case that people in Israel can't expect to get away with things. Israel may go on; most Israelites won't. You still can't simply assume you'll be OK because you belong. Amos's warnings to Ephraim came true when Samaria fell to the **Assyrians** in 722 and its population was transported.

The book of Amos closes with another qualification of the idea that God might totally destroy Israel, which some of his prophecies might seem to have implied. The book began with **Zion**, and it closes with David. If Amos uttered these words in Ephraim itself, it again implicitly reminds Ephraim that it has no future except in association with Zion as the place Yahweh chose and with David as the king Yahweh chose. There'll come a time when David's line is cut down, and a time when the nations can have their way with **Judah** and when the **Edomites** in particular can take over much of Judah's land. But these events won't be the end of the story. From time to time the book of Amos has warned potential readers in Judah that they can't afford to act superior in relation to Ephraim, because Jerusalem escaped conquest by Assyria when Ephraim was conquered, given that Judah is involved in the same contempt for Yahweh as Ephraim. And in due course Jerusalem indeed falls. But the close of the book also offers encouragement to them. It's not the end of the story.

OBADIAH

"Who Could Bring Me Down to Earth?"

¹ Obadiah's vision.

> The Lord Yahweh said this about Edom.
> We have heard a report from Yahweh;
>> an envoy has been sent out among the nations:
> "Rise up—
>> let's rise up against it for battle!"
² Now: I'm making you small among the nations;
>> you're going to be very despised.
³ The arrogance of your mind has deceived you,
>> you who dwell in the clefts of the crag,
>> the height of its abode,
> You're saying within yourself,
>> "Who could bring me down to earth?"

⁴ If you go up high like an eagle,
  if you place your nest among the stars,
 from there I could bring you down
  (Yahweh's declaration).
⁵ If thieves came to you, if robbers came by
    night
   (how you're ruined)
   wouldn't they steal what they needed?
 If grape-pickers came to you,
   wouldn't they leave gleanings?
⁶ How Esau is being ransacked,
   its treasures sought out!
⁷ All the people you were in covenant with
   are sending you off to the border.
 The people you were allied with
   are deceiving you, overpowering you.
 The people who eat your bread
   set a trap beneath you
   (it has no understanding).
⁸ On that day (Yahweh's declaration)
   shall I not eliminate the experts from Edom,
   understanding from Mount Esau?
⁹ Your warriors will be shattered, Teman,
   so people will be cut off from Mount Esau
     through slaughter.
¹⁰ Through the violence to your brother Jacob,
    shame will cover you,
    and you'll be cut off forever.
¹¹ On the day you stood aside,
    on the day foreigners captured his resources,
   and aliens came into his gates, and cast lots for
     Jerusalem,
    you, too, were like one of them.
¹² You shouldn't have looked [in that way] at your
     brother's day,
    the day this alien thing happened to him.
   You shouldn't have rejoiced at the Judahites
    on the day of their perishing.

You shouldn't have talked big
    on the day of distress.
13 You shouldn't have come into my people's gate
    on the day of their disaster;
you shouldn't have looked [in that way],
    you too,
at the evil that happened to him
    on the day of his disaster.
14 You shouldn't have stood at the crossroad
    to cut down his escapees;
you shouldn't have handed over his survivors
    on the day of distress.
15 Because Yahweh's Day is near
    against all the nations.
As you did, it will be done to you;
    your deed will come back upon your head.

16 Because as you [Judahites] drank on my sacred
      mountain,
    all the nations will drink continually.
They'll drink and swallow,
    and they'll be as if they had never been.
17 But on Mount Zion there'll be a group of survivors,
    and it will be holy.
Jacob's household will dispossess
    the people who dispossessed them.
18 Jacob's household will become a fire,
    Joseph's household a flame,
Esau's household straw,
    and they'll burn among them, consume them.
Esau's household will have no survivor,
    because Yahweh has spoken.

19 The Negev will possess Mount Esau;
    the Lowland [will possess] the Philistines.
They'll possess the Ephraimite country
    (that is, the Samarian country),
    and Benjamin [will possess] Gilead.

20   This exile community of forces belonging to the
          Israelites
          [will possess] what [belongs to] the Canaanites as
              far as Zarephat.
      The exile community from Jerusalem which is in
          Sepharad
          will possess the cities of the Negev.
21   Deliverers will go up on Mount Zion
          to govern Mount Esau,
          and the kingship will belong to Yahweh.

The news reported last week that the number of refugees
in the world steadily increases and their plight worsens. No
one wants refugees to settle in the countries where they now
are—neither the host countries nor the people themselves.
Yet three-quarters of the refugee groups registered by the
United Nations have been in exile for five years or more. The
grandchildren of Palestinians who fled from what became
the state of Israel more than sixty years ago still hold onto the
keys of their family homes. People long to go home and wish
out of existence the people who now occupy their homes and
farm their fields.

Ironically, Obadiah presupposes such an experience on the
part of Israel's own ancestors. Presumably this prophecy was
not the only one Obadiah ever uttered, but apparently the
community recognized this one to be really important. One
can guess at the reason. The book presupposes a time much
later than Amos, which it follows; the fall of Jerusalem and
the exile of Judah have now happened. But in theme it links
with the ending of Amos with its reference to Edom, Israel's
neighbor to the southeast. Israel was aware of a family link
with Edom; Israel traced its ancestry back to Jacob and Edom's
ancestry back to Jacob's big brother Esau—hence the prophecy's
references to Esau. Teman was also another name for Edom.
Obadiah's opening reference to what he has heard may connect
with the substantial overlap between Obadiah and Jeremiah

49—the prophet is preaching a sermon on an earlier text, applying **Yahweh**'s earlier word to a later day.

The Prophets refer a number of times to Edom's wrongful treatment of Judah. We don't have Edom's version of events, but it's plausible to think of the **Babylonians** engaging Edomite support in their attack on Jerusalem and/or to imagine Edom having an eye to the main chance for itself. Whereas the Old Testament refers to Yahweh's using Ammon and Moab to chastise Judah, it makes no such "excuses" for Edom. More certainly, the exile and succeeding decades saw gradual Edomite occupation of Judah's southern territory. Yahweh's promise through Obadiah is that Edom won't go unpunished; its takeover of Judahite land won't continue forever. As Mary puts it (Luke 1), lifting up the people who have been down has as the other side of the coin putting down the people in power. Obadiah draws attention to two of Edom's assets that Edom won't actually be able to rely on: its mountainous position and its learning. Edom had a reputation for learning that would find expression in practical expertise.

The way Edom was a thorn in Judah's side in the period after the exile might be enough to explain the focus on Edom here and elsewhere in the Prophets. Yet later, Edom became a cipher for a nation that opposes Yahweh's purpose, such as Rome (like Babylon in the New Testament). The transition to talk about "the nations" toward the end of the prophecy hints at a similar understanding here (the drink to which Obadiah refers is a cup of poison). Similarly Obadiah generalizes the promises concerning Judah. In the period after the exile, Judah is a sad little people, under pressure from all sides. The wider notion of Israel could seem to have no future. Yahweh promises it has one. It will regain its land not only from Edom but from Philistia to the west and from the "Canaanites" or Phoenicians to the northwest. Sepharad perhaps refers to a Jewish community in Turkey. In the period after the exile, **Ephraim** or Samaria was a gray area—

the people there might claim to be worshipers of Yahweh, but the Judahites were not sure they could be trusted religiously or politically. The renewed Israel will embrace them, too.

But the last word concerns Yahweh's reigning in the world. Not Edom, not Judah, not Israel, not a Davidic king, but Yahweh.

JONAH 1:1–2:10

How to Pray from Inside a Fish

[1]Yahweh's message came to Jonah son of Amittai: [2]"Set off, go to the great city of Nineveh and proclaim against it, because their evil has come up before me." [3]But Jonah set off to flee to Tarshish from before Yahweh. He went down to Yafo and found a ship going to Tarshish, paid its fare, and went down into it to go with them to Tarshish from before Yahweh. [4]But Yahweh flung a great wind into the sea, and there was a great storm in the sea, and the ship threatened to break up. [5]The sailors were afraid and cried out each of them to his god. They flung the things in the ship into the sea to lighten it of them, while Jonah went down into the inmost parts of the vessel, lay down, and went to sleep. [6]But the captain went to see him and said to him, "What are you doing, sleeping? Get up, call on your god. Perhaps the god will give a thought to us and we shall not perish."

[7]People said to each other, "Come on, let's cast lots so we can know on whose account this evil has come to us." They cast lots, and the lot fell on Jonah. [8]They said to him, "Will you tell us on whose account this evil has come to us? What's your work? Where do you come from? What's your country? What people are you from?" [9]He said to them, "I'm a Hebrew. I revere Yahweh the God of the heavens, who made the sea and the dry land." [10]The men were greatly afraid, and said to him, "What is this you have done?"—when they knew that he was fleeing from before Yahweh, because he told them. [11]They said to him, "What shall we do to you so that the sea may quiet

down from upon us?" (when the sea was growing stormier). [12]He said to them, "Pick me up and hurl me into the sea, and the sea will quiet down from upon you, because I acknowledge that it was on my account that this great storm came upon you." [13]The men rowed to get back to dry land, but couldn't, because the sea was growing stormier upon them. [14]They called to Yahweh, "Oh, Yahweh, may we not perish for this man's life. Don't set innocent blood upon us. Because you, Yahweh—as you wished, you have acted." [15]They picked Jonah up and hurled him into the sea; and the sea stopped raging. [16]The men greatly revered Yahweh and made a sacrifice to Yahweh and made vows.

[17]Yahweh provided a big fish to swallow Jonah, and Jonah was in the fish's insides three days and three nights. [2:1]Jonah prayed to Yahweh his God from the fish's insides:

2 "I called out of my distress
      to Yahweh and he answered.
   When I called for help from Sheol's belly,
      you listened to my voice.
3 You threw me into the deep,
      into the heart of the seas.
   The river surrounded me;
      all your breakers and waves passed over me.
4 I myself said, 'I have been driven away
      from in front of your eyes.'
   Yet I shall again look
      toward your sacred palace.
5 The waters overwhelmed me, up to my neck,
      the deep surrounded me.
   Reed was wrapped around my head
6   at the roots of the mountains.
   I went down into the earth,
      its bars were about me forever.
   But you brought my life up from the Pit,
      Yahweh my God.
7 When my life was ebbing away from me,
      I was mindful of Yahweh.

152

My plea came to you,
> to your sacred palace.
8 People who pay regard to empty vanities
> forsake their commitment.
9 But I with a voice of thanksgiving will sacrifice to
> you;
> > what I have vowed I shall fulfill—
> > deliverance belongs to Yahweh."

10 Yahweh spoke to the fish, and it vomited Jonah
> onto the dry land.

Last night it was the final class of the term, and for three students it was the end of their time at seminary. Two of them don't know what they'll be doing next, which is reason for some anxiety. Will I miss God's call? Yet the bigger challenge is the possibility that I may deliberately evade God's call. The rector of one of the most flourishing churches in the north of England used to acknowledge that he should never have been there. God had wanted him to go and work abroad, but he had resisted the call. Of course, when we do so, God often rolls his eyes and calls us to something else and blesses our work, as had happened in this rector's life.

I like to picture God rolling his eyes at Jonah when he boarded a ship going the opposite direction from the one to which God pointed. In his case God doesn't give him a different calling and find someone else to go to Nineveh. Sometimes you can get away from God's call; sometimes you can't. Why did Jonah resist? The second half of his story will explain. Preaching judgment to Nineveh, the capital of **Assyria**, may result in its repenting; indeed, Jonah knows that the reason God must have for sending him to preach judgment is a desire to find an excuse for cancelling the judgment. Jonah doesn't want judgment on the great Assyrian oppressor to be cancelled. As Obadiah follows nicely on Amos, then, Jonah follows nicely on Obadiah. Obadiah witnesses to God's toughness, Jonah to

God's desire to show mercy. Jonah wishes he were Obadiah; his story warns Israel not to get too attached to Obadiah's theme. In the story he continues to show his lack of insight into the truth about God. The pagan sailors understand more than he does, even if they too have some pretty primitive ideas.

Jonah was a prophet to whom **Yahweh** gave promises about **Ephraim** regaining territory it had lost (see 2 Kings 14). He lived in the decades just before Amos and Hosea and he's thus the first of the prophets to have a book named after him, but his book differs from theirs in being a story about him, not a collection of his prophecies. I assume it's "just a story," like one of Jesus' parables, but the reason for that assumption isn't that it's impossible to survive for three days inside a fish (the kind of logic Jonah himself would have indulged in). Of course "Yahweh the God of the heavens, who made the sea and the dry land" (as Jonah magnificently calls him) could preserve someone inside a fish. The reason is rather the jokey nature of this story. It resembles many of Jesus' parables. The reason for telling this story about Jonah is that a prophet who gave such a positive promise to Ephraim is the last kind of person to enthuse over Nineveh escaping God's judgment.

Readers can be so preoccupied with the big fish that they miss the significance of the prayer Jonah prays when he's inside it. How does one imagine Jonah praying there? One might have thought he'd be saying "Help, help, help" and "Sorry, sorry, sorry." He's saying neither of those things. He's saying "Thank you, thank you, thank you." The fish is his means of salvation, God's means of getting him back from the middle of the Mediterranean to dry land. So he doesn't need to plead for help. His prayer is a thanksgiving, like ones in the Psalms—it wouldn't have been out of place there. For Jonah, the peril of the deep was all too literal, but in his prayer this talk has become a metaphor, as it is in the Psalms. Like a thanksgiving psalm, his thanksgiving recalls the peril he was in, and speaks of the way death seemed inevitable—it was as if he was already in **Sheol**. He recalls his hopelessness and recalls the way he prayed, and he knows that his prayer did reach Yahweh in his heavenly dwelling. He recalls the way Yahweh answered and he speaks of the confidence he now feels of being able to come to the earthly temple to meet with God again. In the Psalms people often give thanks to God for their deliverance even when it's promised but not yet implemented, which is appropriately the way Jonah gives thanks.

But is there an irony in the prayer? Does his failure to say "Sorry, sorry, sorry" suggest that he still has a lot to learn?

JONAH 3:1–4:11

So What Do You Think?

[1]Yahweh's message came to Jonah a second time: [2]"Set off, go to the great city of Nineveh and proclaim to it the declaration that I'm going to tell you." [3]Jonah set off and went to Nineveh in accordance with Yahweh's message. Now Nineveh was an extraordinarily great city, three days' walk through. [4]Jonah started to go through the city, one day's walk. He proclaimed, "Forty days more, and Nineveh will be overthrown!" [5]The Ninevites believed God. They proclaimed a fast and put on sackcloth, from the most lordly to the least. [6]The message reached the king of Nineveh, and he got up from his throne, took off his robe from upon him, covered himself with sackcloth, and sat on ash. [7]He got people to cry out in Nineveh, "By the decree of the king and his lords: Human being and animal (flock and herd) are not to taste anything. They're not to graze; they're not to drink water. [8]They're to cover themselves in sackcloth, human being and animal, and call on God mightily. They're to turn, each one from his evil way and from the violence that is in their hands. [9]Who knows, God may turn and relent and turn from his anger, and we may not perish."

[10]God saw their actions, that they turned from their evil way, and God relented of the evil that he spoke about doing

to them. He didn't do it. [4:1]But it seemed evil to Jonah, a great evil, and he was furious. [2]He prayed to Yahweh: "Oh, Yahweh, isn't this what I said when I was in my country? Because of this I fled previously to Tarshish, because I knew that you're a God gracious, compassionate, long-tempered, vast in commitment, and relenting about evil. [3]Now, Yahweh, will you take my life from me, because my dying will be better than my living." [4]Yahweh said, "Was it good that you felt fury?"

[5]Jonah had gone out from the city and sat east of the city. He had made a bivouac for himself there and sat under it in the shade until he could see what would happen in the city. [6]Yahweh God provided a qiqayon vine and it grew up over Jonah so as to be a shade over his head to save him from what was evil for him. Jonah felt a great gladness about the qiqayon. [7]But God provided a worm when dawn came up next day and it struck the qiqayon, and it withered; [8]and when the sun rose, God provided a scorching east wind, and the sun struck on Jonah's head. He grew faint and asked for his life, that he might die. He said, "My dying will be better than my living." [9]God said to Jonah, "Was it good that you felt fury about the qiqayon?" He said, "It was good that I felt fury, to the point of death." [10]Yahweh said, "You pitied the qiqayon, for which you didn't labor and which you didn't grow, which came into existence overnight and perished overnight. [11]Should I not pity the great city of Nineveh, in which there are more than 120,000 human beings who don't know their right hand from their left, and many animals?"

Not many people who drink green beer this coming Sunday, St. Patrick's Day, will know who Patrick was. Though he became Ireland's patron saint, he was born in Scotland, in the year 387, but as a teenager was captured by Irish raiders and taken off as a slave. Eventually he escaped and got back to Britain, and was ordained, but then had a vision in which he received letters from Ireland that begged him to "come and walk among us once more." So he went off to that country from which his kidnappers had come. It boggles the mind to think of his achievement in becoming the person credited with making Christ known there.

It boggles the mind to think of Jonah marching into Nineveh and achieving what he achieved. It might initially seem that he has learned from his attempt to avoid doing what Yahweh said, but it will become clear that he has learned nothing. Yet any unwillingness he still feels as Yahweh force-marches him into the Assyrian capital makes no difference to his effectiveness. When you're God's mouthpiece, it may not matter what's in your heart. It matters to you and your own relationship to God, but not in connection with what God achieves through you, which may be unrelated to what is in your heart. It's a reason not to assume that a successful pastor is in close touch with God, and not to assume that an unsuccessful pastor has lost touch with God.

Even the animals are involved in Nineveh's response. They're part of the community; if the city is destroyed, they'll pay the price, too. So Jonah meets with a response that most prophets in Ephraim or Judah would give their eyeteeth for, which is perhaps one of the points about the story ("Won't you Israelites learn from the Ninevites?"). What they needed to do was turn from their previous lifestyle. *Turn* is a word commonly translated "repent," but repentance also implies a change of attitude and a sense of sorrow, and the Ninevites' outward observances show that they repent in this sense, too. They themselves entertain just a little hope that God may be prepared to "turn" or repent, to give up the idea of judgment and act in mercy. They entertain just a little hope that God may be prepared to *relent*, another word commonly translated "repent," but a word that does indicate a change of attitude.

Jonah knows that their tentative hopes are justified, and when God relents, he turns on God in a way that provokes a smile. "I knew you'd do that. That's why I never wanted to come here." And he quotes back at God the words that God had uttered at Sinai about being gracious, compassionate,

157

long-tempered, and vast in commitment (see Exodus 34). They're words that Joel has already quoted and applied to Israel, and Joel has added reference to the possibility of God acting that way toward Israel. Jonah wouldn't mind that application. But to the Assyrians?

Meanwhile Yahweh provides some shade for Jonah (we don't know what a qiqayon was), then adds insult to injury by letting the vine die as quickly as it grew. This act offends Jonah not only because he loses his shade but because he feels sorry for the plant. "Excuse me?" says God. "You feel sorry for the plant? What about the people in Nineveh? And for that matter the animals there (who would be implicated in the city's destruction)?"

The book ends with that question. It doesn't tell us Jonah's answer, but leaves us as readers to answer the question, because it's our answer, not Jonah's, that matters.

MICAH 1:1–2:5

Disaster Reaches the Very Gates

[1]Yahweh's message that came to Micah the Morashtite in the days of Jotham, Ahaz, and Hezekiah, kings of Judah, which he saw concerning Samaria and Jerusalem.

> 2 Listen, peoples, all of you, pay heed,
>> earth and all that lives in it,
>> so that the Lord Yahweh may be a witness against you,
>> the Lord from his sacred palace.
> 3 Because there—Yahweh is going to come out from his place,
>> come down and tread on earth's heights.
> 4 The mountains will melt beneath him, the valleys split,
>> like wax before the fire,
>> like water propelled down a slope.

158

5 All this is for Jacob's rebellion,
   for the household of Israel's offenses.
   What's Jacob's rebellion—is it not Samaria,
   and what's Judah's great high place—is it not
   Jerusalem?

6 I shall make Samaria into a ruin in open country,
   a place for planting a vineyard.
   I shall propel its stones into the ravine,
   expose its foundations.

7 All its images will be smashed, all its earnings
   burned in fire;
   all its idols I shall make into desolation.
   Because it collected [them] from a whore's
   earnings,
   and they'll return to a whore's earnings.

8 Because of this I shall lament and wail,
   I shall go barefoot, stripped.
   I shall make lament like the jackals,
   mourning like the ostriches.

9 Because its wound is incurable,
   because it has come right to Judah.
   It has reached right to my people's gate,
   right to Jerusalem.

10 Don't tell it in Gat, don't weep at all;
   in Bet-le'aphrah roll in dirt.

11 Pass on, you residents of Shaphir, naked in shame;
   the residents of Sa'anan have not gone out.
   Bet-ezel is in lamentation;
   it will take its support from you.

12 Because the residents of Marot
   are sick for something good.
   Because evil has come down from Yahweh
   to Jerusalem's gate.

13 Hitch the chariot to the steed,
   residents of Lachish.
   It was the archetype of offense for Ms. Zion,
   because Israel's rebellions were found in you.

¹⁴ Therefore you'll give parting gifts
  to Moreshet-gat.
The houses of Akzib will be a disappointment
  to Israel's kings.
¹⁵ I shall yet bring a dispossessor to you,
  residents of Mareshah.
Israel's splendor
  will come as far as Adullam.
¹⁶ Shave your head, cut off your hair,
  for the children in whom you delighted.
Extend the shaving of your head like an
   eagle,
  because they've gone into exile from you.

^{2:1} Hey, you people planning wickedness,
  doing evil on their beds.
At morning light they do it,
  because it's in the power of their hand.
² They covet fields and steal them—
  houses, and take them.
They defraud a man of his house,
  a person of his own possession.
³ Therefore Yahweh has said this:
Here am I, against this family I'm planning
   evil
  that you won't free your neck from.
You won't walk tall,
  because it will be a time of evil.
⁴ On that day, someone will lift up a poem
   against you,
  he'll wail with a wail, a wailing (he said).
"We are destroyed, destroyed,
  he has supplanted my people's allocation.
Aaaagh, he removes it from me,
  to a traitor he allocates our fields."
⁵ Therefore there'll be no one for you casting the
   cord by lot
  in Yahweh's congregation.

160

Five years ago my stepdaughter and her husband found themselves in the middle of a coup in Chad in the middle of Africa, where they were working on behalf of Darfuri refugees. They spent the night in the basement of the hotel in the capital, N'Djamena, from where with the bizarreness of technology they were able to call my wife (as she now is) and say that they doubted whether they'd still be alive the next day, and therefore needed to say goodbye. In the event French troops intervened and they lived to tell the tale.

In Micah's day Jerusalem is to have that kind of experience. Micah speaks of disaster reaching the very gates of Jerusalem; he was more right than he may have realized. The book's introduction locates him in the time of Jotham, Ahaz, and Hezekiah, so he is Isaiah's contemporary. In Hezekiah's day, the **Assyrian** army under Sennacherib invaded **Judah** and devastated the country. Places such as Lachish, Judah's second-biggest city, were destroyed. The Assyrian troops proceeded to march on Jerusalem, but never captured it. Second Kings 18–19 tells the story, and Sennacherib's own records note how he shut up Hezekiah in Jerusalem "like a bird in a cage"; but he didn't take the city.

The places Micah lists in the third paragraph are in the lowlands toward the Mediterranean that Sennacherib did devastate. Micah chooses towns whose names can seem to presage their fate. Bet-le'aphrah could almost mean House of Dirt, while Akzib is almost identical to a word meaning disappointment or deception, and Mareshah sounds as if it has something to do with taking possession. Lachish's own name is close to the word for *steed*. It was a strongly fortified city that might stand for reliance on self-sufficiency in respect of self-defense and thus be the epitome of **Israel**'s rebellion against **Yahweh**. Micah offers it an ironic exhortation to mount its horses; it will need them to flee.

Micah came from a little town near Lachish, but like Amos he left his small hometown and fulfilled his prophetic ministry in the city. Whereas Amos worked in Samaria and talks mostly about **Ephraim** but incorporates side glances at Judah, Micah worked in Jerusalem and talks mostly about Judah but incorporates side glances at Ephraim. But whereas Amos's messages became known in Jerusalem (after the fall of Samaria, they will have been preserved and reflected on there), Micah's messages never reached Samaria, as far as we know. His messages about Ephraim were designed for Judah to hear, to undermine any tendency of its people to think they were superior to Ephraim, or to be afraid of Ephraim (as Isaiah makes clear they were), or to think they'd be safe when Samaria fell. Micah's talk about a whore's fees shows how his message also parallels the message Hosea delivered in Samaria. Praying to other gods is a kind of religious adultery, except that it involves paying for what you get and financing the making of images—which will all be destroyed when the city falls.

In passing, the second and third paragraphs noted reasons for Yahweh's judgment: religious faithlessness and reliance on one's own defenses. The final paragraph focuses on community issues. People with resources and power in the community plot how they can extend their resources and power. The punishment will fit the crime. Yahweh will see that they lose their land allocation. The "traitor" will be the person they were themselves trying to cheat out of his or her land. And they themselves will never again have the chance to take part in the allocation of land.

MICAH 2:6–3:12

Papa Don't Preach

> 6 "Don't preach," they preach—
>   they don't preach about these things.
>   Reproaches won't turn away—
> 7 should it be said, Jacob's household?

"Has Yahweh's temper become short,
   are these things his acts?"
Aren't my words good
   with someone who walks upright?
8 Just now my people rises up as an enemy;
      you strip the mantle off the front of the coat
   from people passing by with assurance,
      returning from battle.
9 The women among my people—
      you drive out of her nice house.
   From her infants
      you take my glory forever.
10 Rise up, go,
      because this won't be [your] resting place,
   on account of defilement that will destroy,
      with a grave destruction.
11 If someone were going about
      with wind and deceptive falsehood,
   "I shall preach to you about wine and liquor,"
      he'd be this people's preacher.
12 I definitely intend to assemble Jacob, all of you,
      I definitely intend to gather what remains of
         Israel.
   I shall put them together like sheep in a fold;
      like a flock in the midst of its pasture,
      it will be noisy with people.
13 One who breaks out in front of them is going up;
      they're breaking out, passing through the gate,
      going out through it.
   Their King passes through in front of them,
      Yahweh at their head.

3:1 I said, "Will you listen, heads of Jacob,
      rulers of Israel's household:
      is it not for you to know how to exercise
         government?"
2 They're people who repudiate good
      and give themselves to evil,

who tear the skin from on my people,
    their flesh from on their bones,
3 who eat my people's flesh and strip off their skin,
    and break up their bones,
who cut them up as in a pan,
    like meat inside a pot.
4 Then they'll cry out to Yahweh,
    but he won't answer them.
He'll hide his face from them at that time,
    as they've done evil deeds.

5 Yahweh has said this
    against the prophets who lead my people
      astray:
They chew with their teeth
    and proclaim that things will be well,
but someone who puts nothing in their mouths—
    they declare a sacred battle against him.
6 Therefore there'll be night for you, without
      vision,
    darkness for you, without divination.
The sun will set for the prophets,
    the day will be dark for them.
7 The seers will be ashamed,
    the diviners disgraced.
All of them will cover over their mouth,
    because there's no answer from God.
8 But as for me, I'm full of power, with Yahweh's
      wind,
    and mighty authority,
to declare to Jacob its rebellion,
    to Israel its offense.
9 Will you listen to this, heads of Jacob's household,
    rulers of Israel's household,
you who despise authority,
    and make what's straight crooked,
10 one who builds Zion with bloodshed,
    Jerusalem with crime.

11 Its heads exercise authority for a bribe,
   its priests teach for a fee.
Its prophets divine for money,
   but lean on Yahweh:
"Isn't Yahweh in our midst?—
   evil won't come upon us."
12 Therefore, on account of you,
   Zion will be a field that is plowed.
Jerusalem will become ruins,
   the house's mount a great high place in a forest.

I was in a church service the other week when the congregation applauded enthusiastically at the end of the sermon. Over the fifteen years I have been in the United States, applauding in church is an aspect of Christian practice that I haven't become used to. I don't mean I think it's inherently wrong; it's a cultural difference. Yet I did feel uneasy about applause at the end of that sermon. I was afraid that the preacher had scratched where the congregation itched, told people something confirming what they thought, made them feel comfortable, even made them feel self-righteous. It's said that the preacher's job is to comfort the disturbed and disturb the comfortable.

Micah is preaching in discomforting fashion, and it has got him into trouble with other preacher-prophets, who don't talk the way he does. They tell him he shouldn't do so. Can he seriously mean that God brings about the kind of destructive events that he prophesies or that the community is already experiencing? Yes he can, they're fooling themselves that the worst is over, and these preachers shouldn't be giving people the empty reassurances that they're peddling. It's upright people who can expect to hear good words from God. Micah issues his challenge to the community itself. It's responsible for evaluating its preachers' words and coming to a judgment about who's really bringing God's word.

The nation is its own worst enemy—or rather, it's internally divided, and the people with power and money are behaving like an enemy to the people without power or money. The defilement resulting from such wrongdoing will mean it loses the resting place that **Yahweh** gave it in the land. Yahweh's gathering the members of his flock together sounds like good news, but it's bad news—as their King he's going to break through their defenses in the wrong direction, to lead them out of their city.

Of course the trouble is that preachers get paid, one way or another. They get paid a salary, or get paid for preaching a particular sermon, or perhaps just get paid in the currency of appreciation. So they have something to eat, as the last paragraph notes. You don't get paid for being confrontational and bringing bad news. Or conversely, they're quite willing to tell people who won't put food in their mouths that God is against them. But the day is going to come when Yahweh acts as Micah says, and then the prophets will have nothing to say to their people. They'll be incapable of interpreting what happens.

They no doubt spoke with power and authority, and with at least the outward veneer of people who were possessed by Yahweh's spirit. But there's an ironic link with Micah's comment in the first paragraph about preachers who go about proclaiming a message that is mere wind. The Hebrew word for *wind* and *spirit* is the same word (*ruah*). These prophets will have gone about claiming to speak with the spirit when their words are wind. Micah really does speak in the power of the wind—Yahweh's wind or spirit. There will have been nothing different about the outward form of his words or his demeanor. You can't tell who is the real prophet by looking at him. You have to look at the correlation between his words and the situation to which he speaks. The facts about life in Jerusalem require someone to confront it as a rebellious city. Someone who fails to do so cannot be a true prophet.

An unwillingness to recognize that fact and an insistence on applauding preachers who offer words that people can agree with makes the city's fate more certain. At least Micah got away with preaching his negative sermon, as we know from a story in Jeremiah 26: some people wanted to kill Jeremiah for his negative preaching, but other people reminded them of Micah's words about **Zion** becoming a plowed field, which he had gotten away with, and Jeremiah escaped with his life.

MICAH 4:1–5:9

The New Jerusalem

¹ But at the end of these days
    the mountain of Yahweh's house
will be secure at the head of the mountains,
    elevated above the hills.
Peoples will stream to it;
²   many nations will go and say,
"Come, let's go up to Yahweh's mountain,
    to the house of Jacob's God,
so he may teach us in his ways
    and we may walk in his paths."
Because teaching will go out from Zion,
    Yahweh's word from Jerusalem.
³ He'll decide between many peoples
    and issue reproof for strong nations, even
        far away.
They'll beat their swords into hoes,
    their spears into pruning hooks.
Nation won't take up sword against nation,
    and they'll no more learn war.
⁴ They'll sit, each person
    under his vine and under his fig tree,
with no one disturbing—
    because the mouth of Yahweh Armies has
        spoken.

167

5   Because all the peoples walk,
         each in the name of its god,
      but we ourselves will walk
         in the name of Yahweh our God forever
            and ever.

6   On that day (Yahweh's declaration),
         I shall assemble the lame,
      gather the ones driven out,
         to whom I have done evil.
7   I shall turn the lame into a remainder,
         the outcast into a strong nation.
      Yahweh will reign over them on Mount Zion
         from now and forever.
8   And you, watchtower of the flock,
         citadel, Ms. Zion,
      to you the former rule will arrive and come,
         the kingship of Ms. Jerusalem.
9   Now, why do you issue a shout,
         is there not a King in you?
      Has your Advisor perished,
         that writhing has seized you like a woman
            birthing?
10   Writhe and scream, Ms. Zion,
         like a woman birthing!
      Because you'll now go out from the city
         and dwell in the open country.
      You'll come as far as Babylon,
         but there you'll be saved.
      There Yahweh will restore you
         from the hand of your enemies.

11   But now many nations
         have assembled against you.
      They're saying, "It shall be profaned,
         our eye shall look upon Zion."
12   But they don't know Yahweh's intentions,
         they don't understand his plan.

168

Because he has gathered them
　　like sheaves on the threshing floor.
13　Rise up, thresh, Ms. Zion,
　　because I shall make your horn iron,
　　I shall make your hooves bronze.
You'll crush many peoples,
　　devote their dishonest gain to Yahweh,
　　their resources to the Lord of the entire earth.

5:1　Now, you may form a troop, Ms. Troop—
　　someone has laid siege to us.
They strike Israel's leader
　　on the cheek with a club.
2　But you, Bethlehem in Ephratah,
　　small in being among Judah's clans,
from you will emerge for me someone to be a
　　　ruler in Israel
　　whose emerging is of old, of ancient days.
3　Therefore he'll give them up until the time
　　when the one who is going to birth has given
　　　birth,
and the rest of its relatives
　　return to the Israelites.
4　He'll stand and shepherd with Yahweh's might,
　　in the majesty of the name of Yahweh his God.
They'll live, because now he'll be great,
　　as far as the ends of the earth,
5　　and this will mean things are well.
Assyria, if it comes into our country,
　　if it treads through our fortresses—
we'll set up over it seven shepherds,
　　eight people as generals.
6　They'll shepherd the country of Assyria with the
　　　sword,
　　the country of Nimrod with its gates.
He'll rescue us from Assyria if it comes into our
　　　country,
　　if it treads through our territory.

7   Jacob's remains will become,
        in the midst of many peoples,
    like dew from Yahweh,
        like showers on grass,
    which don't wait for people,
        don't look to human beings.
8   Jacob's remains will become, among the
            nations,
        in the midst of many peoples,
    like a lion among the animals in the forest,
        like a cougar among the flocks of sheep,
    which, when it passes by, tramples and mauls,
        with no one to rescue.
9   Your hand will rise over your adversaries,
        and all your enemies will be cut off.

When I first showed up at the church to which I have belonged for nearly twenty years, three things made me realize that I wanted to join. It had an inviting fellowship, color-blind in its welcome (most members are black, I'm white). It used the Episcopal liturgy and thus affirmed our shared link with the Christian tradition over the centuries. And it manifested a warm spirituality; it was evident that it had a living relationship with Christ. It's just a little congregation, but those are the features that persist, and if we are to attract other people, they'll be the features that attract them.

The Old Testament thinks more in terms of people being attracted to **Israel**, being drawn to recognize that the true God is active there, than in terms of Israel going out to convince people that they should recognize this God. This way of thinking is expressed in Micah's vision of nations flocking to Jerusalem. The prophecy also appears in Isaiah 2; maybe it's original there, or maybe here, or maybe it wasn't associated with a specific prophet and it found its way into the collections of both prophets. Maybe God was happy with that development because it's so important.

Its opening phrase is commonly translated "at the end of the days" or "in the last days," which can give the impression that it explicitly refers to a time way after that of Micah, but the expression rather suggests something to happen at the end of the period the prophet has just been referring to. The preceding chapters have been depressing, and have ended with Zion as a plowed field. But like the opening chapters of Isaiah, the book of Micah alternates warnings with promises. Perhaps there's an element of stick and carrot about the arrangement—people's response decides which type of future they experience. But most readers of the book of Micah would live after the disaster that fulfilled his warnings, and the promise would encourage them with the assurance that God is still to achieve what the vision portrays. Israel usually lived in the shadow of the world of nations that surrounded it, a divided, threatening, and depressing world. It was in no position to make a difference in that world. The prophecy makes astonishing promises to it. God will be the one who makes a difference. God will do so by drawing the world to Jerusalem. Insofar as Israel has to do anything, it's to walk in the name of its God. Of course there's an irony here, because that obligation was one that Israel found hard to fulfill. To the people of God in the twenty-first century, it offers the same hope that it offered Israel, and the same challenge.

The three "Now" prophecies that follow put us back in the middle of the pressures upon the city. First, even in the midst of a life-threatening crisis, Judah is challenged not to be hopeless, because its hope lies in God's presence in its midst. He's the King and Advisor who counts; even if the crisis issues in exile (as it eventually did), it won't be the end of the story. Second, if the nations think they'll have their way with Jerusalem, they'll find they have to rethink things (they'll have to choose between coming to Zion for Yahweh to teach them and to sort out their disputes, and having Judah impose a "solution" on them). Third, there comes the challenge (perhaps ironic) to

Ms. Zion now to become Ms. Troop (that is, to turn herself into an army) in light of the assault on the city and its ruler. Micah is again utilizing his skill with words in that the challenge could as easily be understood to mean "Gash yourself [as a sign of mourning], Ms. Gash." Either way, hope here lies in the fact that God has not finished with the line of David, Bethlehem's famous son; in a different context seven or eight centuries later, Matthew found Micah's promise strangely illuminating when Jesus was born in Bethlehem. God's promise to David goes way back, and God is not going to abandon it. If Yahweh gives Judah up because of its waywardness for a while, the abandonment won't last forever. The day will come when Ms. Zion (the pregnant mother back in the first "Now" prophecy) gives birth to a new David and when Judah's relatives return to their land. The **Assyrians**, who wrought such devastation in **Ephraim**, needn't do the same to Judah.

In effect the closing verses do lay alternative possibilities before nations such as Assyria. Yahweh's desire is that Israel, even though it's now much reduced compared with what it once was, should be like dew or rain to the nations—a means of blessing. But it can alternatively be a means of destruction, like a wild animal. The nations make their choice.

MICAH 5:10–6:16

Faithfulness and Reserve

> [10] On that day (Yahweh's declaration)
> I shall cut down your horses from your midst
> and destroy your chariots.
> [11] I shall cut down the cities in your country,
> demolish all your fortresses.
> [12] I shall cut down the charms from your hand,
> and you'll have no chanters.
> [13] I shall cut down your images
> and your pillars from your midst.

You won't bow down anymore
    to something made by your hands.
14 I shall uproot your posts from your midst
    and destroy your cities.
15 But I shall effect redress in anger and wrath
    on the nations that have not listened.

6:1 Will you listen to what Yahweh has said:
    Get up, contend with the mountains;
        the hills must listen to your voice.
2 Listen to Yahweh's contention, mountains,
        enduring ones, earth's foundations.
Because Yahweh has a contention with his people,
    he has an argument with Israel.
3 "My people, what have I done to you,
    how have I wearied you?—testify against me.
4 Because I got you up out of the country of
        Egypt,
    redeemed you from a household of servants.
I sent before you
    Moses, Aaron, and Miriam.
5 My people, will you be mindful
        of what Balaq king of Moab planned,
        and of what Balaam son of Beor answered him,
    from Acacias to Gilgal,
        for the sake of acknowledging Yahweh's faithful
          acts."

6 By what means shall I approach Yahweh,
    bow down to God on High?
Shall I approach him by means of burnt offerings,
    bullocks a year old?
7 Would Yahweh take pleasure in thousands of rams,
    in myriads of streams of oil?
Should I give my firstborn for my rebellion,
    the fruit of my body for my own offenses?
8 He has told you, people, what's good,
    what Yahweh seeks from you:

> rather, implementing decisions
> > and giving yourself to commitment,
> > and being diffident in how you walk with
> > > your God.

> [9] The voice of Yahweh calls to the city
> > (awe for your name is good sense):
> Listen to the club—
> > and who appointed it [10]still?
> Shall I forget the faithless household,
> > the faithless storehouses,
> > the accursed short measure?
> [11] Shall I be innocent with faithless scales,
> > with a bag of false weights?—
> [12] whose rich people are full of violence,
> > whose residents speak falsehood,
> > and their tongue is deceit in their mouths?
> [13] So I myself am indeed making you sick,
> > > beating you,
> > desolating you for your offenses.
> [14] You—you'll eat but not be full,
> > and you'll have emptiness inside.
> You'll displace, but not save,
> > and what you save I shall give to the sword.
> [15] You—you'll sow but not harvest;
> > you—you'll tread olives, but not rub with oil,
> > and grapes, but not drink wine.
> [16] You have kept Omri's laws,
> > every practice of Ahab's household,
> walked by their policies,
> > for the sake of my making you a desolation,
> your residents a hissing;
> > you'll bear the reviling of my people.

We're getting ready for Holy Week and Easter at church. So on Friday we'll be cutting down palm branches (living in California is different from living in England). On Saturday we'll be making palm crosses from them and on Sunday we shall parade around with these. I'm told that Sunday School children are excited about the foot-washing service we shall have on Maundy Thursday, and I'm also planning the Easter Day celebration. It will be much simpler than the Easter Vigil we had in England, but there'll be some lighting of an Easter Candle and some special words and some walking in procession.

If we're not careful we'll fall foul of Micah's slamming critique of **Judah**. Its people brought burnt offerings of year-old bullocks; Micah could imagine them bringing thousands of rams, using rivers of oil for anointing, even seeking to atone for their wrongdoing by sacrificing their children (there were times when Judahites did so). It's hard for Western people to imagine people bringing such offerings, because we have different ways of devising worship that costs a lot of money in the size of buildings and the salaries we pay, and a lot of time in planning and rehearsing.

"You make it so complicated," God says. "What I'm interested in is simple." He specifies two things. "First, I wish you'd make **decisions** in a way that expresses **giving of yourselves** to commitment." God wants to see **authority** exercised, but exercised in a way that embodies the commitment of people to one another. The exercise of authority usually works in favor of the people exercising it. As a minimum they live in better houses and have better health plans; they may more directly see that decisions get taken in ways that improve their position.

The other thing God looks for is diffidence in the way people walk with him. Whereas the first priority concerns relationships within the community, the second concerns relationships with God (so Jesus' summary of the **Torah** in terms of commitment to God and to one's neighbor corresponds to these two expectations). Whereas the first priority picks up common themes in the Prophets, the command about diffidence before God uses a rare word, but related contexts suggest it means reserve, the opposite of arrogance or presumption. Judahites assumed that they knew what would count as appropriate worship, as they knew what would count as wise political policies. Maybe they asked for God's guidance at the beginning of a cabinet meeting, but then they used their intelligence. What else can one do? But it's easy for us to use intelligence and creativity in a way that imposes the results of our thinking on God.

The section starts there. Judah was seeking to safeguard its future by developing its defenses and developing its military resources, its intelligence resources (chanters and charmers), and its spiritual resources (images and pillars). None of these actions counts as deference to **Yahweh**. Won't the people apply their minds to the way things had been when they faced crises in the past? Haven't they listened to their own stories about Yahweh's acts of **faithfulness** that brought them out of **Egypt**, through the wilderness, and into the promised land?

The section ends with a critique that relates to Yahweh's expectation of community life characterized by an exercise of power that embodies mutual faithfulness. You only have to look at what happens in the market to see the failure here, Micah declares. Consider what merchants do and get away with because the authorities collude (because the merchants are also the authorities). In a cutting critique, Micah declares that Judah's lifestyle corresponds to **Ephraim**'s in the days of Omri and his notorious son Ahab. It's as if Judah is deliberately setting itself up to be made into a desolation, like Ephraim. So the people are not only faithless. They're stupid. Yahweh has been wielding the club against them, but they won't listen to its message. They'll put in all manner of effort to guarantee their own future, but none of it will work. They'll end up reviled by Yahweh's people as the cause of their country's desolation.

MICAH 7:1–20

Lament, Prayer, Expectation, and Worship for the City

¹ Oh, for me, because I've become
    like the gatherings of summer fruit,
    like the gleanings of the vintage.
There's no cluster to eat,
    or early fig that my appetite could fancy.
² The committed person has perished from the
      country,
    there's no one upright among the people.
All of them lie in wait for blood;
    one person hunts his brother with a net.
³ Both hands are on evil, to do it well:
    the official asking, and the leader, with a reward.
The important man speaks his appetite's desire
    and they weave it together.
⁴ The best of them is like a brier,
    the most upright worse than a thorn hedge.
The day your lookouts described,
    the day of your appointment, is going to come;
    now the disarray they described will happen.
⁵ You people, don't believe a neighbor,
    don't trust a friend.
From the one who sleeps in your embrace
    guard the opening of your mouth.
⁶ Because son demeans father,
    daughter rises up against her mother,
daughter-in-law against her mother-in-law;
    a person's enemies are the people in his household.
⁷ But I shall look to Yahweh,
    I shall wait for my God who saves me;
    my God will listen to me.

⁸ Don't celebrate over me, my enemy;
    if I have fallen, I'm getting up.
If I sit in darkness,
    Yahweh will be my light.

9   I shall carry Yahweh's wrath
        if I have offended against him,
    until he contends for me
        and makes a decision for me.
    He'll bring me out into the light,
        I shall look at his faithfulness,
10 My enemy will see,
        and shame will cover her,
    the one who says to me,
        "Where is he, Yahweh, your God?"
    My eyes will look on her;
        now she'll be for trampling like mud in the streets.
11 A day for mending your walls—
        that will be a day when your boundary moves far
            away.
12 That day one will come to you
        from Assyria and the cities of Egypt,
    from Egypt as far as the River,
        to sea from sea, to mountain from mountain.
13 But the earth will become a desolation because of
            its inhabitants,
        as the fruit of their deeds.

14 Shepherd your people with your club,
        your very own flock,
    dwelling by itself in a forest
        in the midst of farmland.
    May they graze in Bashan and Gilead
        as in days of old,
15   as in the days when you came out of the country
            of Egypt.

    When I show it my wonders, 16nations will see
        and be ashamed of all their might.
    They'll put their hand to their mouth,
        their ears will go deaf.
17 They'll lick the dirt like a snake,
        like things that crawl on the earth.

178

> May they come trembling out of their strongholds
>   to Yahweh our God,
>   may they be in dread and awe of you.
> [18] Who is a God like you, one who carries
>   waywardness
>   and passes over rebellion for the remains of his
>   own possession?
>   He doesn't hold onto his anger forever,
>   because he delights in commitment;
> [19] he'll again have compassion on us and trample on
>   our wayward acts;
>   he'll throw all our offenses into the depths of
>   the sea.
> [20] You'll show truthfulness to Jacob,
>   commitment to Abraham,
>   as you swore to our ancestors from days of old.

A mile north of our house and half a mile west of our church on Friday, two men in their twenties and a four-year-old boy were the victims of a non-fatal shooting in an incident that looks gang-related. Local people wonder whether there's a link with the fatal shooting of another man two months ago, and of another man who was standing in the wrong place at the wrong time three weeks previously, on Christmas Day. It's not surprising that older members of our church are afraid to go out at night (though most of these shootings happened during the day). Meanwhile, a local newspaper commented on the fact that in a recent election the winning representative for this area was the person who had most money to spend on the campaign.

It's easy to be depressed about the city. This final section of Micah starts there, though it opens with an image from elsewhere. The prophet feels like a poor person going out to the fields at harvest time, and finding that there's nothing to glean. The reapers have done such a fine job that there's nothing to collect. So the prophet goes around the city looking

179

for committed people or upright people and can find none. One and all, people are interested only in trampling one another. Once again Micah indicts the people with responsibility in the city, who can use their position in order to do well for themselves, but he also notes that whether he looks at community relations or the family, things look equally depressing and discouraging.

Yet in the midst of this first paragraph it becomes clear that he isn't merely bemoaning the situation to no one in particular, but lamenting it to God, as the one who has warned the city through his lookouts (the prophets) and who's going to bring about the day he's appointed for it. His bringing God into the picture continues as he speaks of looking to God for protection. He needs to be able to do so because of his personal danger. One who speaks the truth as he does can expect the people who are the objects of his critique to make him another of their victims.

In the second paragraph, the prophet puts words in the city's own mouth. It will in due course be destroyed in fulfillment of those warnings that it has ignored. But it can pray that its fall won't be the end of its story, and that the peoples who are the means of God's acting against it—who so act for their own sake, not because they see themselves as God's executors—will get their comeuppance. The words the prophecy puts on the city's lips include a recognition of its wrongdoing (in effect, they acknowledge that Micah was right). They're not merely a self-willed determination to survive the calamity. They're a statement of expectancy in God. Thus they meet with a response from God that affirms their expectation. There'll be a day for destruction, but there'll be a day for rebuilding and a day when the people scattered from the city all over the known world will be free to return when the nations themselves receive their own reward.

The city again speaks, urging **Yahweh** to do more. In Micah's day, and even more in later times, **Judah** was a sad little enclave around Jerusalem. On its behalf the prophecy asks God to restore its wider pasturage, using his shepherd's club to protect its people from those who'd oppose such a restoration, acting the way he did when he came out of **Egypt**, bringing them with him. Once more God responds, promising to show such wonders again and confound the nations again.

The city has the last word. Maybe it envisages the nations coming trembling out of their strongholds in a negative fear of God, or maybe in a positive submission to God. The former would fit the immediate context; the latter would fit Micah's earlier vision of the nations coming to Jerusalem. Maybe they decide. If they come in awed submission, they become the beneficiaries of God's mercy, which dominates the book's final lines, as the prophecy closes its prophecy and its prayer with worship.

NAHUM 1:1–2:9

The Empire Writes Back

1 The pronouncement about Nineveh, the book of
   the vision of Nahum the Elkoshite.

2 Yahweh is a God who is passionate and takes redress;
   Yahweh takes redress and is a master of fury.
   Yahweh takes redress on his adversaries,
   maintains it toward his enemies.
3 Yahweh is long-tempered but big in strength,
   and certainly doesn't treat people as innocent.
   Yahweh—his way is in the whirlwind and storm,
   the cloud is the dust from his feet.
4 He blasts the sea and withers it,
   dries up all the rivers.
   Bashan and Carmel languish,
   Lebanon's bud languishes.
5 Mountains quake before him,
   the hills melt.

181

The earth lifts before him,
 the world and all the people who live in it.
⁶ Before his wrath, who can stand,
 and who can rise against his angry burning?
His fury pours out like fire,
 and rocks shatter because of him.
⁷ Yahweh is good, a stronghold on the day of trouble,
 and he acknowledges people who take refuge
  with him.
⁸ With a sweeping flood he makes an end of
  someone's place,
 pursues his enemies into darkness.
⁹ What do you plan for Yahweh?—he makes an end;
 trouble doesn't rise twice.
¹⁰ Because they're tangled among thorns,
 and drunk as with their drink,
  they're consumed like straw that is fully dry.

¹¹ From you has gone out
 one who plans evil against Yahweh,
 one who counsels wickedness.
¹² Yahweh has said this:
 if they're thriving and even so many,
even so they're sheared and are passing away;
 whereas I afflicted you, I shall afflict you no more.
¹³ So now, I shall break its yoke from on you,
 tear off your shackles.

¹⁴ Yahweh has commanded against you:
 nothing more from your name will be sown.
From your god's house I shall cut off
 carved image and cast image.
I shall make your grave,
 because you're insignificant.
¹⁵ There, on the mountains the feet of a herald,
 proclaiming good fortune:
celebrate your pilgrimage, Judah,
 fulfill your vows.

Because wickedness will no more pass through you,
the whole of it is cut off.

2:1 A shatterer has gone up against you—
guard the guard posts.
Watch the road, gird up your loins,
fortify your strength all you can.
2 Because Yahweh is restoring Jacob's majesty,
like Israel's majesty.
Because wasters have wasted them,
ravaged their branches.
3 His warriors' shield is painted red,
the soldiers clad in scarlet.
The chariotry is with flashing fire on the day it's
made ready,
the junipers are brandished.
4 In the streets the chariotry race,
they rush about in the squares,
their appearance like torches,
they speed like lightning streaks.
5 He musters his nobles, they fall as they go;
they hurry to its wall, the siege shelter is made
ready.
6 The river gates open, the palace melts;
7it's decreed, it's exiled, it's taken up.
Its servant girls lament like the voice of doves,
beating on their breasts.
8 Nineveh was like a pool of water of old, but they're
fleeing;
"Stop, stop"—but no one can turn them.
9 Plunder silver, plunder gold,
there's no limit to the things prepared,
the splendor from all the things that people hold
in high regard.

Some years ago, British Indian novelist Salman Rushdie published a piece in the London *Times* about writers in Britain's former colonial empire. In a riff on the movie title *The Empire*

Strikes Back, the piece was entitled "The Empire Writes Back." Such writers assert, argue for, and demonstrate the independent viability and importance of work emerging from their once-colonial cultures and resisting the framework of thinking imposed on them in their imperial past. They assert their countries' independence as not merely a matter of government but of thinking and self-understanding.

In Nahum's day, **Judah** is effectively an **Assyrian** colony. There is no body of Assyrians resident in Jerusalem, directly controlling affairs there, but Assyria controls its relations with other peoples from its capital, Nineveh, and extracts taxes for the privilege of being part of the Assyrian Empire. Judah's position is thus a little like Kenya's or Malaysia's when they were seeking independence from Britain in the 1950s.

In the Twelve Prophets so far, the center of gravity has lain in the eighth century BC, the heyday of Assyrian power, the time of Hosea, Amos, Jonah, and Micah (and also Isaiah ben Amoz). In Nahum, Habakkuk, and Zephaniah (and Jeremiah) the focus moves into the seventh century BC, the years of Assyria's decline; it was eventually taken over by **Babylon**. Nahum's job is to declare that Assyria's fall will indeed happen. He was proved right, which will likely be one reason why this little collection of his prophecies was included in the Scriptures. "Elkoshite" indicates where Nahum comes from, but we don't know where the city of Elkosh was.

Prophets such as Nahum give no encouragement to Judah to attempt violent resistance to Assyria, though it's not because they think violence is wrong but because the task of the people of God is to trust in God and let him sort out their future. They have in common with modern colonial writers a passion to discourage their people from simply accepting their fate as inevitable. They want to encourage hope in their people, and that is Nahum's aim.

The prophets can see a power such as Assyria as both God's agent and God's enemy. It's God's agent because it's God's means of chastising **Israel** for rebelling against God. But Assyria acts in this way not because it wants to serve God but because it wants to extend its power and wealth. Nahum declares that God is not one who simply sits on the side when an empire oppresses others for such reasons, even if it assures itself it's also bringing benefits to the people it conquers. Nahum takes up the style and some of the words from God's self-revelation in Exodus 34, in which God declares himself to be gracious and forgiving, and points out that this revelation doesn't mean **Yahweh** is indifferent when nations behave in a way that demands redress. Yahweh has passion to arouse in those circumstances. How stupid to make plans against Yahweh! He also has an army to muster. Nahum may be referring to the army of another nation that Yahweh will marshal (in which case, the literal referent will be Babylon, which will in due course take on Assyria). But more likely he's referring to Yahweh's heavenly forces.

Grammatically, his prophecies sometimes address Assyria, sometimes Judah. His actual audience is Judah, the people directly encouraged when God speaks of acknowledging people who take refuge with him. But Judah is also able to overhear what God is saying to Assyria, for its further encouragement.

NAHUM 2:10–3:19

The Fall of the Bloody City

¹⁰ Emptiness, just emptiness, devastation;
    the spirit melts, the knees knock.
All bodies tremble,
    the faces of all of them have collected a flush.
¹¹ So where is the lions' dwelling,
    the pasture for the cougars,
where the lion walked, the lioness,
    the lion's cub, with no one disturbing,

¹² the lion tearing enough for its cubs,
and strangling for its lionesses,
filling its lairs with prey,
its dwellings with prey?
¹³ Here am I toward you
(a declaration of Yahweh Armies):
I shall burn its chariotry in smoke,
the sword will devour your cougars.
I shall cut off your prey from the earth;
your aides' voice will no more be listened to.
³:¹ Hey, city of bloodshed, all of it deception,
full of plunder, where prey doesn't depart!
² The sound of the whip,
the sound of the rumble of a wheel,
a horse galloping,
a chariot jumping,
³ cavalry going up, sword flashing,
spear glittering, a multitude slain,
a heap of corpses, no end of the bodies,
people fall over their bodies.

⁴ Because of the abundant whorings of the
whore,
the graceful goodness of the expert in
charms,
who sells nations with her whorings,
clans with her charms,
⁵ here am I toward you (a declaration of Yahweh
Armies):
I shall expose your skirts over your face.
I shall show the nations your nakedness,
kingdoms your humiliation.
⁶ I shall throw abominations over you,
demean you and make a spectacle of you;
⁷ all who see you will flee from you;
they'll say,
"Nineveh is ruined, who will mourn for her,
where shall I look for people to comfort her?"

8   Are you better than Thebes, which was sitting on
        the Nile,
        water surrounding it,
    whose rampart was the sea,
        its wall made from the sea?
9   Mighty Sudan and Egypt without end,
        Put and Libya were your help.
10 Even it was for exile, it went into captivity;
        even its babies were smashed at the head of
            every street.
    For its honorable men people cast lots,
        all its important people were bound in chains.
11 Even you'll become drunk, you'll be in hiding;
        even you'll look for a refuge from the enemy.
12 All your fortresses are fig trees, with the first
            fruit;
        if people shake them, they fall into the mouth
            of an eater.
13 There, your company is women in your midst,
        to your enemies the gates of your country
            are wide open,
        fire is consuming your gate bars.
14 Draw siege water for yourself,
        strengthen your fortresses,
    tread the clay, trample the mud,
        take hold of the brick mold!
15 Fire will devour you there,
        the sword will put an end to you.
    It will devour you like the grasshopper,
        multiply like the grasshopper.
    They multiply like the locust;
16   you made your merchants more than the stars
            in the heavens.
    The grasshopper strips and flies;
17   your guards are like a pile of grubs
            that settle on walls on a cold day.
    When the sun comes out, they flee;
        their place, where they are, isn't known.

¹⁸ Your shepherds have gone to sleep, king of Assyria;
    your nobles settle down.
Your people have scattered over the hills,
    and there's no one gathering them.
¹⁹ There's no healing for your wound;
    your injury is severe.
All who hear the report of you clap their hands at
    you,
    because to whom has evil from you not passed,
        constantly?

The British Empire began with Elizabeth I and lasted until Elizabeth II. Much of its early achievement was based on slavery, though it would be nice to think that there was a moral link between slavery's abolition in the empire and the empire's reaching its heyday in the nineteenth century. But it got tired in the twentieth century and gave up, and the twentieth century belonged to the United States. Nowadays it's sometimes said that the United States is tired and will hardly continue to be the world's sole superpower and police officer; atrocities associated with the Iraq War contribute to a sense of moral tiredness with this role. My American wife thinks the Chinese will simply come and ask for their money . . .

You could say that **Assyria** was tired in Nahum's day and that he didn't require a special revelation from God to see that the empire's days were numbered, but maybe that's only evident with hindsight. It doesn't look as if Nahum thought that either Assyria or **Judah** believed Assyria's downfall to be inevitable or imminent. Like other prophets, Nahum has a conviction born from the awareness that God has spoken to him and the awareness that the empire must fall for theological and moral reasons.

Nahum thus continues to bring Judah good news concerning the putting down of the superpower. At the moment, nations like Judah are its prey; they'll then be safe. Nahum goes on to describe the chaotic violence that the bloody city brings to the different parts of its empire when it sends off its army. He berates Nineveh for the immorality of its focus on trade and its reliance on its information resources. In doing so, he takes up the convention of describing a city as a woman; so the city becomes a whore who is exposed for her trade.

In 663 the Assyrians themselves had captured Thebes on the Nile, a city that looked impregnable. If Thebes can fall, is any city safe? Nahum describes Nineveh's fall as if it's happening before his eyes—which in his vision, it is. Its fortifications look impressive, but they'll fall like ripe fruit from a tree. It will look as if it has no defenses at all, as if it's an unwalled village. Its army looks brave, but it will collapse with the stereotypical fear of a woman. Its leaders will turn out to be totally incompetent. Its king won't know what to do.

Nahum here names Assyria for the only time in the book. Further, although the book's introduction told us that Nineveh was its subject, the city was named just once in the first section and once in this last section. The prophecy thus lies open to being applied to other empires as well as Assyria and other cities as well as Nineveh, which is another implication and result of its being included in Scripture. Within Israel's experience, the good news in due course will be that its warnings apply to Babylon as they applied to Nineveh. Isaiah 40–55 takes up Nahum's earlier comments about the feet of a herald on the mountains bringing good news, and takes up the description of Ms. Nineveh's reliance on its experts, and applies them to Ms. Babylon. The bad news is that the description of Nineveh's fate can also apply to Ms. Jerusalem, which is also a bloody city whose infants will be smashed at the head of every street.

HABAKKUK 1:1–2:1

You Can't Do That!

¹ The pronouncement that Habakkuk the prophet saw.

² How long have I called for help, Yahweh, and you
    don't listen?
    I cry out to you, "Violence," but you don't
    deliver.

³ Why do you make me watch wickedness,
    why do you look at oppression?
    Destruction and violence are in front of me;
    there has been contention, and strife arises.

⁴ Therefore teaching ceases,
    judgment never issues.
    Because the faithless person encircles the faithful;
    therefore judgment issues deformed.

⁵ Watch the nations,
    look, and be utterly astounded.
    Because I'm going to do something in your days
    that you wouldn't believe if it were told.

⁶ Because here am I, I'm going to raise up the
    Kaldeans,
    that fierce, quick-moving nation
    that goes to the far reaches of the earth,
    to possess dwellings that don't belong to it.

⁷ It's terrible and fearful;
    from itself its authority and dignity issues.

⁸ Its horses are swifter than leopards,
    keener than wolves at evening; its steeds gallop.
    Its steeds come from afar,
    they fly like an eagle hastening to devour.

⁹ All of it comes for violence,
    the thrust of their faces is forward;
    it collects captives like sand.

¹⁰ That nation derides kings,
    rulers are a laugh to it.
    That nation laughs at every fortress,
    fortifies earth and captures it.

¹¹ Then the wind sweeps on and passes through,
    and it becomes guilty, because its strength is
    its god.

¹² Aren't you from of old, Yahweh—
     my God, my holiness? You don't die.
   Yahweh, you have made [Babylon] for judgment;
     my crag, you have established it to reprove.
¹³ Your eyes are too pure to watch evil,
     you can't look at oppression.
   Why do you look at the treacherous,
     stay still when the faithless person devours the
       faithful?
¹⁴ You've made humanity like the fish in the sea,
     like moving things that have no ruler.
¹⁵ [The faithless person] has brought all of them up
       with a hook,
     drags them away in his net.
   He gathers them in his trawl;
     therefore he celebrates and rejoices.
¹⁶ Therefore he sacrifices to his net,
     burns an offering to his trawl.
   Because through them his portion is rich,
     his food luxuriant.
¹⁷ Is he therefore to empty his net,
     continually to slay nations and not pity?
^{2:1} On my watch I shall take my stand,
     station myself at my post.
   I shall look to see what he'll speak through me,
     what I shall reply to my reproof.

I've twice mentioned the plight of the Darfuri refugees in Chad. It's ten years since the slaughter of hundreds of thousands of them in Sudan and the flight of hundreds of thousands more. My stepdaughter and her husband give their lives to making their plight known and getting some international action, but see no movement on that front. In two weeks there begins a hundred-days "fast" of identifying with the Darfuri: they get a thousand calories per day, so for the "fast" for one day each week we will eat only what they eat. My wife is inclined to ask in anguish why God seems to have abandoned the Darfuri, so in addition to fasting we shall be crying out to God each of these hundred days and urging him to listen to our cry on these people's behalf.

Habakkuk is starting from a similar anguish about his people's situation. The time is similar to that presupposed by Nahum; **Assyria** exercises oppressive rule over **Judah**. But the way he speaks about violence and oppression suggests that his concern relates to Judah's own internal life, like Amos or Micah, or contemporaries such as Jeremiah or Zephaniah. We're told nothing about him apart from his name and the fact that he was a prophet. Further, in the entire book there's only one line that indicates the historical context, the reference to the **Kaldeans**; the paucity of such references makes for a parallel with Nahum. The issue the book raises isn't confined to the particular time when Habakkuk lived, and his identity isn't very important; it's the discussion of the issue that counts. The faithless often hem in the **faithful**, surround them like attacking animals. Judgment is often exercised in a way that ignores the **Torah**'s teaching; judgment goes out deformed. God is supposed to be on the side of the powerless, but he often does nothing about it.

A distinctive feature of Habakkuk is that it takes the form of a dialog between the prophet and God. Habakkuk's opening protest parallels protests in the Psalms. While those protests speak in the name of the people who are faithful but are being treated wrongly, they may presuppose that other people identify with their protests. Here in Habakkuk that identification is explicit; Habakkuk protests not for himself but for people he sees being wronged in a situation where he's in no position to do anything about it. Being a prophet doesn't give him any power to take any action. Again, the protests in a psalm may presuppose that someone who hears the protester speaking in the temple has the vocation of bringing a response from God. Here in Habakkuk it's explicit that God responds. Habakkuk is both the person who prays and the person who reports God's answer.

The response is that God indeed intends to take action against the wrongdoing in the city. It's where the Kaldeans come in. The answer is the one prophets regularly give, the one that will be vindicated by events when the Kaldeans invade Judah, besiege Jerusalem, and eventually destroy the city. This army's power and ruthlessness will sort matters out for the city. While the prospect might seem just as bad news for the victims of wrongdoing as for the wrongdoers themselves, in the event at least it meant that the people in power were taken off into **exile** while the ordinary people were able to reclaim the land that the powerful people had swindled them out of.

Habakkuk has a different worry. His response to God's declaration first affirms some truths about God and acknowledges the good news in God's acting by means of **Babylon**, but then points out that this action raises a further question. God's own words have pointed to the ruthless nature of the Babylonian military machine. Babylon in its military might is its own god. Can God simply use it in the way he intends? Do two wrongs (the wrongdoing of the people in power in Jerusalem and the wrongdoing of the Babylonians) make a right? The Babylonians, too, are the faithless devouring the faithful. They're just like people involved in fishing who are amassing "victims" in their dragnet. Using Babylon to rescue powerless Judahites is a bit like using North Korea to rescue the Darfuri.

Habakkuk then declares his intention to wait to see how God will reply. Being a prophet doesn't mean God is at your beck and call. You don't have a hotline. You may have to wait for God to speak. Habakkuk then refers to what God will speak *through* him and how he (Habakkuk) will *answer* his own rebuke. We might have thought we were just reading about a conversation between Habakkuk and God, with Habakkuk trying to sort out a question that's important to him. The section's closing words make more explicit that his book isn't merely the transcript of a private transaction between Habakkuk and God but something composed for his people, something that deals with issues they're raising.

HABAKKUK 2:2–20

On Violence to the Earth

² Yahweh answered me:

"Write the vision, make it plain on tablets,
  so that someone who reads it out can run with it.
³ Because there's yet a vision about the appointed time,
  it testifies about the time, and it won't deceive.
  If it's slow, wait for it,
  because it will definitely come, it won't lag.
⁴ There: his appetite within him is swollen, not upright,
  whereas the faithful person will live by his truthfulness.
⁵ How much more does wine betray the arrogant man,
  one who's let his appetite be as wide as Sheol.
  He won't abide,
  the one who is like death but isn't full,
  the one who collects to himself all the nations,
  gathers to himself all the peoples.
⁶ Won't these people, all of them, raise a poem about him,
  mocking, questions, about him:
  'Oh: one who accumulates what's not his—how long,
  one who makes debts heavy for himself'?
⁷ Won't your creditors suddenly arise,
  won't the people who make you tremble wake up,
  and you'll turn into plunder for them.

8   Because you're one who despoiled many nations,
         what's left of the peoples will despoil you,
     on account of the human bloodshed and the
             violence against the country,
         the town and all the people who live in it.
9   Oh, one who acquires dishonest gain, an evil to his
         household,
         to set his nest on high, to escape from the hand
             of evil!
10   You have planned shame for your household,
         cutting off many peoples and making yourself
             guilty.
11   Because a stone will cry out from the wall,
         and the beam from the wood will answer it.
12   Oh, one who builds a city through bloodshed
         who establishes a town through wrongdoing!—
13   there, isn't it from Yahweh Armies?—
         and peoples labored for the fire,
         nations toiled for emptiness.
14   Because the earth will be full
         so as to acknowledge Yahweh's splendor,
         as the waters cover over the sea.
15   Oh, one who makes his neighbor drink,
         pouring out your wrath and your drunken
             anger,
         in order to look at their naked bodies.
16   You're being filled with humiliation rather than
         splendor;
         drink, and show your uncircumcision, you too.
     The chalice in Yahweh's right hand will come
             around to you,
         and humiliation in place of your splendor.
17   Because your violence upon Lebanon will cover
             you,
         the destruction of animals, which terrifies them,
     on account of human bloodshed and violence to
             the earth,
         the town and all who live in it.

195

¹⁸ What use is a carved image when its maker has
    shaped it,
  an image, which teaches lies—
when the one who shaped it trusts in it,
    in making dumb idols?
¹⁹ Oh, one who says to wood, 'Wake up,'
    'Get up,' to dumb stone, so it may teach.
Yes, it's cased in gold and silver,
    but there isn't any breath in it.
²⁰ But Yahweh is in his sacred palace—
    be silent before him, all the earth."

Last night we watched a movie about a billionaire from the United States who's acquired the right to turn an unspoiled stretch of Scottish coastland into a magnificent golf course and hotel complex. The work doesn't please the ordinary smallholders and people who make their living by fishing, who have long had the area to themselves; they're inclined to call down curses on the billionaire and on their own government for allowing it. I also happened to read an article about a billionaire who arouses similar reactions from many of her fellow Australians for the work of her mining company. The Scots and the Australians feel that there's something wrong with the despoiling of their land for the sake of making a profit.

Habakkuk declares that **Yahweh** feels the same about the **Babylonians**—though it's again worth noting that he doesn't name the despoilers, so his words can be effortlessly reapplied. They're morally no better than **Assyria** (or **Judah** itself), and they'll get their comeuppance like Assyria.

When you live under a superpower, it's hard to imagine that it won't retain its position forever. With the benefit of hindsight in light of the rise and fall of more than half a dozen superpowers since Habakkuk's day, it's easier for us to remember that empires rise and fall, yet imagining the current superpower's fall is hard both for the underling and for the superpower itself. Habakkuk knows only about Assyria, the waning first Middle Eastern empire, and about Babylon, on the way to replacing it. Perhaps Babylon's power will stand forever? Oh no it won't, says Yahweh—not merely because of some inexorable law of politics and history but because Yahweh says so. It may take time, but it will come (actually Babylon ended up ruling the Middle East for a shorter time than Assyria, or **Persia** as its successor). Greed, self-indulgence, ruthlessness, arrogance, bloodshed: they'll get their reward. The superpower may harness the labor of its underlings to build it up, but Yahweh will ensure that their hard work brings it no profit. And Yahweh's bringing about the superpower's fall will lead to Yahweh's majesty being recognized all over the world.

On the other hand, **faithful** people will live by their truthfulness. In Romans 1, Paul quotes these words as "the just will live by faith," and makes them key to understanding the gospel. As often happens, he thus uses the words in a different sense from the one they have in their original context, but makes a good Old Testament point (as Paul notes elsewhere, faith was key to Abraham's relationship with God) even though it's not the point this passage makes. Habakkuk's words also reappear in Hebrews 10, with a meaning nearer to Habakkuk's own. When you live under the oppressive authority of a superpower, it's easy to believe that might is right, that power is all that counts. Take the long view, Habakkuk says. Faithful people will prove that truthfulness, honesty, reliability, and steadfastness do issue in a life characterized by blessing, good fortune, and **well-being**. It's not always true. People do get martyred. But it's reliable enough as a generalization to make it worth living by.

The section goes on to note the superpower's contempt for the world itself. The violence on Lebanon refers to felling its trees for building and war-making; it brings back to my mind the movie's scenes of earthmovers uprooting trees on the

Scottish coast. Destroying forests also destroys the refuges of animals who get scared by the human invasion; the deer won't frolic over that countryside anymore. The superpower's dumb idols might let it get away with such action, but in reality the world belongs to the One who sits enthroned in the heavens, before whom a little less arrogance would be wise.

HABAKKUK 3:1–19

A Vision That God Must and Will Turn to Reality

1   A plea by Habakkuk the prophet; on
    "Laments."

2   Yahweh, I've heard a report of you;
    I'm in awe of your action.
  As the years approach, bring it to life;
    as the years approach, cause it to be
      acknowledged;
    in the turmoil, be mindful of compassion.

3   God comes from Teman,
    the Holy One from Mount Paran. (Rise)
  His majesty has covered the heavens,
    his praise has filled the earth.
4   His brightness comes like dawn,
    its rays come from his hand,
    and there is the hiding place of his power.
5   Before him epidemic comes,
    plague comes out at his feet.
6   He has stood and shaken the earth;
    he has looked, and agitated nations.
  Ancient mountains have shattered,
    age-old hills sank down.
  The age-old ways are his,
7   in place of the wickedness that I have seen.
  Cushan's tents shake,
    the dwellings of Midian's country.

8   Are you wrathful at the Rivers, Yahweh,
        is your anger at the Rivers, is your wrath at
            the Sea,
    when you mount on your horses,
        your chariots that bring deliverance?
9   You totally bare your bow;
        your clubs are sworn, by your word. (Rise)
    With Rivers you split the earth;
10   when they see you, mountains writhe.
    A torrent of water has passed by,
        the Deep has given its voice.
    The sun has raised its hands in the height,
11   the moon has stood on high.
    Your arrows go to give light,
        the flash of your spear to give brightness.
12 In rage you stride on the earth,
        in anger you trample nations.
13 You have gone out for the deliverance of your
            people,
        for the deliverance of your anointed.
    You have shattered the head of the faithless household,
        laying it bare, foundation to neck.
14 You have pierced his head with his clubs
        when his warriors were storming out,
    to scatter me in their exultation,
        as if to devour a lowly man in hiding.
15 You have made your way through the sea with
            your horses,
        with a stirring of many waters.

16 I heard and my insides quaked,
        at the sound my lips quivered.
    Rot comes into my bones;
        in my place I tremble,
    while I rest for the day of distress
        to come up for the people who invade us.
17 Because the fig tree may not bud
        and there may be no produce on the vines,

199

the product of the olive may disappoint
  and the fields may not produce food,
someone may cut off the flock from the fold
  and there may be no cattle in the stalls:
[18] yet I shall exult in Yahweh,
  rejoice in the God who delivers me.
[19] The Lord Yahweh is my strength,
  he makes my feet like the deer's,
  enables me to tread on the high places.

The leader's; with strings.

Guisma is one of the girls in a Darfuri refugee camp in Chad, among the people whose plight I mentioned in connection with Habakkuk's opening chapter. During the last ten years, Guisma has gone from living with her brothers and parents in their village in Darfur, to seeing two older brothers killed during the attack on their home, another younger brother die during the escape to Chad, and a little sister die in the refugee camp that is now Guisma's home. My stepdaughter comments that Guisma is a beautiful girl, but her eyes have seen much more than any girl should have seen. She has reason for grieving over what has happened to her through the acts of the nation of which her people used to be part, and for grieving over the rest of the world's tolerance of what has happened to her and her people.

Habakkuk grieves about his nation and about his nation's overlords, but his book closes with a vision of God doing something about it. The opening and closing lines suggest that the vision and the prayer associated with it had been used in worship, like a psalm (the interjection "Rise" also recurs in the Psalms, but we don't know what it signified). Habakkuk has received a message about **Yahweh**'s action; his prayer is that Yahweh will bring the message to life in the present. In the context of the turmoil in his nation and in international events, he urges Yahweh to be mindful of the vision he has given Habakkuk and of the compassion for people that the vision implies, and thus to act on the basis of it.

In his vision he has seen a repetition of the way God has acted in the past. He has seen Yahweh once more making the journey to Canaan from his home in Sinai, with the reverberations in nature that this coming evokes. It's another reenactment of the victory over nature's rebellious forces that Yahweh also won at the Red Sea. On this occasion the object of Yahweh's wrath is the great empire, "the nations," and the head of this faithless household. And the aim of Yahweh's action is the delivering of the people headed by Yahweh's anointed, the king on David's throne.

While the vision opens up a frightening prospect for the superpower, its shocking nature has a frightening effect on Habakkuk himself. Yet the sense of horror can be accompanied by a sense of anticipation. It's hard to stay tranquil and serene when you live in the midst of the violence of a city like Jerusalem or that of a modern city. In a sense you shouldn't do so. But at another level you can. Habakkuk is realistic; he can't do anything about the situation in his city, or about the superpower's oppression of his people. Yet he commits himself to being composed. The disturbing vision is also a basis for hope. He has seen Yahweh acting. The reality in the vision is going to become reality in the external world. The superpower exults in its domination of people like him. But he has a basis for continuing to exult in Yahweh, even if in the short term an invading army wreaks the kind of devastation that armies bring.

ZEPHANIAH 1:1–18

How Do You Change a Culture?

[1]Yahweh's message that came to Zephaniah son of Cushi son of Gedaliah son of Amariah son of Hezekiah, in the days of Josiah son of Amon, king of Judah.

² I shall totally sweep away everything
  from on the face of the ground (Yahweh's
    declaration).
³ I shall sweep away human beings and animals;
  I shall sweep away the birds in the heavens,
  and those who make the faithless fall.
I shall cut off humanity
  from on the face of the ground (Yahweh's
    declaration).

⁴ I shall stretch out my hand against Judah,
  and against all the people who live in Jerusalem.
I shall cut off from this place all remains of the
    Master,
  the names of the priestlings with the priests,
⁵ the people who bow down on the roofs
  to the army in the heavens,
who bow down (who swear) to Yahweh
  and swear by their King,
⁶ who turn away from following Yahweh
  and who don't inquire of Yahweh nor look to
    him.
⁷ Silence before the Lord Yahweh,
  because Yahweh's Day is coming near.
Because Yahweh has prepared a sacrifice,
  sanctified the people he summoned.
⁸ On the day of Yahweh's sacrifice
  I shall attend to the officials,
to the king's sons,
  and to all the people wearing foreign clothing.
⁹ I shall attend to all the people who leap on the
    threshold
  on that day,
who fill their lord's house
  through violence and deceit.

¹⁰ On that day there'll be (Yahweh's declaration)
  the sound of an outcry from the Fish Gate,

202

a howl from the Mishneh,
a great shattering from the Hills.
11 Wail, you who live in the Crushing-cup,
because the entire trading people has perished,
all those who weigh out silver have been cut off.
12 At that time
I shall search Jerusalem with lamps.
I shall attend to the people
who are relaxing on their lees,
who are saying to themselves,
"Yahweh won't do good and he won't do evil."
13 Their resources will be for plundering,
their houses will be for wasting.
They'll build houses but not live [there],
plant vineyards but not drink their wine.
14 Yahweh's great day is coming near,
coming near very quickly.
The sound of Yahweh's Day is fierce;
the warrior is going to shriek there.
15 That day will be a wrathful day,
a day of trouble and distress,
a day of devastation and desolation,
a day of darkness and gloom,
a day of cloud and shadow,
16 a day of horn blast and battle shout,
against the fortified cities,
and against the lofty corner towers.
17 I shall bring distress to the people, they'll walk like
the blind,
because they've offended against Yahweh.
Their blood will be poured out like dirt,
their marrow like feces.
18 Neither their silver nor their gold
will be able to save them.
On Yahweh's wrathful day, in his passionate fire,
the entire country will be consumed.
Because he'll make an end, yes, how terrible,
of all the people who live in the country.

This past Wednesday would have been John Lennon and Yoko Ono's forty-fourth wedding anniversary, but in 1980 Lennon was shot outside their New York apartment. On Wednesday evening Yoko Ono posted four antigun messages with an image of the blood-splattered glasses that John was wearing when he was shot. Over a million people have been killed by guns in the United States since Lennon's death. The same week, the senate majority leader announced that the main gun-control bill advancing in the Senate wouldn't include a proposed ban on assault weapons and high-capacity gun magazines. The parents of victims of a recent school shooting wept at the news. Then yesterday was the anniversary of the shooting by police, in a street between our house and our church, of a boy they had been told was armed.

How do you change a culture in its attitude to violence? It's a subject the Prophets regularly fret over. Zephaniah refers to people who fill their lord's house through violence and deceit, which makes them sound like mafia underlings. Maybe Zephaniah refers to people filling their Lord's house. Certainly their violence goes along with twisted views about religion. Zephaniah lives in a time when **Judah** is deeply influenced by the traditional religion of the area, which had reasserted itself strongly between the time of Isaiah and Micah in the eighth century and the time of Zephaniah and Jeremiah in the seventh. People pray to the **Master**, who could (allegedly) ensure that nature flourished. They prayed to the planetary and star gods, who (allegedly) controlled events on earth. They prayed to the King, which in this context refers to the King of the realm of Death who was (allegedly) responsible for their loved ones who had passed. They dressed for worship in a way that reflected the alien nature of their religion. Leaping on the threshold is some kind of ritual. But to be safe, they prayed to **Yahweh**, too. Or didn't; maybe Zephaniah's point is that they go through the motions of worship in bowing down to Yahweh, but don't actually look to him for what they need.

Whether they put it into words or not, the implication of their practice is that they don't believe Yahweh is one who makes things happen, either good things or bad things.

The first device Zephaniah tries in order to change the culture is one other Prophets use to get people's attention. He declares that Yahweh is going to bring judgment on the world. The people of God like to hear about that judgment. One can imagine Zephaniah going to the crowded temple courtyards on a festival occasion. One can imagine his declaration fitting one of the emphases of the festival when Zephaniah was preaching. His message parallels Nahum's. But the judgment of which he speaks is worryingly total. It involves the whole world, not just the (other) nations. After making this point he makes explicit that Jerusalem will indeed be among the victims when Yahweh reaches out. The Mishneh, the Hills, and the Crushing-cup are regions of the city; the last may be so named because of its bowl-like shape, but the kind of bowl after which it's named suggests its destiny. The festival is "the Lord's Day," when many sacrifices were offered. Zephaniah warns people about another kind of "Lord's Day" involving another kind of sacrifice.

ZEPHANIAH 2:1–15

Where to Look

¹ Pile together, pile it, nation that isn't wanted,
    ²before the decree's birth (the day like chaff),
    before Yahweh's angry burning doesn't come upon
        you,
    before Yahweh's Day doesn't come upon you.
³ Look to Yahweh, all you lowly people in the country,
    who have implemented his decision.
    Look in faithfulness, look in lowliness;
        perhaps you can hide on the day of Yahweh's
        anger.

205

⁴ Because Gaza will become abandoned,
  Ashqelon a desolation.
 Ashdod will be dispossessed at midday,
  Eqron uprooted.
⁵ Hey, you people who live in the region by the sea,
  the nation of Kerethites!
 Yahweh's message is against you,
  Canaan, country of the Philistines!
 I shall wipe you out, without inhabitant.
⁶ The region by the sea will become pastures,
  shepherds' cisterns, pens for flocks.
⁷ It will be a region for the remains of Judah's
    household;
   on these they'll graze.
 In Ashqelon's houses
  they'll lie down in the evening.
 Because Yahweh their God will attend to them,
  and restore their fortunes.
⁸ I have heard Moab's reviling,
  the insults of Ammon
 who have reviled my people,
  talked big over their territory.
⁹ Therefore, as I live
   (a declaration of Yahweh Armies, Israel's
     God),
 because Moab will become like Sodom,
  the Ammonites like Gomorrah:
 the possession of chickweed and a salt pit,
  desolation forever.
¹⁰ This is what they'll have instead of their majesty,
  because they reviled and talked big
 at the people belonging to Yahweh Armies.
¹¹ Yahweh will be fearsome against them,
  because he's reducing all earth's gods.
 All the nations' shores will bow down to him,
  each from its place.
¹² You Sudanese, too,
  will be slain by my sword.

¹³ And he'll stretch out his hand against the north,
    and wipe out Assyria.
He'll make Nineveh a desolation,
    dry like the wilderness.
¹⁴ Flocks will lie down in its midst,
    every creature in the nation.
Both jackdaw and owl will stay in its pillars,
    the sound will sing in the windows.
Devastation will be in the threshold,
    because the cedar is stripped.
¹⁵ This is the exultant city, one that sits with assurance,
    saying to itself, "I'm the one, there is no other."
Aaaagh! It has become a waste,
    a lair for wild creatures.
Everyone who passes by it hisses
    and shakes his hand.

As part of our liturgy for Palm Sunday and Passion Sunday this past weekend, we did a corporate reading of the crucifixion story. It's always a powerful event. I had not previously noticed that the Prayer Book permits you to omit both the creed and the confession after the Palm Sunday liturgy, and this idea seemed odd, so I ignored the rubric. Reading the crucifixion story surely makes you want to say the creed? And the reading involves a renewed acknowledgment that we belong to the crowd that cries out "Crucify him!" Surely you want to repent after that reading? When Jesus warns people not to weep for him but for themselves and for their children, surely you realize you had better do so?

As well as threatening people with the Lord's Day, Zephaniah has a second way of seeking to change his culture. It builds on the first. He urges his people to repent. The story of Jonah shows that a prophet doesn't have to issue that exhortation. He may leave people to work out that repentance is the appropriate response to a warning about judgment. But he may make the move, and Zephaniah does so.

207

It's no standard exhortation to repent. His opening words about "piling it up" make for a strange beginning, and they would have unhappy resonances for his hearers. They refer to collecting stubble, the rubbish that's left after the harvest. You do so in order to burn it or let it blow away. A nation that's only rubbish is a nation **Yahweh** doesn't want. They're chaff on the way to burning, the burning that is birthed by Yahweh's decree.

Zephaniah goes on to urge people to look to Yahweh, to turn to Yahweh. The people he addresses are the ordinary people in the country, those who have been living by Yahweh's standards. We could have formed the impression that the nation is rotten through and through, but Zephaniah implies it's not so. Yet when the day of disaster comes, it will swallow up people who don't deserve it as well as people who do. (We don't know what eventually happened to Zephaniah but we do know what happened to contemporary prophets such as Jeremiah and Ezekiel—they didn't escape sharing in the fate of their people, even though they didn't deserve it.) So they'd be wise to turn to Yahweh as a further expression of their **faithfulness** and neediness and pray that he may hide them from the disaster on that day. And we have noted that on the whole the ordinary people and the country people did have a less disastrous time than the leaders and the other people in Jerusalem, as they escaped **exile** and were maybe able to reclaim the land that had been appropriated by the powerful and the rich.

So is Zephaniah really urging his listeners to repent? As usual one needs to remember that the people to whom the prophets *seem* to be speaking may not be the only ones with whom they're seeking to communicate. If Zephaniah is preaching in the temple courtyard, then the people he has attacked (the people who use violence and who look to other gods) are listening to him. Indirectly he's addressing them and saying, "You need to become people who look to Yahweh in faithfulness and lowliness." Yes, they need to repent. It looks as if they did so. King Josiah led them in a great cleanup of the temple worship, and the judgment of which Zephaniah spoke didn't come about. Alas, the reform was short-lived, and a few decades later, Jerusalem fell.

Before launching his attack on **Judah**, Zephaniah spoke of Yahweh's sweeping away everything. After exhorting people to look to Yahweh, he returns to speaking of Yahweh's action against the peoples who surrounded Judah and/or controlled its destiny. There are positive implications to his message. There's also a warning. If this disaster will come to these nations, what will happen to people who acknowledged Yahweh and then turned away from Yahweh?

ZEPHANIAH 3:1–20

God in the Midst

1 Hey, rebellious and defiled one,
    oppressive city!
2 It has not listened to a voice,
    it has not accepted discipline.
  It has not trusted in Yahweh,
    it has not come near to its God.
3 Its officials in its midst
    are roaring lions.
  Its rulers are wolves at evening;
    they don't gnaw until morning.
4 Its prophets are arrogant, people of perfidy;
    its priests profane what's sacred, they violate
      Torah.

5 Yahweh is faithful in its midst;
    he doesn't do wrong.
  Morning by morning he gives his decision,
    at daybreak he doesn't fail,
    but the wrongdoer doesn't acknowledge shame.

⁶ "I'm cutting off nations,
    their corner towers are becoming desolate.
I'm ruining their streets,
    so that no one passes through.
Their cities are coming to stand without people,
    with no inhabitant.
⁷ I said, 'You'll surely be in awe of me,
    you'll accept discipline.'
Then its abode wouldn't be cut off,
    all that I attended to for it.
On the contrary, they've been eager
    to make all their deeds corrupt.

⁸ Therefore wait for me (Yahweh's declaration),
    for the day when I stand up as a witness.
Because it's my decision to gather nations,
    for me to assemble kingdoms,
to pour out on them my wrath,
    all my angry burning.
Because in my passionate fire
    the entire earth will be consumed.
⁹ Because then I shall restore to the peoples
    purified speech,
so that all of them call on Yahweh's name,
    so that they serve him with united strength.
¹⁰ From beyond Sudan's rivers my suppliants,
    my scattered community, will bring my offering.
¹¹ On that day, they won't be ashamed of all their deeds,
    with which they rebelled against me.
Because then I shall remove from your midst
    the people exulting in your majesty.
You'll no more be very superior
    on my sacred mountain.
¹² I shall leave remaining in your midst a lowly,
        poor people,
    and they'll find refuge in Yahweh's name.
¹³ The remains of Israel won't do wrong,
    and won't speak falsehood.

210

There won't be present in their mouth
    a deceitful tongue.
Because they're the ones who'll graze and lie down,
    with no one disturbing."

14 Resound, Ms. Zion,
    shout, Israel.
Celebrate and exult with all your heart,
    Ms. Jerusalem.
15 Yahweh is reversing the decisions concerning you,
    he's turning back your enemy.
Yahweh, Israel's King, is in your midst;
    you needn't be afraid of evil anymore.
16 On that day it will be said to Jerusalem,
    Don't be afraid, Zion;
    your hands shouldn't droop.
17 Yahweh your God is in your midst,
    a warrior who delivers.
He'll celebrate over you with rejoicing,
    he'll hold his peace in his love,
    he'll be glad over you with resounding.
18 The people who grieve on account of the set events—
    I'm gathering them from you;
    upon you they've been a burden, a reviling.
19 Here am I, I'm going to deal with all your
        oppressors
    at that time.
I shall deliver the lame,
    gather the ones driven out.
I shall change their shame into praise and renown
    in the entire earth.
20 At that time I shall bring you—
    yes, at the time I shall gather you.
Because I shall make you an object of praise and
        renown
    among all the peoples of the earth,
when I restore your fortunes before your eyes
    (Yahweh has said).

Last night we watched a film about Sholem Aleichem (Solomon Rabinovich was his real name), best known as the author of the stories that were turned into the musical *Fiddler on the Roof*. He was born in the Ukraine in the mid-nineteenth century, where Jewish communities were poor but reasonably secure. In the late nineteenth century came an experience of pogrom that led to mass emigration to the United States. It was in support of Jews affected by the pogroms that Emma Lazarus wrote the lines inscribed at the base of the Statue of Liberty, "Give me your tired, your poor/Your huddled masses yearning to breathe free." The Jewish community in the United States then flourished over succeeding decades so as to gain a leading place in the nation. The story is one embodiment of Zephaniah's promise that **Yahweh** would deliver the lame and the people driven out, and change their shame into praise and renown.

Zephaniah naturally focuses on the community in Jerusalem itself, beginning once more from the degenerate aspects of the city's life. A key motif is the expression "in the midst" or "from the midst," which comes more times in this chapter than in any other in the Old Testament. Initially it's another way of expressing Zephaniah's prophetic critique: the city's officials "in its midst" are roaring lions. They're supposed to serve their people, but they consume them (not gnawing until morning implies eating up everything overnight). In contrast, Yahweh "in its midst" does the right thing in relation to people. He operates each day like a **faithful** leader, not a faithless one. It's both good news and bad news. If you want to see the implications, Yahweh says, think again about what I'm doing to those other nations. I thought you'd be sensible enough to learn the lesson and thereby avoid that fate, but you declined.

The third paragraph extends the parallel between what Yahweh will do to the nations and what Yahweh will do for **Judah**. It begins with what looks like the nations' total destruction, but then segues into talk of their speech being purified so that they call on Yahweh's name. Likewise the devastating judgment on Judah will turn out not to be the end, because Yahweh will bring back survivors of his scattered people so they too can bring their offerings to Yahweh. The judgment will turn out to be a cleansing that removes the powerful who are faithless and arrogant "from your midst." It will leave "in your midst" a lowly and poor people who'll live honorably in their relationships with one another. As usual, it's not that the lowly people become the **remnant** because they're faithful; it's by God's mercy that they're the remnant, and as a result they're called to be faithful.

So Yahweh, **Israel's** King, is "in your midst" and you need no more be afraid of imperial powers such as **Assyria**. Yahweh your God is "in your midst." It's a basis for hope. The people who grieve on account of the set events (the festivals) are perhaps people who focus on the losses of the past. The warning encourages them to believe in what Yahweh is now doing. Only here does the Old Testament apply the nouns "rejoicing" and "resounding" to Yahweh, words that picture Yahweh celebrating with the uninhibited enthusiasm that Jerusalem shows at a festival. Yahweh's being able also to hold his peace perhaps reflects the fact that he no longer needs to rage at his people. If Yahweh will so rejoice over the city, it can surely rejoice itself.

HAGGAI 1:1–15a

Concerning Remodeling Priorities

[1]In the second year of King Darius, in the sixth month, on the first day of the month, Yahweh's message came by means of Haggai the prophet to Zerubbabel son of Shealtiel, governor of Judah, and to Joshua son of Jehosadaq, senior priest: [2]Yahweh Armies has said this: This people has said, "The time hasn't come" (the time for building Yahweh's house). [3]Yahweh's message came by means of Haggai the prophet: [4]Is it the time

for you yourselves to live in your paneled houses, and this house is desolate? [5]So now Yahweh Armies has said this: Apply your mind to your ways. [6]You have sown much but brought in little. You eat but without having enough. You drink but without getting drunk. You dress but without a person getting warm. And the people who earn wages earn them for a purse with holes. [7]Yahweh Armies has said this: Apply your mind to your ways. [8]Go up to the mountain and bring wood and build the house, and I shall look at it and find honor, Yahweh has said. [9]You looked for much, but there—little. You brought it home, and I'd blow on it. On account of what (a declaration of Yahweh Armies)? On account of my house that is desolate, and you're running each person to his own house. [10]Therefore above you the heavens have withheld dew, and the earth has withheld its yield, [11]and I have summoned drought onto the earth, the mountains, the grain, the new wine, the fresh oil, all that the ground produces, human beings, animals and all the labor of your hands.

[12]Zerubbabel son of Shealtiel and Joshua son of Jehosadaq, the senior priest, and all the remains of the people listened to the voice of Yahweh their God, and because of Haggai the prophet, as Yahweh their God sent him. So the people were in awe of Yahweh. [13]And Haggai, Yahweh's aide in Yahweh's work, said to the people, I am with you (Yahweh's declaration). [14]And Yahweh aroused the spirit of Zerubbabel son of Shealtiel, governor of Judah, and the spirit of Joshua son of Jehosadaq, senior priest, and the spirit of all the remains of the people, and they came and did work on the house of Yahweh Armies, their God, [15]on the twenty-fourth day of the sixth month.

I've mentioned that there's a problem with one of the walls in our apartment. The problems aren't confined to our particular bit of wall. Ideally some radical work needs to be done to the building's drainage so that such problems don't recur. But the work will be expensive, so we're all discussing whether we want to do the radical work, which would raise financial difficulties for some of us and raise questions about priorities for others. Shall we rather take the risk of making piecemeal repairs when need arises?

Thinking about this issue has given me a bit more sympathy for people in Jerusalem in Haggai's day. They're the **remains** of **Judah**, the remnant, the people who are left of the magnificent people of **Israel** whose great days seem to be long ago. Events have moved on a century from the time of Zephaniah. His warnings have come true, and Jerusalem has been destroyed and its leaders taken into **exile**. Some people in the city had escaped exile; some came back when the old superpower, **Babylon**, gave way to the new one, **Persia**. The book thus begins with a reference to the Persian king, Darius. An earlier prophet's book would be dated by the reigns of Israelite kings, but there's no Israelite king. Zerubbabel did belong to the royal line (Shealtiel was the son of King Jehoiakin) so he was qualified to be made king; he's governor appointed by the Persians, but it's quite something that a Davidic prince is exercising authority in Jerusalem. The mention of Joshua reflects how the joint leadership of a governor and a high priest is now a feature of Judah's life.

The Jerusalemites had begun to rebuild the temple but then given up because of tensions with their neighbors and opposition from them; the book of Ezra tells the story. Now Haggai (and Zechariah, whose book comes next) urges them to take up the work again. Haggai doesn't refer to opposition as the people's problem, but to their focusing on their own houses rather than that of **Yahweh Armies**. They've repaired their own houses, which was certainly needed ("paneled" needn't imply great luxury, though it does imply something reasonably nice). They've left Yahweh's house in its broken-down state.

The prophet's confrontation makes for a contrast with that of earlier prophets. When David wanted to build Yahweh a house because he felt guilty about his own nice house, Yahweh questioned his desire for several reasons. In the different situation 500 years later when the people's attitude raises different questions, Yahweh's own attitude is different. Yahweh challenges people to review their own priorities and suggests that their economic problems reflect their priorities. Paul will be following Haggai when he promises the Corinthians that people who give generously will receive all that they need (2 Corinthians 9).

HAGGAI 1:15b–2:23

A New Splendor

[15b]In the second year of King Darius, [2:1]in the seventh [month], on the twenty-first of the month, Yahweh's message came by means of Haggai the prophet: [2]Will you say to Zerubbabel son of Shealtiel, governor of Judah, and to Joshua son of Jehosadaq, senior priest, and to the remains of the people: [3]Who among you remains who saw this house in its former splendor? How do you see it now? In comparison with it, isn't it just nothing in your eyes? [4]But now, be strong, Zerubbabel (Yahweh's declaration); be strong, Joshua son of Jehosadaq, senior priest; be strong, all you people of the country (Yahweh's declaration). Act, because I'm with you (a declaration of Yahweh Armies), [5]the thing that I sealed with you when you got out of Egypt. My spirit remains among you. Don't be afraid. [6]Because Yahweh Armies has said this: Once more, shortly, I'm going to shake the heavens and the earth, the sea and the dry land. [7]I shall shake all the nations, and the things held in high regard belonging to all the nations will come. I shall fill this house with splendor (Yahweh Armies has said). [8]Mine is the silver and mine is the gold (a declaration of Yahweh Armies). [9]The splendor of this later house will be greater than the earlier one (Yahweh Armies has said). In this place I shall give **well-being** (a declaration of Yahweh Armies).

[10]On the twenty-fourth of the ninth in the second year of Darius, Yahweh's message came to Haggai the prophet. [11]Yahweh Armies said this: Will you ask the priests for teaching: [12]If someone carries sacred meat in the fold of his garment and touches bread or stew or wine or oil or any other

food with the fold, does it become sacred? The priests responded, "No." [13]Haggai said, "If someone taboo because of a body touches any of these, does it become taboo?" The priests responded, "It becomes taboo." [14]Haggai responded, So is this people, so is this nation before me (Yahweh's declaration), and so is the action of their hands. What they present there is taboo.

[15]But now, will you apply your mind, from this day and onward, before the setting of stone on stone in Yahweh's palace. [16]From when these things happened, someone came to a twenty-measure heap, and there'd be ten; someone came to the wine vat to skim off fifty measures, there'd be ten. [17]I struck you down with blight, mildew, and hail, all the work of your hands, but you were not with me (Yahweh's declaration). [18]Will you apply your mind from this day and onward, from the twenty-fourth day of the ninth, from the day when Yahweh's palace was founded—apply your mind: [19]is there still seed in the barn? Whereas until now the vine, fig tree, pomegranate, and olive tree have not borne, from this day I shall bless you.

[20]Yahweh's message came a second time to Haggai on the twenty-fourth of the month: [21]Say to Zerubbabel, governor of Judah: I'm going to shake the heavens and the earth [22]and overturn the throne of the regimes and destroy the strength of the nations' regimes, and overturn chariotry and its drivers. Horses and their riders will come down, each by his brother's sword. [23]On that day (a declaration of Yahweh Armies), I shall take you, Zerubbabel son of Shealtiel, my servant (Yahweh's declaration) and make you like a signet, because I have chosen you (a declaration of Yahweh Armies).

Last night we had our Maundy Thursday service, with Eucharist and a sermon and foot-washing, and eleven people were there; it was if anything a slightly pleasing turnout. If we get a few more tonight for our Good Friday service, I shall be pleased. This week, we have been finalizing our annual report to the diocese, and I had to count the number of people who had been to church over the past year. It was ten percent down on the previous year. Two or three decades ago, there'd be more than a hundred people in church on a Sunday; now it's less than half that number. We've done wonderful work restoring the inside of the church building this year and we've had one or two new people start coming, and one or two start coming back, but will the church ever see its former glory?

It was hard for the **Judahites** to imagine its former glory returning to the temple. The answer to the question "How many of you saw that glory?" would be "Only a handful," because it's nearly seventy years since the temple was destroyed. But everybody knew how glorious it was said to have been, and perhaps people's impression of its splendor would have become enhanced over the years. You couldn't blame people for being gloomy about the idea that they could restore it at all, let alone to that splendor.

They have to remember a few things. There's the fact that **Yahweh Armies** is with them, which in the Old Testament doesn't mean that they merely have a *feeling* of God's presence but that they experience God present and acting. To put it another way, God's spirit is with them, as was the case at the exodus (contrary to the assumption Christians sometimes have that God's spirit was not among **Israel** in the Old Testament). That presence, too, meant not merely a feeling but a dynamic reality.

The covenant that God sealed with them back then still holds. So they can have confidence that the work they put into rebuilding the temple will be fruitful. But when we finished remodeling our church building last year, we knew we also needed to attend to the remodeling of the church people, and Haggai goes on to that fact. The congregation can bring pure offerings into the temple, but if they themselves aren't pure or the temple building isn't pure, the impurity will spread to the offerings. Both people and temple have been rendered impure by their association with the worship of other gods, the worship that prophets such as Zephaniah condemned. The people and the temple need to be cleansed of such defilement and kept clean.

They already have evidence of **Yahweh**'s fulfilling his promise of blessing. We know from Haggai's first message that they had been having a hard time; here the third paragraph indicates that the tide has turned since they started work on the temple. There's seed in the barn. The fruit trees have borne fruit. Yes, the tide has turned.

The final prophecy declares that this development is just a harbinger of blessing to come. Like other prophets, Haggai asserts that the empire (which in his case was the greatest the world had known) won't stand. Like David, Zerubbabel is Yahweh's chosen and Yahweh's servant, and Yahweh is going to treat him like the signet ring with which a king seals things. Haggai doesn't say he'll ever be king (Darius is the only king) nor that he'll lead the forces that will topple Darius, as David might have done, but he'll be Yahweh's true representative.

Yahweh didn't make Persia fall in the lifetime of Haggai or Zerubbabel, nor did he make the second temple more glorious than the first. Apparently these facts didn't trouble the Judahites who held onto Haggai's prophecies. They knew that prophets' messages were sometimes larger than life, for ill and for good. They did see the temple rebuilt and reconsecrated, and they knew that Haggai's ministry had been decisively important in making it happen. I imagine that Haggai uttered other prophecies, but that this fact explains why these prophecies were preserved as especially important. If there had been no Haggai and Zechariah, there'd have been no temple building. There was thus no doubt that Yahweh called Haggai and worked through him. The Judahites knew that God sometimes has a change of mind about prophecies, so maybe they assumed that Persia's persistence was just an example. When Persia fell, two centuries later, perhaps they said to one another,

"You see, Haggai was right that it would come, the same as he was right about the other things."

ZECHARIAH 1:1–21

A World Too Peaceful

¹In the eighth month of the second year of Darius, Yahweh's message came to Zechariah son of Berekiah son of Iddo.
²Yahweh was very angry with the ancestors of you all. ³You're to say to them, Yahweh Armies has said this: Turn back to me (a declaration of Yahweh Armies) and I shall turn back to you (Yahweh Armies has said). ⁴Don't become like your ancestors, to whom the earlier prophets called, "Yahweh Armies has said this: Will you turn back from your evil ways," but they didn't listen or pay heed to me (Yahweh's declaration). ⁵Your ancestors: where are they? The prophets: do they live forever? ⁶Yet my words and my laws that I commanded my servants the prophets: did they not overtake your ancestors? And they turned back and said, "As Yahweh Armies schemed to do to us in accordance with our ways and our deeds, so he has done with us."
⁷On the twenty-fourth day of the eleventh month (the month of Shebat) in the second year of Darius, Yahweh's message came to Zechariah son of Berekiah son of Iddo. ⁸I saw by night: there, a man riding on a red horse. He was standing among myrtle trees, which were in a valley. Behind him were red, brown, and white horses. ⁹I said, "What are these, my lord?" The aide who was speaking with me said, "I'll show you what those are." ¹⁰The man who was standing among the myrtle trees responded, "These are ones Yahweh sent to go around in the earth." ¹¹They responded to Yahweh's aide who was standing among the myrtle trees, "We have been going around in the earth. There, all the earth is dwelling quiet." ¹²Yahweh's aide responded, "Yahweh Armies, how long will you not have compassion on Jerusalem and on Judah's cities, with which you have been wrathful these seventy years?" ¹³Yahweh responded to the aide who was speaking with me

with good words, comforting words. [14]The aide who was speaking with me said to me, "Proclaim: Yahweh Armies has said this: I have felt a great passion for Jerusalem and Zion, [15]and I—I have been feeling a great anger against the nations that are at ease, because I was a bit angry, but they helped it become evil. [16]Therefore Yahweh has said this: I'm turning back to Jerusalem in compassion. My house will be built up in it (a declaration of Yahweh Armies), and a cord will be stretched over Jerusalem. [17]Proclaim further: Yahweh Armies has said this: My cities will again flow with good things. Yahweh will again comfort Zion and again choose Jerusalem.

[18]I lifted my eyes and looked: there, four horns. [19]I said to the aide who was speaking with me, "What are these?" He said to me, "These are the horns that scattered Judah, Israel, and Jerusalem." [20]And Yahweh Armies showed me four smiths. [21]I said, "What are these coming to do?" He said, "These are the horns that scattered Judah to such an extent that no one raised his head. But these [smiths] have come to disturb them by throwing down the horns of the nations that raised a horn against the country of Judah, to scatter it."

In our prayers this morning my wife prayed about the fact that North Korea has its rockets on standby to attack the United States because our drones have been active over South Korea. United States officials said that North Korea's declarations shouldn't be dismissed as mere talk. Its rhetoric was similar to the way people in the United States and Israel talk about running out of peaceful options for settling things with Iran and conclude that we have no alternative to bombing Iran. There was another country about which Kathleen prayed; it could have been one of many. The world can seem so unsettled, like a powder keg.

Zechariah's problem is that the world is too settled. Haggai and Zechariah were contemporaries (they appear together in the book of Ezra) and a couple of months previously Haggai had spoken of **Yahweh** overturning the superpower. The men on horses stand for the agents Darius uses to keep him informed on the situation in different parts of his empire, like the Pony Express. They're a supernatural version whose job is to report back to **Yahweh Armies** on the situation in the world. Zechariah overhears their report. For Darius the good news is that the rebellions that had greeted his accession are over; there are now no signs of disturbance. But there's thus no sign that Yahweh is bringing about the overturning of the superpower.

One aspect of the good news is that the prophets and their people are not the only ones who'd be troubled by the absence of disturbing news. The **aide** is troubled, and in his capacity as a member of the heavenly cabinet he's in a position to protest to Yahweh and then to tell Zechariah what Yahweh says. The answer comes in the form of reassurances about Yahweh's good intentions, turning back, passion, compassion, comfort, election, and anger. Yahweh's passion signifies the depth of Yahweh's feelings about Jerusalem. The word often denotes Yahweh's jealousy, and even in English *jealous* and *zealous* are similar words. Compassion denotes Yahweh's motherly feelings for the city. Comfort has two aspects: it suggests both words of reassurance and actions that back up the words and change the situation. Election reaffirms the special status of the city that is related to Yahweh's intention of using it as the location from which to exercise authority in the world. Anger is good news, too, because Yahweh's being angry with his people's oppressors, no longer with his people themselves, means deliverance will follow. It will issue in the rebuilding of both temple and city.

Yahweh gives no promises about timing; indeed, he implicitly warns against making inferences about how and why things will work out. He refers to the interaction between his desires and the desires of human agencies. Yes, he had become angry with Jerusalem, and the superpower (then **Babylon**) had been the means of expressing that anger. But Babylon wasn't like a judge whose own agenda doesn't come into the court's verdicts and sentencing. Babylon was implementing its own agenda, and it had "helped it become **evil**." Elsewhere the Old Testament comments that Babylon had been tougher on **Judah** than Yahweh wanted; here Zechariah implies that Judah's suffering had gone on longer than Yahweh needed it to do. But Yahweh's working via human agents needn't involve maneuvering them into acting in ways other than the ones to which they're inclined, and Yahweh is always prepared to take the long view. He'll bring about his purpose for Jerusalem's comfort and the new superpower's fall, but he gives no promises about the timing.

The vision of the horns sets Zechariah's promises on an even broader canvas. The reference to Judah, **Israel**, and Jerusalem suggests reference to the entire history of the people's relationship with the superpowers (**Assyria**, Babylon, and now **Persia**), and the four horns suggest the completeness of that imperial rule. The four smiths then suggest a comparable completeness of agencies whereby the superpowers will be put down. Not only is there no promise about timing; there's also no revelation about who'll do the work of these four visionary smiths. But the work will be done.

In the meantime, what the people of Judah need to do is turn back to Yahweh. Their ancestors took a long time to learn this lesson—they were people who worshiped other gods, saw Jerusalem fall, but then expressed their repentance in the prayers that comprise the book of Lamentations. The present generation will be wise to learn from their story.

ZECHARIAH 2:1–3:10

Plenty of Guilt to Go Around

¹I lifted my eyes and looked: there, a man, with a measuring line in his hand. ²I said, "Where are you going?" He said to me, "To measure Jerusalem, to see exactly what's its breadth and

length." ³But there: the aide who was speaking with me was going out, and another aide was going out to meet him. ⁴He said to him, "Run, speak to that young man, and say: 'Jerusalem will be inhabited as unwalled villages because of the abundance of people and animals in its midst. ⁵And I myself shall be for it (Yahweh's declaration) a wall of fire around, and I shall be splendor in its midst.'"

⁶Hey, hey, flee from the northern country (Yahweh's declaration), because I'm scattering you like the four winds of the heavens (Yahweh's declaration). ⁷Hey, Zion, escape, you who live in Ms. Babylon. ⁸Because Yahweh Armies has said this (after splendor sent me) regarding the nations who plundered you: "The one touching you was touching the apple of my eye. ⁹Because here am I, I'm going to lift my hand against them. They'll become plunder for their servants." And you'll acknowledge that Yahweh Armies sent me.

¹⁰"Resound, celebrate, Ms. Zion, because here am I—I'm coming to dwell in your midst (Yahweh's declaration). ¹¹Many nations will attach themselves to Yahweh on that day and will become my people, and I shall dwell in your midst." And you'll acknowledge that Yahweh sent me to you. ¹²And Yahweh will possess Judah as his share on the sacred ground, and will again choose Jerusalem. ¹³Hush, all flesh, before Yahweh, because he has roused himself from his sacred abode.

³:¹He showed me Joshua the senior priest standing before Yahweh's aide, and the accuser standing at his right to accuse him. ²Yahweh said to the accuser, "Yahweh rebuke you, accuser, Yahweh who chose Jerusalem rebuke you. Isn't this a burning stick snatched from the fire?" ³Joshua was wearing filthy clothes as he was standing before the aide. ⁴[Yahweh] spoke up to the beings who were standing before him, "Take the filthy clothes off him," and said to him, "Look: I've transferred your waywardness from you, and you may wear fine robes. ⁵And I've said, 'They're to put a pure turban on his head.'" They put the pure turban on his head and dressed him in clothes as Yahweh's aide was standing by. ⁶Yahweh's aide testified against Joshua: ⁷"Yahweh Armies has said this: If you walk in my ways and keep my charge, you yourself will both govern my house

and guard my courtyards, and I shall grant to you movement among these who are standing by. ⁸Will you listen, Joshua, senior priest, you and your fellows who are sitting before you, because those are people who constitute a sign. Because here am I, I'm going to bring my servant Branch. ⁹Because here's the stone that I've put before Joshua. On one stone are seven eyes. Here am I, I'm going to make its engraving (a declaration of Yahweh Armies), and I shall remove this country's waywardness in one day. ¹⁰On that day (a declaration of Yahweh Armies) you'll call, each person his neighbor, under his vine and under his fig tree."

There's plenty of guilt to go around. On the way to church today we drove past the spot where a teenager was shot by police a year and a week ago. It was partly the youth's fault if he was engaged in a robbery. It was partly the fault of the man who called the police and told them the youth was armed when he wasn't. It may have been partly the fault of the police, even if they were understandably scared. It was partly our fault as a community, the people on whose behalf the police act and who expect the police to protect us.

In Judah there's plenty of guilt to go around, but wherever it resides, Yahweh is committed to dealing with it. In Zechariah's vision, Joshua is on trial. Like any king, Yahweh meets on a regular basis with his staff, and like the king in many traditional societies, he also functions as supreme court. Joshua is accused of being unclean. Perhaps having been in exile made him impure, not because foreign countries themselves are unclean, but because exile put him in contact with the worship of foreign gods. Perhaps Joshua or his family had worshiped other gods. Perhaps Joshua stands for the priesthood; there were certainly priests who had been involved in such worship. There's no dispute about the fact of uncleanness. The question is, what's the court to do about it?

Like a president, the King has the right to issue pardon, but there are people who think the King should take a tough line. Idolaters shouldn't get away with their faithlessness. It would undermine the importance of faithfulness. Yahweh's staff includes a kind of official prosecutor whose job is to press charges, though the vision may imply he gets too enthusiastic about his job. Yahweh has decided that this occasion is one of those times when he must risk making an exception. Joshua is to be restored in his position as senior priest.

The accuser is right that you have to be careful about issuing a royal pardon. It mustn't encourage the recipient to be casual about commitment to Yahweh. But yes, there's plenty of guilt to go around, and Joshua's pardon is a sign that the whole community can be pardoned. Yes, the reestablishment of the priesthood as a whole is a sign of God's grace and God's commitment (the stone may be the jewel sitting on the senior priest's headdress). At the moment the "tree" of David is cut down, but Yahweh is going to make it produce a new Branch (we'd call him the Messiah, but that word doesn't come in this connection in the Old Testament) and bring the new age when people will relax under their vine and fig tree.

The vision in the first paragraph develops God's promise in another way as it takes up again Yahweh's promise about Jerusalem's restoration. The young man is like a city employee who has to plan the rebuilding of the city's walls. Walls? What use are they when the city will be growing so fast they can never keep up? And why do you need walls when you have God's protection and God's fire within?

There's a link between this promise of exponential growth and the words that follow. While many Judahites have returned to Jerusalem, many others have stayed in **Babylon**, which might seem more attractive than returning to Jerusalem. Zechariah declares that it's not as safe as it might seem. The **Persians'** takeover in Babylon, which made that return possible, had been more peaceful than one might have expected, and than earlier prophets envisaged, but there had been subsequent rebellion there. More is to follow, and the Persians will be seeking to teach Babylon a lesson. Yahweh, too, has not finished with Babylon. Judahites will find themselves scattering from there. They'd be wise to leave while they have the chance. Jerusalem, after all, is the city Yahweh chose. Babylon may have looked like the center of the world. Actually Jerusalem is.

ZECHARIAH 4:1–5:11

A Lamp Stand, a Flying Scroll, and a Flying Container

[1]The aide who was speaking with me came back and woke me up like someone who wakes up from sleep. [2]He said to me, "What are you looking at?" I said, "I looked, and there—a lamp stand of gold, all of it, and its bowl on top of it, and its seven lamps on it, with seven spouts each for the lamps that were on top of it, [3]and two olive trees by it, one to the right of the bowl and one to its left." [4]I responded to the aide who was speaking with me, "What are these, my lord?" [5]The aide who spoke with me responded to me, "Do you not know what these are?" I said, "No, my lord." [6]He responded to me:

(This is Yahweh's message to Zerubbabel: "Not by resources, not by strength, but by my spirit—Yahweh Armies has said. [7]Who are you, big mountain, before Zerubbabel? Into level ground! He'll take out the top stone, with shouts of 'Grace, grace to it!'" [8]Yahweh's message came to me: [9]"Zerubbabel's hands have founded this house and they'll finish it off, and you'll acknowledge that Yahweh Armies sent me to you all. [10]Because who despises the day of little things? They'll celebrate when they see the metal stone in Zerubbabel's hand.")

"These seven are Yahweh's eyes ranging through all the earth." [11]I responded to him, "What are these two olive trees on the right of the lamp stand and on its left?" [12]I responded to him a second time, "What are the two ears of the olive trees that pour out gold from themselves by means of the two gold pipes?" [13]He said to me, "Do you not know what these are?" I said, "No, my lord." [14]He said, "These are the two sons of fresh oil who stand by the Lord of All the Earth."

^{5:1}I again lifted my eyes and looked—there, a flying scroll. ²He said to me, "What are you looking at?" I said, "I'm looking at a flying scroll. Its length is twenty cubits and its width ten cubits." ³He said to me, "This is the oath that is going out over the face of the entire country. Because anyone who steals (from this side, according to it) has gone innocent, and anyone who swears (from the other side, according to it) has gone innocent. ⁴I'm causing it to go out (a declaration of Yahweh Armies) and it will come into the thief's house and the house of the person who swears by my name for falsehood. It will lodge inside his house and consume it, both its timbers and its stones."

⁵The aide who spoke with me went out and said to me, "Do lift up your eyes and look. What's this going out?" ⁶I said, "What is it?" He said, "This is the container that is going out." He said, "This is the appearance of them in the entire country." ⁷And there, a lead disk lifted, and it was a woman sitting inside the container. ⁸He said, "This is Faithlessness." He propelled her inside the container and propelled the lead disk to its mouth. ⁹I lifted my eyes and looked, and there—two women going out with wind in their wings (they had wings like a stork's wings). They carried the container between the earth and the heavens. ¹⁰I said to the aide who was speaking with me, "Where are they making the container go?" ¹¹He said to me, "To build it a house in the country of Shinar. It will be set in place. [The container] will be put down there on its place."

Two friends of ours have been working for eighteen years in a part of their own African country that isn't predominantly Christian and seeing little fruit. In a recent letter they described how their landlady had told them of her disappointment that her fifteen-year-old coconut tree never yielded fruit. The tree is so tall that its leaves hang in front of their kitchen on the second floor. So one of them took its leaves in her hand one day and spoke words of blessing. Right afterwards the tree began to bloom and produce fruit. Our friends wondered if this event was a sign from God to indicate that they were soon to see much fruit in their ministry. "We know that neither the planters nor those who water are important, but the Lord of the Harvest!"

Planters and waterers do matter, and resources and strength are important to Zerubbabel in connection with the temple-building project. Yet you can have all the resources and strength in the world and get nowhere. You can also have no resources or strength and find that extraordinary things happen. Yahweh's promise is that a divine dynamic will be involved in what happens, as is surely needed. Zerubbabel may be David's descendant, but he doesn't have David's resources or strength. The mound of rubbish to which Zechariah refers isn't simply a metaphorical one. You couldn't blame people for seeing this as a day of little things and for being skeptical about whether rebuilding work would ever be finished. The story in Ezra-Nehemiah shows how Yahweh's promises through Zechariah found fulfillment. (The metal stone is the inscribed tablet that was incorporated in a sanctuary building to mark its completion.)

The promises to Zerubbabel sit inside another vision, of a lamp stand. Its lamps represent Yahweh's eyes shining out over the entire world. One implication of this image is that Yahweh knows all about what's happening, which is both bad news and good news depending on your circumstances and commitments. Another implication is that Yahweh has his eye on things so that he's ready to take action—again for good or ill depending on your circumstances and commitments. The shining out of light from the lamp stand requires oil, which comes from two olive trees. The olive trees presumably stand for the community's two leaders, Zerubbabel and Joshua. If Zerubbabel was daunted by the size of the task that lay ahead of the community, then not untypically God not only promises that it will be completed but also makes it more demanding, or points out that Zerubbabel hasn't noticed how demanding it is. While God can work in the world without human mediation, God also works via human agents; the governor and senior priest are such agents. One has more responsibility for the city, the other for the temple. Both responsibilities relate to God's concerns; the division isn't between sacred and secular or church and state. They exercise a joint leadership with different foci.

The final paragraphs draw attention to two further aspects of the renewal the community needs. They express two regular concerns of the Prophets. On one hand, the community needs to become a place characterized by honesty, by the basic commitments expressed in the Ten Commandments. At the moment it could seem that people get away with ignoring these commitments. The message of the scroll is that God has taken an oath to pay serious heed to such infractions. So people need to get their act together.

The scroll's focus on people's relationship with one another is complemented by the container's focus on people's relationship with God. The woman embodying faithlessness stands for the worship of other gods (maybe it's a woman because, as we know from Jeremiah, the worship of a goddess, the Queen of Heaven, was a particular issue in Jerusalem). The good news is that such worship is taken far away to where it belongs, as the image of the goddess is set up in **Babylon**. It's also another way of saying to the **Judahites**, "Don't you see that your religious practice is in place there, but not here?"

ZECHARIAH 6:1–7:14

Who Are You Fasting For?

¹I lifted my eyes again and looked, and there—four chariots going out from between two mountains; the mountains were mountains of bronze. ²In the first chariot the horses were red, in the second chariot the horses were black, ³in the third chariot the horses were white, in the fourth chariot the horses were dappled, strong. ⁴I responded to the aide who

was speaking with me, "What are these, my lord?" [5]The aide responded to me, "These are the four winds of the heavens leaving after standing by the Lord of All the Earth." [6]The one where the black horses are—they were leaving for the northern country. The white left after them. The dappled left for the southern country. [7]So the strong left. When they sought to go, so as to go about through the earth, he said, "Go, go about through the earth." So they went about through the earth. [8]He cried out to me and spoke to me: "Look, the ones leaving for the northern country have settled my spirit in the northern country."

[9]Yahweh's message came to me: [10]Receive [silver and gold] from the exile community, from Helday, Tobiah, and Jeda'yah. You yourself are to come on that day, you're to come to the house of Josiah son of Zephaniah, when they've come from Babylon. [11]You're to receive silver and gold and make crowns and put [one] on the head of Joshua son of Jehosadaq the senior priest, [12]and say to him, Yahweh Armies has said this: There's the man whose name is Branch. From his place he'll branch out and build Yahweh's palace. [13]He's the one who'll build Yahweh's palace. He's the one who'll put on majesty, and sit and rule on his throne. A priest will be by his throne, and there'll be peaceful counsel between the two of them. [14]For Helem, Tobiah, Jeda'yah, and Hen son of Zephaniah, the crowns will be a memorial in Yahweh's palace. [15]Distant people will come and build in Yahweh's palace, and you'll acknowledge that Yahweh Armies sent me to you. It will happen if you really do listen to the voice of Yahweh your God.

[7:1]In the fourth year of King Darius, Yahweh's message came to Zechariah, on the fourth of the ninth month, Kislev. [2]Bethel-sarezer and Regem-melek and his men sent to supplicate Yahweh [3]by saying to the priests at the house of Yahweh Armies and to the prophets, "Should I weep in the fifth month, consecrating myself, as I have done these how many years?" [4]A message from Yahweh Armies came to me: [5]Say to all the people of the country and to the priests, When you fasted and lamented in the fifth and the seventh even these seventy years, did you really fast for me? [6]And when you eat and drink, is it

not you who eat and you who drink? ⁷Are not these the words
that Yahweh proclaimed by means of the earlier prophets
when Jerusalem was peopled and at ease, and its cities around
it, and the Negev and the Lowland were peopled?

⁸Yahweh's message came to Zechariah: ⁹Yahweh Armies has
said this: Exercise truthful authority, exercise commitment
and compassion each person with his brother. ¹⁰Don't oppress
widow and orphan, alien and lowly. Don't plan evil, each
person against his brother in his heart. ¹¹But they refused to
pay heed and presented a stubborn shoulder. They stopped
their ears from listening. ¹²They made their mind concrete
so as not to listen to the teaching and words that Yahweh
Armies sent by his spirit by means of the earlier prophets, and
great wrath came from Yahweh Armies. ¹³As he called but they
didn't listen, so they'll call and I shall not listen, Yahweh
Armies said. ¹⁴And I blasted them away to all the nations that
they had not known. The country was desolate behind them
from anyone passing through and coming back. They made a
country that was held in high regard into a desolation.

Whereas I weighed 147 pounds when I was in my twenties,
three or four years ago I faced the fact that my weight had gone
beyond 160 and decided to give up my morning coffee cake,
my afternoon scone, and my suppertime piece of fruit pie.
With vigilance I can stick at 155, which I'm happy about in
order to avoid becoming one of those men with a pot belly. On
the other hand, in connection with Habakkuk I mentioned
our fast on behalf of the Darfuri refugees, which we start next
week. It's designed as an act of identification with the Darfuri.
We're making it also the embodiment of a cry to God on their
behalf.

There are many reasons for fasting, as well as many levels
of fasting. Here, some people raise a question about the
way they've been weeping and dedicating themselves to God;
Zechariah's response implies that these are observances to
which they've been committed since the fall of Jerusalem

seventy years previously. Zechariah gives various answers—in other words, the question stimulates a number of observations about such practices of self-discipline. His first response raises the question about who they were really fasting for. My discipline over what I eat is a purely selfish gesture, but there's nothing wrong with such discipline, unless you're fooling yourself or think you're fooling God about your reasons.

Zechariah goes on to hint that their discipline was self-centered in another sense, by noting the priorities that the Prophets had regularly put before people who were serious in living for God rather than living for themselves. If you aren't making a priority of the principles expressed in the section's last paragraph, then it shows you're living for yourself, not for God. Your discipline about eating and your lamenting the broken-down state of Jerusalem becomes just part of a life lived for self and not for God.

Why did the envoys raise the question? The date, the fourth year of Darius, is halfway through the four years it took to rebuild the temple, which Zechariah here describes as "Yahweh's palace." Its restoration is progressing before people's eyes. Local opposition to the project has been overcome through appeal to Darius. Is the time for weeping and fasting over?

The halfway nature of the community's situation is also suggested by the vision occupying the first paragraph of this section, and by Yahweh's message in the second paragraph. The vision has some parallels with Zechariah's first vision, but its point is different. It focuses more on the chariots than on the horses that power them. The mountains stand for the place where Yahweh Armies lives, and the chariots are Yahweh's means of implementing his purpose in the world. One chariot goes south, because Egypt had also been a destination for Judahites fleeing when the Babylonians invaded, but two chariots go north, toward Babylon, the main location of the exiles. We don't hear what happened to the first chariot (might it be waiting to leave, depending on what people do?).

The idea of settling Yahweh's spirit in Babylon is perhaps explained in the next paragraph, about gifts that have come from the exile community in Babylon. Yahweh is inspiring people in Babylon to be involved in the temple project and to send gifts in connection with it. The gifts are to be made into crowns. One is explicitly for Zerubbabel as the current representative of the Davidic "tree." The other is presumably for Joshua as the senior priest, but Zechariah doesn't explicitly make this point, which fits with the message's implication that Zerubbabel is the person with authority in the city; Joshua has authority in connection with worship, though the two of them are to work together harmoniously. Even Zerubbabel still isn't called king; only Darius has that title.

We don't know anything else about the men who bring the gifts; the point about them is that they're a kind of first-fruits or advance guard heralding the arrival of many more Judahites who are yet going to return from Babylon to get involved in the restoration of Jerusalem. Zechariah's words are thus an encouragement to the people in Jerusalem, but also a challenge and encouragement to the rest of the Judahites in Babylon if the message reaches them.

ZECHARIAH 8:1–23

Make Me a Blessing

[1]A message from Yahweh Armies came to me. [2]Yahweh Armies has said this: I feel a great passion for Zion. I feel a fierce passion for it. [3]Yahweh has said this: I'm returning to Zion and I shall dwell in the midst of Jerusalem. Jerusalem will be called "Truthful City," and the mountain of Yahweh Armies "Sacred Mountain." [4]Yahweh Armies has said this: There'll yet be old men and women in Jerusalem's squares, each with his cane in his hand because of the abundance of his days. [5]The city's squares will be full of boys and girls playing in its squares. [6]Yahweh Armies has said this: Because it will be fantastic in the

eyes of the remains of this people in those days, will it be fantastic in my eyes (a declaration of Yahweh Armies)? [7]Yahweh Armies has said this: Here am I, I'm going to deliver my people from the eastern country and from the western country, [8]and bring them, and they'll dwell in the midst of Jerusalem. They'll be a people for me and I shall be God for them, in truth and faithfulness.

[9]Yahweh Armies has said this: Your hands are to be strong, you who are listening to these words in these days, from the mouth of the prophets who lived in the day when the house of Yahweh Armies was founded, for building the palace. [10]Because before those days there were no wages for a human being and there were no wages for an animal. For anyone going out or coming in, there was no peace from the adversary. I had set all human beings one against his neighbor. [11]But now I'm not acting toward these remains as in earlier days (a declaration of Yahweh Armies), [12]because the sowing is in peace, the vine will give its fruit, the earth will give its produce, the heavens will give their dew. I shall let the remains of this people possess all these things. [13]As you became a belittling among the nations, Judah's household and Israel's household, so I shall deliver you and you'll become a blessing. Don't be afraid. Your hands are to be strong.

[14]Because Yahweh Armies has said this: As I schemed to do evil to you when your ancestors infuriated me (Yahweh Armies said) and didn't relent, [15]so I have again schemed in these days to do good to Jerusalem and to Judah's household. Don't be afraid. [16]These are the things that you're to do. Speak the truth each to his neighbor. Implement truthfulness and judgment that make for peace in your gates. [17]Don't decide in your heart each person on evil against his neighbor. Don't give yourself to a false oath. Because all these are things that I repudiate (Yahweh's declaration).

[18]The message of Yahweh Armies came to me. [19]Yahweh Armies has said this: The fast of the fourth and the fast of the fifth and the fast of the seventh and the fast of the tenth will become for Judah's household celebration and rejoicing, good festival occasions. So give yourselves to truthfulness and peace.

²⁰Yahweh Armies has said this: Peoples and residents of many cities will yet come, ²¹and the inhabitants of one will go to one another saying, "Let's go, let's go to supplicate Yahweh and seek help from Yahweh Armies. I myself intend to go, yes." ²²Many peoples will come, powerful nations, to seek help from Yahweh Armies in Jerusalem and to supplicate Yahweh. ²³Yahweh Armies has said this: In those days, when ten people from all the nations' tongues will take hold, they'll take hold of the hem of a Judahite individual's coat, saying "We want to go with you, because we've heard that God is with you."

From time to time our congregation or its church council discusses ways of attracting more people to church, and we talk about getting children into Sunday School and thereby drawing their parents, or having more barbecues, or having livelier music. On the other hand, there are aspects of our church that might put some people off, such as too much reading of the Bible or too many prayers that are the same every week. Yet these are also among the features that drew the present members of the church. In those discussions someone will then draw attention to other factors that originally drew these present members—the warmth of the welcome, the sense of fellowship, the reality of the spiritual life.

The ending of the first half of Zechariah fits with that last dynamic. While both Old Testament and New assume that God reaches the world through his people, it's sometimes said that the Old Testament's approach is centripetal while the New Testament's is centrifugal—that is, in the Old Testament God's plan is to draw the nations in to **Israel**, while in the New Testament God's plan is to send his people out to the nations. It's an oversimplification; God uses Israel's **exile** to spread knowledge of the **Torah** around the world, and 1 Corinthians 14 assumes that people will be drawn into the church by seeing God active there; they come in to worship because they perceive that "God is really among you." It sounds almost like an echo of the last line in this section of Zechariah. But there's something in the contrast.

Zechariah knows that it's God's business to reveal himself to the world and thus draw the world, and that he'll do so through his people. They need to be wary of standing in the way of that process, as they can easily do by the kind of activity Zechariah mentions that embodies faithlessness to one another or to God. It's God who'll bring about his self-revelation through the wonder of his restoring Jerusalem. Zechariah here describes it in terms of the city's transformation and the fulfillment of his creation purpose for humanity, as they're able to live full human lives from childhood to old age. **Yahweh** is going to draw **Judahites** scattered over the world to come to live in Jerusalem again. He's going to dwell in their midst. He'll realize his intent that the feeble **remains** of Israel should be his people and that he should be their God. They're going to be characterized by truth and **faithfulness** in relation to him and to one another. As a whole it's a crazy vision, God admits, but its craziness doesn't mean it won't happen, because he's passionate about Jerusalem. And whereas he had made Jerusalem a belittling (that is, people would pray, "May you be put down like Jerusalem"), his action will turn it into a blessing (that is, people will pray, "May God bless our city the way he has blessed Jerusalem").

They don't have to burden themselves with responsibility for making God's self-revelation happen. But as well as not standing in its way, they're responsible for living in light of God's promises. God won't rebuild the city by doing a miracle that they simply watch. It won't be like the Red Sea event, when God defeated the **Egyptian** army on his own. In light of God's promises, their job is to get on with the project of building Yahweh a palace in the assurance that it can be completed. They have encouragement beyond Yahweh's simple promises. As Haggai has been able to note, since they began the building project both the economic situation and the security situation are better than they were. It's no coincidence. Oh, and by the way, to go back to the question with which chapter 7 started, you can give up your fasting, because celebration is going to be more appropriate.

Those of us who are Gentiles come to be followers of Jesus by grabbing hold of the coat of Jews such as Peter and Paul, and Yahweh's promise through Zechariah thus keeps finding fulfillment.

ZECHARIAH 9:1–17

The King on a Donkey

¹ A pronouncement.

Yahweh's message is against the country of Hadrach,
  Damascus will be its resting place.
Because the eyes of humanity will be toward
    Yahweh,
  and all Israel's clans.
² Hamat, too, which borders on it;
  Tyre, and Sidon, because it's very clever.
³ Tyre has built itself a stronghold,
  heaped up silver like dirt,
  gold like the mud in the streets;
⁴   there, the Lord Yahweh will dispossess it.
  He'll strike down its resources into the sea;
  it will be consumed by fire itself.
⁵ Ashqelon will see and be afraid, Gaza will writhe
    much,
  and Eqron, because its trust will have withered.
  King will perish from Gaza,
  Ashqelon won't be inhabited.
⁶ A mongrel will live in Ashdod;
  I shall cut off the majesty of the Philistines.
⁷ But I shall remove its blood from its mouth,
  and its abominations from between its teeth.

What remains of it, too, will belong to our God,
  and become like a clan in Judah,
  while Eqron will be like the Jebusites.
8 I shall camp for my house as a watch
  against anyone passing through or coming back.
No oppressor will pass through against them again,
  because now I shall have looked with my eyes.

9 Celebrate greatly, Ms. Zion;
  shout, Ms. Jerusalem.
There, your king will come to you;
  he'll be faithful and one who finds deliverance,
lowly and riding on a donkey,
  on an ass, the child of a she-ass.
10 I shall cut off chariotry from Ephraim
  and horse from Jerusalem.
The bow of war will be cut off;
  he'll speak of peace to the nations.
His rule will be from sea to sea,
  from the River to the ends of the earth.

11 Yes, you [Jerusalem], by your covenant blood:
  I'm sending off your captives
  from the pit where there's no water.
12 Get back to the fortress, hopeful prisoners;
  yes, today I'm going to announce:
  I shall give back double to you.
13 Because I'm directing Judah for myself as a bow,
  I'm loading Ephraim.
I shall arouse your sons, Zion,
  against your sons, Greece,
  and make you like a warrior's sword.
14 Yahweh—he'll appear over them,
  his arrow will go out like lightning.
The Lord Yahweh will sound like a horn
  and go in southern storms.
15 Yahweh Armies will shield over them;
  they'll consume and tread down slingstones.

> They'll drink, yell as with wine,
>> be full like a bowl, like the altar's corners.
> [16] Yahweh our God will deliver them
>> on that day, like sheep.
> Because they're crown jewels glittering on his land,
>> [17]because how great is their goodness,
>> how great is their beauty!
> Grain will make the young men flourish,
>> new wine the young women.

On Palm Sunday the Patriarch of Moscow used to ride a "donkey" (actually a horse draped with a white cloth) from the Kremlin to the cathedral. There are towns in New Jersey and Alabama and elsewhere where people have revived that tradition, though I doubt if they realize whose example they're following. People may even lead the donkey into church (ridden by a child), which seems risky. A Canadian pastor comments that in his church it's wise to keep your distance from the donkey, especially from her hind legs, which can powerfully kick backward.

A horse is mainly a military animal; hence the promise that Jerusalem's king will cut off horses and chariots from both **Ephraim** and **Judah**. It's like a Hummer or a half-track armored vehicle. A donkey is more like a pickup truck. Every family needs one for its work on the farm or in the city. Zechariah hasn't previously spoken of Judah's ruler in terms of his being king; we have noted that the only king he has mentioned is Darius. Here the prophecy does speak of Jerusalem having its own king again, but it doesn't give any indications of a context to which it belongs, as earlier chapters did. It isn't exactly timeless, but it doesn't tell us what period it belongs to or what period it refers to.

This king won't be like Darius or like any other king the Judahites have known. He'll be just a regular guy on a regular animal. There's no pointer that the prophecy refers to Zerubbabel, but he'd give you the right idea. There's a sense in which this will be a strange kind of king. A king's first job (like a president's) is to be commander-in-chief of the armed forces and to see that his people are defended from their enemies. But Yahweh is going to terminate war-making on the part of Ephraim and Judah, as on the other peoples' part. The king of Israel will be able to rule the world without needing to use force.

The first paragraph resembles prophecies of earlier prophets, not previous prophecies in Zechariah. It declares how Yahweh will deal with the nations that surround Judah, working from the northeast to the northwest to the west and southwest. Yahweh intends to expose the inadequacy and pretension of human strength and expertise. But Yahweh's action isn't merely punitive. Yahweh intends to treat these other peoples as he has treated Judah, which extends to the way he'll leave some remains, so that they can be cleaned up so as to become like a clan within Judah. They will have a position like the original inhabitants of Jerusalem who were able to stay in their city in association with Israel on the basis of their coming to acknowledge Yahweh. But there'll be no more nonsense of nations such as Persia invading Judah. Judah having its king will be part of its restoration and of the fulfillment of Yahweh's promise to David, Yahweh's vision for a kingship that focuses on faithfulness, and Yahweh's commitment to ruling all the nations.

The third paragraph apparently pulls back and complements the first paragraph in portraying the violent way Yahweh's purpose will be achieved. But it begins with a promise to Jerusalem that he'll complete the process whereby he restores the city by bringing its exiles back. He'll do so because of the city's covenant blood—that is, because of his relationship with Israel that was sealed by a sacrifice at Sinai. Here the object of that restoration is to turn Israel into a fighting force that Yahweh can use. Greece is the power that eventually replaces

Persia as superpower, but tension between Persia and Greece begins a few decades after Zechariah's own day, in the fifth century, the time of Ezra and Nehemiah. Yahweh envisages using Israel against Greece. But it's not a declaration that gives Israel the right to decide to make war on Greece, which would incidentally be a foolish venture. The prophecy warns pacifists off from thinking that God cannot undertake violent action, but it warns warmongers off from thinking they can decide when to take such action. The Jerusalemite rebellion against Antiochus Epiphanes and the victory the rebels won in fulfillment of more specific promises in Daniel might be an example of the fulfillment of this promise.

ZECHARIAH 10:1–11:17

Lying, Neglectful, Loathsome, and Stupid Shepherds

¹ Ask for rain from Yahweh at the time of the spring
  rain;
    Yahweh is the one who sends lightning flashes,
  and gives them a downpour of rain,
    growth in the countryside for each one.
² Because the effigies have spoken wickedness,
    the diviners have seen falsehood.
  They speak lying dreams,
    they comfort with emptiness.
  Therefore people have strayed like a flock,
    they suffer because there's no shepherd.
³ "Against the shepherds my anger has blazed,
    I shall attend to the big guys."

  Because Yahweh Armies is attending
    to his flock, Judah's household.
  He'll make them like his majestic horse in battle;
    ⁴from [Judah will emerge] cornerstone,
  from it tent peg, from it battle bow,
    from it will emerge every overseer, together.

5   They'll be like warriors,
        trampling in the mud of the streets, in battle.
    They'll do battle, because Yahweh will be with them;
        they'll shame the people riding horses.

6   So I shall make Judah's household warriors,
        and deliver Joseph's household.
    I shall restore them, because I've had compassion
            on them;
        they'll be as if I had not rejected them.
    Because I am Yahweh,
        their God, and I shall answer them.
7   Ephraim will be an actual warrior;
        its heart will rejoice as with wine.
    Their children will see and rejoice;
        their heart will be joyful in Yahweh.
8   I shall whistle to them and gather them,
        because I have redeemed them
        and they'll become many, as they were many.
9   Though I sow them among the nations,
        in far-off places they'll be mindful of me;
        they'll live along with their children, and come back.
10 I shall bring them back from the country of Egypt,
        gather them from Assyria.
    Though I bring them to the country of Gilead and
            Lebanon,
        [room] won't be found for them.
11 [Yahweh] will pass through the confining sea,
        strike the sea of waves,
        and all the Nile's deeps will dry up.
    The rising of Assyria will be put down,
        Egypt's club will pass away.
12 I shall make them warlike through Yahweh,
        and in his name they'll go about
        (Yahweh's declaration).

11:1 Open your doors, Lebanon,
        so fire can consume your cedars!

2 Howl, cypresses, because the cedar is falling,
  when the mighty are being destroyed!
Howl, Bashan oaks,
  because the fortified forest is falling.
3 The sound of the shepherds' wailing,
  because their wealth is destroyed!
The sound of the lions' roar,
  because Jordan's majesty is destroyed!

[4]Yahweh my God said this: "Tend the sheep to be slaughtered, [5]whose acquirers will slaughter them and won't be guilty, whose sellers will say, 'Yahweh be worshiped! I shall be rich,' and whose shepherds won't have pity on them. [6]Because I shall no more have pity on the country's inhabitants (Yahweh's declaration). There, I'm going to make people vulnerable, each to his neighbor's hand and to his king's hand. They'll crush the country, and I shall not rescue it from their hand."

[7]So I tended the sheep to be slaughtered, therefore the lowliest of the flock. I got myself two staffs. I called one "Beauty," and the other I called "Binders." So I tended the sheep. [8]I got rid of the three shepherds in one month. My heart lost patience with them, and also their heart loathed me. [9]So I said, "I shall not tend you. The one who dies may die and the one who gets cut off may get cut off, and the ones who remain, each may eat the flesh of her neighbor." [10]I got my staff "Beauty" and broke it, to revoke my covenant that I sealed with all the peoples. [11]So it was revoked on that day, and the lowliest of the sheep, who were keeping watch toward me, thus acknowledged that it was Yahweh's message. [12]I said to them, "If it's good in your eyes, give me my pay; if not, withhold it." They weighed out my pay, thirty silver [pieces]. [13]Yahweh said to me, "Throw it to the potter" (the worthy magnificence that I was worth to them). So I took the thirty silver [pieces] and threw them to the potter in Yahweh's house. [14]And I broke my second staff, Binders, to revoke the brotherhood between Judah and Israel.

[15]Yahweh said to me again, Get yourself the implements of a stupid shepherd. [16]Because here I am, I'm going to raise

up a shepherd in the country who won't attend to the ones who are cut off or look for the young one or heal the injured or sustain the one who stands firm, but will eat the flesh of the fat one and tear off their hooves.

17 Hey, worthless shepherds, abandoning the flock:
        a sword on your arm and on your right eye!
    May his arm quite wither,
        his right eye go quite blind!

On Thursday we celebrated some "anniversaries" in our seminary—the completion of five, ten, fifteen, twenty, twenty-five, thirty, even thirty-five years of service on the part of different faculty and staff (fifteen for me). Laudatory words were said about people's service to the seminary that enables it to seek to fulfill its commitment to the "manifold ministries of Christ and his church." Did we deserve it? Not so much. Hardly anyone is undertaking their work for unselfish reasons. Nearly all of us are undertaking it because we want to or need to earn a salary. We prefer this job to working somewhere else or to being out of work. It's the same with pastors.

So we're in grave danger of being guilty of the same sin and open to the same condemnation that this prophecy heaps on Israel's pastors. The people suffer because there are no shepherds. Actually there were shepherds, but they failed to do their job. The shepherds (the kings, prophets, and priests) were supposed to guide the people. Either they were acting like diviners, the kind who relied on effigies (images of family members who had passed, whom one would seek to consult on the assumption that they might know things that their living relatives couldn't know). Or they were simply not speaking against this popular way of seeking guidance and help. Either way, they compromise the fact that Yahweh is the one who makes it rain, which is the decisive factor that can't be taken for granted in getting things to grow in Canaan. They're guilty guides, though the message presupposes that their failure doesn't let the people off the hook. They need to listen to more reliable guides like this prophecy, which goes on to elaborate the preceding promise about Yahweh transforming **Judah** into a war machine he can use. Judah's inclination is not to be warlike, but in Yahweh's hands it will prove capable of putting down far more powerful forces, as happened at the beginning of its story. The same promise applies to **Ephraim**. It's even more implausible. Ephraim disappeared centuries ago. But God will once again overcome the imprisoning and tumultuous forces embodied by the Tigris and Euphrates and the Nile. The poetic lines about the trees of Lebanon, Bashan, and the Jordan valley make the point in another way by describing Yahweh putting down the arrogant forces that the trees symbolize.

The enigmatic prose prophecy returns to the theme of shepherds. Its talk of breaking a staff and of revoking a covenant suggests that it is a retrospective on the history of Judah and Ephraim, the history lying behind the promises in the poetry. The "I" of the prophecy then represents the sequence of prophets who have ministered in Ephraim and Judah over the years, ministering to a flock that was on the way to the slaughter that came with the fall of Samaria and of Jerusalem at the hands of **Assyria** and **Babylon**. The two staffs stand for two aspects of the one nature of Israel, but the fact that there are two of them heralds the fact that their unity is fragile.

A prophet would have ambivalent feelings about the slaughter, desiring to care for the sheep and protect them but recognizing that by their lifestyle they had signed their own death warrant. Not only so: the abrogation of the covenant with them was a disaster for "all the peoples," because the covenant with Israel was designed to be a means of bringing the nations into a covenant relationship with Yahweh. We can't identify three specific leaders who were disposed of; maybe the three stand for kings, prophets, and priests in general. All were judged when Samaria and Jerusalem fell. With irony, this prophet invites people to pay him for his message of judgment, as they were used to paying prophets, and they do so, but he doesn't really prophesy for money so he makes his fee a donation to the temple funds.

The last part of the section involves another parable; maybe both parables were acted out. It involves the prophet playing the part of a shepherd whose treatment of the sheep is the exact opposite of what it's supposed to be. It will not be the end of the story.

ZECHARIAH 12:1–13:6

On the Stabbing of Prophets, True and False

¹ A pronouncement.

> Yahweh's message concerning Israel,
>   a declaration of Yahweh,
> the one who stretched out the heavens, who
>   founded the earth,
>   who shaped the spirit of humanity within it.

²There, I'm going to make Jerusalem a chalice that causes reeling to all the peoples around. They'll also be against Judah during the blockade against Jerusalem. ³On that day, I shall make Jerusalem a stone hard to lift for all the peoples. All who lift it will seriously injure themselves when all the nations of the earth gather against it. ⁴On that day (Yahweh's declaration), I shall strike every horse with panic and its rider with madness. Over Judah's household I shall open my eyes, but every horse belonging to the peoples I shall strike with blindness. ⁵Judah's clans will say to themselves, "Jerusalem's residents are my strength, through Yahweh Armies, their God." ⁶On that day, I shall make Judah's clans like a fire pot among trees, like a fiery torch among sheaves. They'll consume all the peoples around, to the right and the left. And Jerusalem will again live in its place, in Jerusalem.

[7]Yahweh will deliver Judah's tents first, so that the glory of David's household and the glory of Jerusalem's population will not be greater than Judah. [8]On that day Yahweh will shield over Jerusalem's population. A person among them who is liable to fall will be like David on that day, and David's household will be like gods, like Yahweh's aide going before them.

[9]On that day I shall seek to destroy all the nations that come against Jerusalem, [10]but I shall pour out on David's household and on Jerusalem's population a spirit of grace and of prayers for grace. They'll look to me concerning someone they've stabbed, and they'll lament over him with the lamentation for an only son, and express distress for him like the distress over a firstborn. [11]On that day the lamentation in Jerusalem will be great, like the lamentation for Hadad-rimmon in the Vale of Megiddo. [12]The country will lament, family by family by itself, the family of David's household by itself and their women by themselves, the family of Nathan's household by itself and their women by themselves, [13]the family of Levi's household by itself and their women by themselves, the family of the Shimeites by itself and their women by themselves, [14]all the remaining families family by family by itself and their women by themselves.

[13:1]On that day there'll be a fountain opened for David's household and Jerusalem's residents, for purification and cleansing. [2]And on that day (a declaration of Yahweh Armies) I shall cut off the names of the images from the country. They won't be mentioned again. Also the prophets and the unclean spirit I shall cause to pass away from the country. [3]When a person prophesies again, his father and mother, who brought him to birth, will say, "You shall not live, because you've spoken falsehood in Yahweh's name." His father and mother, who brought him to birth, will stab him when he prophesies. [4]On that day the prophets will be ashamed, each one, of his vision when he prophesies. They won't wear a garment of hair so as to deceive. [5]He'll say, "I'm not a prophet, I'm a man who works the ground, because a man acquired me from my youth." [6]If someone says to him, "What are these wounds between your hands?" he'll say, "I was wounded in my friends' house."

The other day I sat on a plane editing *Daniel and the Twelve Prophets for Everyone* and the man next to me, noticing I was reading Hebrew, told me that he was Jewish and wondered what I was doing. Another man overheard our conversation and started ranting about how the Jews are the source of all our troubles and that we wouldn't be fighting wars in the Middle East if it were not for them and that they totally control the country. They are our enemies, he said. Eventually I gave up trying to discuss the questions with him as there seemed no possibility of dialogue. Afterwards my wife said she wished she'd said, "Well, if they are our enemies, aren't we supposed to love our enemies?" Would that remark have given him something to think about? How do you get people to think differently?

This section describes God taking action to that end. It takes God to do so, though God may use a word of ours in this connection. While the prophet knows that his words alone aren't going to achieve anything along those lines, he may hope that God will use them; but God will need to pour out on the people a spirit of grace and of prayers for grace. The spirit of grace means a different attitude toward someone else; the prayers for grace mean prayers for grace to be shown to oneself. The two go together. You can't pray for grace unless you are prepared to show grace.

As with the three shepherds in the previous chapter, we can't identify a person who's been stabbed. The paragraph is reminiscent of the vision in Isaiah 53 of a servant of Yahweh who's been attacked by people who now realize how wrong they were. There and here, the prophecy is describing the kind of thing that happens to prophets when they're bringing God's word. As usual, then, the passage's omitting to clarify who it describes helps us by implying that its significance isn't confined to one context. Any community reading it must ask whether the passage issues a challenge. It sets before us a vision of serious sorrow for the wrong we've done to someone—

especially in God's name. (Hadad-rimmon was a Canaanite god, the kind of god with whom there were associated mourning rites, but we don't know any more about them.)

The introduction "on that day" regularly suggests the beginning of a different prophecy, but here the promise of a fountain for purification and cleansing follows well on that vision of people pleading for grace and mourning for the person they wounded or killed. If the victim was a person such as a prophet, then the succeeding lines also follow well, though in a more paradoxical way. It's a reminder that many, maybe most, of the prophets mentioned in the Old Testament were what we would call false prophets. So whereas for us *prophets* is a good word, in the Old Testament it's not. So the context of this paragraph suggests it refers to prophets who encouraged the use of images and who engaged in self-laceration, like the Master's prophets in 1 Kings 18. In other words, they were inspired by or involved with an unclean spirit—because worship by means of images makes a person unclean. Things would be clearer if these prophets prophesied in the name of other gods, but they prophesy in Yahweh's name, and go about wearing the garb that true prophets sometimes wore—or alternatively they deny being a prophet and claim to be only a farmer, like Amos. Their parents should be the first not only to disown them but to treat them the way the section has described people treating a true prophet. As far as we can tell, Israel didn't assume that such injunctions were designed for literal implementation (it was mainly true prophets who got executed). But this fact increases rather than decreases the force of their declaration concerning how terrible is the wrongdoing involved.

The section's opening reasserts Yahweh's promise that the nations are going to pay for their attacks on Judah. The attacks will turn out to resemble taking a drink and discovering that it is spiked and makes you fall over, or trying to lift weights and finding you've hurt yourself. It will mean assuming that you have great military resources (horses and riders) but finding that they can't see where they're going (while Yahweh keeps his eye on Judah), or thinking you're going to set the city on fire but finding that it sets you on fire.

There'll be unusual mutuality of relationships within the land. They'll obtain between the capital city and the other parts of the country; Judah can rely on and trust Jerusalem, while Jerusalem and its royal house will not be lording it over the other parts of the country. They'll also obtain within the city itself, where the weak won't go to the wall or be open to trampling by the administration; the royal administration will be fantastically strong, but the ordinary people will themselves be like David, so watch out.

ZECHARIAH 13:7–14:21

What Goes Around Comes Around (Forever?)

> 7 Sword, arise against my shepherd,
>   against a man who is my aide
>   (a declaration of Yahweh Armies).
>   Strike down my shepherd, the flock is to scatter;
>   I shall turn my hand against the little ones.
> 8 In all the country (Yahweh's declaration)
>   two parts in it will be cut off, will perish.
>   A third will be left in it,
> 9   but I shall bring the third into the fire.
>   I shall smelt them as one smelts silver,
>   test them as one tests gold.
>   It will call in my name
>   and I myself shall answer it,
>   I shall say, "It is my people,"
>   and it will say, "Yahweh is my God."

14:1 There, a day of Yahweh is coming, and your spoil [Jerusalem] will be allocated in your midst. 2 I shall gather all the nations to Jerusalem for war. The city will be captured, the houses will be plundered, the women will be ravished, and half the city will

251

go out into exile. But the rest of the people will not be cut off from the city, [3]and Yahweh will go out and make war on those nations, as he makes war on a day of engagement. [4]On that day his feet will stand on the Mount of Olives which faces Jerusalem to the east. The Mount of Olives will split in half from east to west, a very big canyon; half of the mountain will move away northward, half of it southward. [5]You people will flee by the valley between my mountains, because the valley between the mountains will reach to Asal. You will flee as you fled from the earthquake in the days of Uzziah, king of Judah. But Yahweh my God will come—all the holy ones will be with you.

[6]On that day there won't be light from the glorious ones, which will dwindle. [7]There'll be one day (it is known to Yahweh), not day and not night; at evening time it will be light. [8]On that day living waters will go out from Jerusalem, half of them to the eastern sea, half of them to the western sea. It will happen in summer and winter. [9]Yahweh will be king over all the earth. On that day Yahweh will be one and his name one. [10]The entire country will turn around like the steppe, from Geba to Rimmon south of Jerusalem, but [Jerusalem] will arise and stay in its place from the Benjamin Gate to the place of the First Gate, to the Corner Gate, and from Hananel's Tower to the king's winepresses. [11]People will live in it, and annihilation will not occur anymore. Jerusalem will live in assurance.

[12]But this will be the epidemic that Yahweh will impose on all the peoples that made war against Jerusalem: making someone's flesh waste away while he stands on his feet; his eyes will waste away in their sockets, and his tongue will waste away in their mouth. [13]On that day a great panic from Yahweh will come upon them. They will take hold, each person, of his neighbor's hand, and his hand will rise against his neighbor's hand. [14]Judah, too, will make war at Jerusalem. The resources of all the nations around will be gathered—gold and silver and clothing, a great abundance. [15]Such will be the epidemic affecting horse, mule, camel, donkey, and every animal that will be in those camps, like this epidemic.

[16]But everyone who is left from all the nations that come against Jerusalem will go up year by year to bow down to the King, Yahweh Armies, and to observe the Sukkot festival. [17]Whichever does not go up from the families of the earth to Jerusalem to bow down to the King, Yahweh Armies, there'll be no rain on it. [18]If Egypt's family doesn't go up and doesn't come, there'll be none on them; there'll be the epidemic that Yahweh imposes on the [other] nations that don't go up to observe the Sukkot festival. [19]Such will be the offense of Egypt and the offense of all the nations that don't go up to observe the Sukkot festival.

[20]On that day, upon a horse's bells will be "Sacred to Yahweh." The pots in Yahweh's house will be like the basins in front of the altar. [21]Every pot in Jerusalem and Judah will be sacred to Yahweh Armies. All the people who offer sacrifice will come and take some of them and cook in them. There'll be no more trader in the house of Yahweh Armies on that day.

I've been reading an article by a Libyan whose father had been living abroad but was excited by the coup that overturned the Libyan monarchy in 1969 and resulted in the rule of Muʿammar al-Gadhafi. He returned to Libya but was eventually arrested, and after some years died in confinement. Then last night we watched a "based on fact" movie about the storming of the U.S. embassy in Tehran in 1979 and the rescue of some U.S. personnel from the Canadian embassy, which reminded me of the way Westerners had rejoiced when the Shah was deposed and replaced by Ayatollah Khomeini. We soon changed our minds about that development, too. Revolutions have a way of turning sour. Patterns repeat themselves in history.

Maybe that helps with a question about these closing chapters in Zechariah. The prophet's way of speaking suggests he is thinking about events that are about to happen. Yet his language also reflects how things have turned out in the past. The opening poetic lines would remind his audience of Jerusalem's fall in 587; they reuse imagery from Ezekiel in this connection. The event involved the capture and disabling of the Davidic king, **Yahweh**'s shepherd and servant, and the devastating of his people. Yet it didn't mean their annihilation. Yahweh allowed enough of them to survive to form the beginnings of a new people for whom the old covenant relationship could be reasserted. They would be Yahweh's people; Yahweh would be their God. As the devastation happened, so has the restoration. Yet the prophecy presents this scenario as still to unfold, suggesting that it is a pattern that will repeat itself.

The subsequent prose prophecy has the same implication. Its language again takes up earlier messages from God such as those of Ezekiel. The nations again gather around Jerusalem. Again Jerusalem will fall, its property become plunder, its women be raped. War involves such happenings. It could seem like the end of the story, but it won't be. Often the Prophets describe Yahweh as intervening when it seems all is lost and effecting an unpredictable deliverance, perhaps doing something that looks miraculous, as happens here, and accompanying his people along with his heavenly army. We don't know where Asal was or anything more about the earthquake in Uzziah's day, but Amos 1 also refers to it; it was evidently spectacular.

So Yahweh is both the one who brings about the crisis and the one who limits its toll. The next paragraph takes the marvelous nature of the picture further. The light of sun and moon will disappear because Yahweh will introduce continuous daylight, and there'll be a parallel transformation of the water resources for the country, and a transformation of its topography so that instead of a random chain of mountains with Jerusalem in their midst, there's a plain with Jerusalem standing out from it. Yahweh will exercise sovereignty in the whole world. Thus it will be clear that there is one Yahweh. While that fact implies there is one God, implies monotheistic beliefs, this formulation is not one that interests the Bible. In the Old Testament, the important question is not how many gods there are but who is God. From the beginning the Old

Testament asserts that Yahweh is God. His is the one name that people are to recognize. Near the end of the Old Testament, the world recognizes that name.

The second half of the passage paints the scenario once more, offering another picture of a crisis coming to Jerusalem and of Yahweh's acting against the hostile forces. It adds a new note that resonates with earlier chapters in the book. As the judgment on Jerusalem does not mean complete annihilation, so it will be with the judgment on Jerusalem's attackers. Yet the focus doesn't lie on mercy toward them. The trouble with killing people is that it doesn't mean they acknowledge the truth—in fact, it makes that recognition impossible. The survival of people from the nations means they'll come to recognize Yahweh, the one Yahweh, their real king. They had better. The reason for the special comment on **Egypt** may be the fact of which Egypt was proud, that it didn't need rain because it had the Nile. It will still be hit by an epidemic.

Much of the final chapter's picture is wildly metaphorical. The closing verses are also metaphorical, but they give a nice down-to-earth impression of how things will be "on that day." Sacredness will permeate every detail of the city's life. The pattern of sin and judgment, of restoration and falling away, of attack and deliverance, won't go on forever.

MALACHI 1:1–14

Easygoing Pastors

[1]A pronouncement. Yahweh's message to Israel by means of Malachi.

[2]I have given myself to you, Yahweh said. But you say, "How have you given yourself to us?" Isn't Esau Jacob's brother (Yahweh's declaration)? But I gave myself to Jacob [3]and repudiated Esau. I am making his mountains a desolation, his own possession for wilderness jackals. [4]Because Edom says, "We've been crushed, but we'll build the ruins again," Yahweh

255

Armies has said this: Those people may build, but I myself shall demolish. They'll be called "Faithless Territory," the people Yahweh was wrathful with forever. [5]Your own eyes will see it. You yourselves will say, "Yahweh is great, beyond Israel's territory!"

[6]A son honors his father, a servant his Lord. If I'm a father, where's the honor for me? If I'm a Lord, where's the awe for me? said Yahweh Armies to you priests who disdain my name. You say, "How have we disdained your name?" [7]You're presenting defiled food on my altar. You say, "How have we defiled you?" By your saying, "Yahweh's table can be disdained." [8]When you present something blind for sacrifice, there's no evil. When you present something lame or sick, there's no evil. Do offer it to your governor. Would he be pleased with you? Would he accept you? (Yahweh Armies has said). [9]Now, do entreat Yahweh so that he shows favor to us. This has come from your hand. Will he accept any of you? (Yahweh Armies has said).

[10]Who indeed is there among you who'll shut the doors and not light a fire on my altar to no end! I find no delight in you (Yahweh Armies has said) and I shall not be pleased with an offering from your hand. [11]Because from the sun's rising to its setting my name is great among the nations and in every place incense is offered to my name, and a pure offering, because my name is great among the nations (Yahweh Armies has said). [12]But you are profaning it when you say, "The Lord's table is defiled, and its fruit, its food, can be disdained," [13]or say, "This is a weariness," and blow it off (Yahweh Armies has said), or bring something stolen or lame or sick, and bring it as the offering. Shall I be pleased with it from your hand (Yahweh has said)? [14]Cursed is the cheat when there's a male in his flock but he promises and sacrifices to the Lord something spoiled. Because I am a great king (Yahweh Armies has said) and my name is held in awe among the nations.

My wife likes to reminisce about the church she belonged to in Seattle, and specifically about its men's Bible study group (to which she did not belong). The Bible study group met on Monday night, which is counterintuitive because every real American male wants to watch Monday Night Football, but the result was that men had to decide whether they were prepared to take their commitment to Christ seriously enough to want to make that sacrifice. At work next day it then also meant that the question "What did you think of the game?" met with the answer, "Oh I didn't see it, but we had this fantastic time at Bible study . . ."

Malachi would nod in approval. He knows that **Yahweh** deserves the best and that sacrifice is supposed to involve sacrifice. Offering Yahweh animals that aren't much use to you says something significant about your attitude to Yahweh.

The temple is now rebuilt and functioning; Malachi works in a context later than Haggai and Zechariah, after the completion of the rebuilding related in Ezra 1–6. But people's reluctance to take God with total seriousness corresponds to the attitude Haggai confronted. It would be better to give up worship altogether than offer God such unworthy worship, God says. In a further barbed comment, Malachi makes an unfavorable contrast between the sacrificial worship the priests encourage in the temple and the incense offering made by **Judahites** in the Dispersion, who couldn't offer the "proper" sacrifices. Jerusalemites would be inclined to feel superior to Judahites who hadn't come "home." Malachi turns such attitudes on their head. The priests fail to lay proper expectations before the people, and thus show favor to them. They wouldn't see themselves as disdaining Yahweh, but that was the implication of their attitude and the attitude they encouraged. Perhaps they thought they were being pastoral in making allowance for the toughness of people's situation. But their easygoing stance will actually exact a cost of the people. When the priests declare God's blessing on the people and their flocks, farms, and families, the blessing won't follow. Indeed, the opposite will happen.

Whereas the prophet feels that people are neglecting God, they feel God is neglecting them. The opening reference to Jacob and Esau/**Edom** points to an aspect of their case. Genesis declares that God chose Jacob over his elder brother Esau. The Hebrew words for *gave myself to* and *repudiate* are usually translated "love" and "hate," but these English words give a misleading impression. God was deciding to use Jacob rather than Esau as the means of fulfilling his purpose. It didn't imply that Jacob was "elect" and Esau wasn't, any more than when Jesus chose some people to be his disciples. In Malachi's time, Judah represents Jacob and Edom represents Esau, and the trouble is that Edom is doing well at Judah's expense— it took over much of Judah's territory. It's a funny way to indicate that we are your chosen people, Judah comments. Yahweh doesn't dispute the point; he simply promises that the situation won't continue. Ironically, the way Yahweh fulfilled this promise was not by destroying Edom but by Edom's coming to be absorbed by the Jewish people and thus to acknowledge Yahweh.

MALACHI 2:1–16

Two Neglected Covenants

[1]So now to you priests, this command. [2]If you don't listen and don't take it into your thinking to give honor to my name (Yahweh Armies has said), I shall send off a curse among you. I shall curse your blessings. Indeed, I have cursed it, because you don't take it into your thinking. [3]Here am I, I'm going to blast your seed. I'm going to spread feces on your faces, the feces from your festival sacrifice. Someone will carry you out to them. [4]And you'll acknowledge that I sent off this command to you so that it might be my covenant with Levi (Yahweh Armies has said). [5]My covenant with him was life and well-being, and I gave them to him, with revering. He did revere me. He was in awe of my name.

⁶ True teaching was in his mouth;
wrongdoing wasn't found on his lips.
In peace and uprightness he walked with me,
and he turned many from waywardness.
⁷ Because a priest's lips guard knowledge;
people look for teaching from his mouth,
because he is an aide of Yahweh Armies,
⁸but you have turned from the way.
You've made many people fall through your
teaching;
you've ruined the covenant of Levi
(Yahweh Armies has said).

⁹I myself in turn am making you shameful and low to the entire people, on account of the fact that you don't guard my ways but show favor in the teaching.

¹⁰Don't we have one father, all of us? Didn't one God create us? Why do we break faith, each with his brother, in profaning our ancestors' covenant? ¹¹Judah has broken faith. Outrage has been committed in Israel and in Jerusalem, because Judah has profaned what is sacred to Yahweh, which he gives himself to, and married the daughter of a strange god. ¹²May Yahweh cut off the person who does this (anyone who arises and anyone who responds) from Jacob's tents, even one who presents an offering to Yahweh Armies. ¹³You do this second thing: covering Yahweh's altar with tears, weeping and wailing because he is no longer regarding the offering or accepting it with favor from your hand. ¹⁴You've said, "On account of what?" On account of the fact that Yahweh is a witness between you and the wife of your youth, with whom you've broken faith, when she was your partner and your covenanted woman. ¹⁵Didn't One make [us], and isn't the remains of the spirit his? And what is the One looking for? Godly offspring. So you'll guard yourself in your spirit. A person is not to break faith with the wife of your youth. ¹⁶When he's hostile so as to divorce (Yahweh the God of Israel has said), he makes violence a cover over his clothing (Yahweh Armies has said). So you will guard yourself in your spirit and not break faith.

One of our neighbors is angry and distraught; her son-in-law has just informed his wife, our neighbor's daughter, that he's leaving her. They have three school-age children. It seems irresponsible, almost juvenile. It reminded me of a recent documentary about the reggae singer Bob Marley, whose wife Rita spoke of the way she coped with his philandering. She knew she was his rock, his stability, she said. He would always come back. A friend of mine who is a recovering alcoholic tells me that the spouses of alcoholics have to be prepared to let their spouses go, to surrender them to drink; only when they've done so and the spouse has reached rock bottom will it be possible for them to come back.

Although we may rightly be horrified at divorce statistics and people's reluctance to commit themselves in marriage, it may be a strange comfort to realize that something along these lines has always been so, even if the profile of the problem changes. While the fact that the temple is functioning indicates that Malachi lived after Haggai and Zechariah, his need to confront the problem of mixed marriages implies that he lived before Ezra and Nehemiah, who took steps to deal with the issue.

There are several aspects to the problem as Malachi sees it. There's the fact that men are abandoning the "wives of their youth." Perhaps his words reflect the fact that marriages would commonly be arranged when the boy and girl were very young; one can imagine a man using this fact as an excuse for abandoning his wife when they are older, as men do in a Western context. But even if the marriage was arranged when the couple were very young, it led into a mutual commitment. The testimony of people in our own time whose marriages were arranged is that having an arranged marriage is no bar to developing a relationship of love. The two people became "partners." They entered into a covenantal relationship. Yahweh was a witness to the promises they made. Their unity was made more real by its context in their mutual relationship with the "One" God, which was designed to be the means of bringing to birth the "godly offspring" on whom the future of **Israel** belonged. So giving up on the marriage involves "breaking faith"—breaking faith with Yahweh as well as with your spouse. But Malachi is especially concerned with the violence that is often involved in divorce, when it means a husband simply throws his wife out.

There's likely a link between these general comments on divorce and the comments on "marrying the daughters of a strange god." In other words, the men were abandoning their **Judahite** wives to marry (for example) a Moabite, perhaps because their Judahite wife was unable to have children. If a Moabite woman made a commitment to Yahweh, like Ruth, then there need be no problem about marrying a Moabite in itself. Like Ezra and Nehemiah, Malachi has in mind women who keep their adherence to their present god, which compromises the commitment of the family and imperils Israel's future as Yahweh's people.

In the first part of the chapter, Malachi extends his critique of the priests, the clan of **Levi**. That initial critique presupposed that their job was not confined to offering sacrifices on people's behalf. Here Malachi makes explicit that it included teaching them about the proper nature of the worship they offered. Teaching was integral to the original covenant relationship between Yahweh and Levi—Yahweh made a commitment to Levi and his successors and they had a responsibility to him. Their ancestor had been faithful in his ministry; his descendants are not. They'll pay for their faithlessness in unpleasant ways. When they supervised the killing and offering of an animal, there were unpleasant bits of it that had to be disposed of. They'll find themselves accompanying these bits.

MALACHI 2:17–4:6

A Full and Frank Exchange of Views

[17]You've wearied Yahweh with your words. You've said, "How have we wearied him?" When you say, "Everyone who does evil

is good in Yahweh's eyes. In them he takes delight." Or "Where is the God who exercises authority?" [3:1]Here am I, I'm going to send my aide, and he'll clear the way before me. Suddenly there'll come to his palace the Lord for whom you are looking.

So the covenant aide for whom you long—there, he's coming (Yahweh Armies has said). [2]But who's going to endure the day of his coming? Who's going to stand when he appears? Because he'll be like a smelter's fire or like launderer's soap. [3]He'll sit smelting and purifying silver. He'll purify the Levites and refine them like gold and silver, and they'll be Yahweh's, people who present an offering in faithfulness. [4]The offering of Judah and Jerusalem will please Yahweh as in the days gone by, in former years.

[5]So I shall come near to you to exercise authority and be an eager witness against the diviners, the adulterers, the people who swear falsely, the people who defraud the employee of his wages, and the widow and orphan, and who turn aside the alien, and who are not in awe of me (Yahweh Armies has said). [6]Because I am Yahweh, I haven't changed, and you're Jacob's descendants, you haven't come to an end. [7]From your ancestors' days you've turned away from my laws and not kept them. Come back to me and I shall come back to you (Yahweh Armies has said).

You'll say, "How shall we come back?" [8]Does a person cheat God? Because you're cheating me. You'll say, "How have we cheated you?" In tithe and contribution. [9]You're subjected to a curse, but you're cheating me—the nation, all of it. [10]Bring the entire tithe into the storehouse, so that there may be food in my house, and do test me by this (Yahweh Armies has said), if I don't open the heavens' floodgates and empty out blessing on you until there's no need. [11]I shall blast the devourer for you, and it won't destroy the fruit of the ground for you, and the vine in the open country won't miscarry for you (Yahweh Armies has said). [12]All the nations will count you fortunate, because you'll be a delightful land (Yahweh Armies has said).

[13]You've made your words tough against me (Yahweh has said). You'll say, "What have we said against you?" [14]You've said, "Serving God is futile. What was the gain when we kept

his charge and walked in gloom before Yahweh Armies? [15]So now we count the arrogant fortunate. The people who act in faithlessness have both been built up, and have also tested God and escaped."

[16]Then the people who were in awe of Yahweh talked, each with his neighbor, and Yahweh took heed and listened, and a remembrance scroll was written before him regarding the people who were in awe of Yahweh and who esteemed his name. [17]For me they'll be a special possession (Yahweh Armies has said) for the day that I'm making. I shall have pity on them as someone has pity on his son who serves him. [18]You'll again see the difference between the faithful and the faithless, between the one who serves God over against the one who has not served him.

[4:1]Because there—the day's coming, burning like an oven, when all the arrogant and all the people who act in faithlessness are stubble, and the day that's coming will burn them up (Yahweh Armies has said) so that it doesn't leave them root or branch. [2]But there will rise for you who are in awe of my name a faithful sun with healing in its rays. You'll go out and jump like well-fed bullocks. [3]You'll trample on the faithless, because they'll be ashes under the soles of your feet, on that day that I'm making (Yahweh Armies has said).

[4]Be mindful of Moses my servant's teaching, which I commanded him for all Israel at Horeb, laws and decisions. [5]There, I'm sending you Elijah the prophet before the coming of the great and awe-inspiring Day of Yahweh. [6]He'll turn back the mind of parents to their children and the mind of children to their parents, so that I don't come and strike the country with annihilation.

Yesterday one of my Asian students responded to something I had said in class. When we were discussing the extreme nature of the way people talk to God in the Psalms or Job talks to God, and the way God talks back, I suggested that this bluntness reflects the confidence that **Israelites** have in talking to God because the relationship is like that of children and parents. I would always have wanted my children to be able to say anything to me and to batter on my chest if it seemed necessary. If there's a strong relationship between parents and children, it should be possible for them to do so. The Asian student pointed out that this assumption about forthright speaking on the part of children doesn't fit the understandings of family in her culture. It made me wonder whether it would have fitted Israelite culture.

Reading Malachi reinforces the impression that God and Israel could be pretty straight with each other. This last section of the book continues the mutual confrontation and questioning that has characterized the book from the beginning. Admittedly the first complaint speaks *about* God rather than *to* God—another occasional feature of the way Israel operates in the Old Testament, as if it didn't realize God might be listening even if he wasn't directly addressed. It's a standard Israelite and Christian complaint—why doesn't God intervene if he is supposed to be sovereign in the world?

On this occasion God responds, "OK, I'll intervene, but you may not like it." Like 1 Peter 4 warning the church that judgment will begin at God's household, Malachi warns **Judah** that God's acting to implement his righteous purpose in the world will be an uncomfortable experience for God's people, like smelting, even if its work will finally be positive. There's a link with **Yahweh**'s subsequent comment, "I haven't changed," and "you haven't come to an end." Throughout Israel's story Israel has been inclined to weary Yahweh by the way it conducts its life. It's amazing that it continues in existence, but it does so, notwithstanding the chastisements and the cutting down to size.

Maybe there's an unspoken implication that the people of Judah haven't changed, either. They are, after all, Jacob's descendants. It's not surprising that they're cheating God by failing to bring in their tithes and contributions that made the temple worship possible. The Hebrew word for *cheat* is unusual, and it's also similar to the name *Jacob*, belonging to the brother who cheated Esau out of his birthright as firstborn. The link also subverts any inclination on Judah's part to think they were superior to Esau/**Edom**, on the basis of the way Malachi's book began.

The complaint about God recurs in the middle of the section. Serving God is pointless. It doesn't get you anywhere. This time it leads into a description of an appropriate response to the experience of God not acting in the way we need. People talked to one another. It was a different kind of talking from the complaint, talk by people who continued to be in awe of Yahweh, to be committed to Yahweh, to trust in Yahweh. They didn't hide from the reality of their hardship but neither were they in danger of giving up on Yahweh. Yahweh could take a different stance to them from the one he took to the people who surrendered to cynicism. He takes steps to make sure they're not forgotten.

In the meantime, the first important thing is to be mindful of Moses' teaching (the **Torah**). Malachi didn't identify the "covenant aide" of whom he spoke earlier in this section. Perhaps the implication is that people will know him when they see him. But maybe the last verses of the book identify him as Elijah returning (in a sense John the Baptizer fulfilled this role).

Solemnly, the last word in the Old Testament is *annihilation*. It's the word that most often refers to God's command to the Israelites regarding the annihilation of the Canaanites. The Hebrew Bible tells people to repeat the verse about God sending Elijah after this worrisome ending, so that the book ends on a note that affirms God's involvement with us. But people who are sure that they belong to God need that reminder that the judgment of God starts with God's household.

GLOSSARY

aide

An aide is a supernatural agent through whom God may appear and work in the world. English translations refer to them as "angels," but this suggests ethereal winged figures wearing diaphanous white dresses. Aides are humanlike figures; hence it is possible to give them hospitality without realizing who they are (Hebrews 13). They have no wings, hence their need of a stairway or ramp between heaven and earth (Genesis 28). They appear in order to act or speak on God's behalf and so fully represent God that they can speak as if they *are* God (Genesis 22). They are involved in dynamic, forceful action in the world (Psalms 34 and 35). They bring the reality of God's presence, action, and voice, without bringing such a real presence that it would electrocute mere mortals or shatter their hearing.

Assyria, Assyrians

The first great Middle Eastern superpower, the Assyrians spread their empire westward into Syria-Palestine in the eighth century, the time of Amos and Isaiah. They made **Ephraim** part of their empire; then when Ephraim kept trying to assert independence, they invaded Ephraim, destroyed its capital at Samaria, transported its people, and settled people from other parts of their empire in their place. They also invaded **Judah** and devastated much of the country, but didn't take Jerusalem. Prophets such as Amos and Isaiah describe how **Yahweh** was thus using Assyria as a means of disciplining **Israel**.

authority, authoritative

English translations commonly translate the Hebrew *mishpat* with words such as "judgment" or "justice," but the word suggests exercising authority and making decisions in a broader sense. It's a word for *government*. In principle, then, the word has positive implications, though it is quite possible for people in authority to make decisions in an unjust way. It's a king's job to exercise authority in accordance with **faithfulness** to God and people and in a way that brings deliverance. Exercising authority means making decisions and acting decisively on behalf of people in need and of people wronged by others. Thus speaking of God as judge implies good news (unless you are a major wrongdoer). God's "decisions" can also denote God's authoritative declarations concerning human behavior and about what he intends to do.

Babylon, Babylonians

A minor power in the context of the earlier of the Twelve Prophets, in the time of Nahum, Habakkuk, and Zephaniah Babylon took over as the regional superpower from **Assyria** and kept that position for nearly a century until conquered by **Persia**. Prophets such as these three describe how **Yahweh** was using the Babylonians as a means of disciplining **Judah**. Their creation stories, law codes, and more philosophical writings help us understand aspects of the Old Testament's equivalent writings while their astrological religion also forms background to aspects of polemic in the Prophets.

decision, see authority

Edom, Edomites

Edom is **Judah**'s southeastern neighbor, occupying an area to the southeast of the Dead Sea. As **Israel** traces its ancestry back to Jacob, it traces Edom's ancestry back to Jacob's brother Esau. The Old Testament critiques Edom in particular for its inclination to take advantage of Judah's vulnerability and for its support of the **Babylonians** when they captured Jerusalem. Subsequently the Edomites occupied considerable parts of southern Judah.

Egypt, Egyptians

As **Israel**'s big southern neighbor, Egypt appears in four connections in Daniel and the Twelve Prophets. Israel's story as a nation begins in Egypt, from which **Yahweh** delivered them to bring them to Canaan. In the eighth and seventh century **Judah** was inclined to look to Egypt for help when it was under threat from **Assyria** or **Babylon**. In the exile, it became a place of refuge; henceforth there was a significant Jewish community in Egypt. In the period to which Daniel's visions refer, Judah was sometimes under **Seleucid** control, sometimes under the control of the Ptolemies in Egypt.

Ephraim, Ephraimites

After the reign of David and Solomon, the nation of **Israel** split into two. Most of the twelve Israelite clans set up an independent state in the north, separate from **Judah** and Jerusalem and from the line of David. Because it was the bigger of the two states, politically it kept the name Israel, which is confusing because Israel is still the name of the whole people of God. In the Prophets, it is sometimes difficult to tell whether "Israel" refers to the people of God as a whole or just to the northern state. Sometimes the state is referred to by the name of Ephraim, one of its dominant clans, so I use this term to refer to that northern state to try to reduce the confusion.

evil

The Old Testament uses this word in a similar fashion to the way English uses the word *bad*—it can refer both to the bad things that people do and the bad things that happen to them, both to morally bad actions and to bad experiences. Prophets can thus speak of God doing evil in the sense of bringing calamity to people. They sometimes use the word with both connotations in the same context, pointing toward the fact that bad things often happen because people do bad things—though they know that this is not invariably so.

exile

At the end of the seventh century **Babylon** became the major power in **Judah**'s world, but Judah was inclined to rebel against its authority. As part of a campaign to get Judah to submit properly to its authority, in 597 and in 587 BC the Babylonians transported many people from Jerusalem to Babylon. They made a special point of transporting people in leadership positions, such as members of the royal family and the court, priests, and prophets. These people were thus compelled to live in Babylonia for the next fifty years or so. Through the same period, people back in Judah were also under Babylonian authority. They were not physically in exile, but they were also living *in* the exile as a period of time.

faithfulness, faithful

In English Bibles the Hebrew word for *faithfulness* (*sedaqah*) is usually translated "righteousness," but it denotes a particular slant on what we might mean by righteousness. It means doing the right thing by the people with whom one is in a relationship, the members of one's community. Thus it is really closer to "faithfulness" than "righteousness."

give oneself, giving of oneself

I use this expression in many passages to translate the Hebrew word traditionally translated "love," because whereas the latter word in English easily suggests an emotion, the Hebrew word denotes an attitude and action at least as much as an emotion.

Greece, Greek

In 336 BC Greek forces under Alexander the Great took control of the Persian Empire, but after Alexander's death in 333 his empire split up. The largest part, to the north and east of Palestine, was ruled by one of his generals, Seleucus, and his successors. **Judah** was under its control for much of the next two centuries, though it was at the extreme southwestern border of this empire and sometimes came under the control of the Ptolemaic Empire in Egypt (ruled by successors of another of Alexander's officers). In 167 the **Seleucid** ruler Antiochus Epiphanes attempted to ban observance of the **Torah** and persecuted the faithful community in Jerusalem, but they rebelled and experienced a great deliverance.

Israel, Israelites

Originally, Israel was the new name God gave Abraham's grandson, Jacob. His twelve sons were then forefathers of the twelve clans that comprise the people Israel. In the time of Saul and David these twelve clans became more of a political entity. So Israel was both the people of God and a nation or state like other nations or states. After Solomon's day, this state split into two separate states, **Ephraim** and **Judah**. Because Ephraim was far the bigger, it often continued to be referred to as Israel. So if one is thinking of the people of God, Judah is part of Israel. If one is thinking politically, Judah isn't part of Israel. Once Ephraim has gone out of existence, then for practical purposes Judah *is* Israel, as the people of God.

Judah, Judahites

One of the twelve sons of Jacob and the clan that traces its ancestry to him, then the dominant clan in the southern of the two states after the time of Solomon. Effectively Judah *was* **Israel** after the fall of **Ephraim**.

Kaldeans

Kaldea was an area southeast of **Babylon** from which the kings who ruled Babylonia came in the time Babylonia ruled **Judah**. Thus the Old Testament refers to the **Babylonian**s as the Kaldeans.

Levi, Levites

Within the clan of Levi, the descendants of Aaron are the priests, the people who have specific responsibilities in connection with offering the community's sacrifices and helping individuals to offer their sacrifices by performing some aspects of the offering such as the sprinkling of the animal's blood. The other Levites fulfill a support and administrative role in the temple and are also involved in teaching the people and in other aspects of leading worship.

Master, Masters

The Hebrew word is *ba'al*, an ordinary word for a master, lord, or owner, but the word is also used to describe a Canaanite god. It is thus parallel to the word *Lord*, used to describe **Yahweh**. So like *Lord*, *Master* can be a proper name, as it is treated in translations when they transliterate the word as *Baal*. The Old Testament generally uses *Master* for a Canaanite god and *Lord* for the real God, Yahweh, to make the difference clear. Like many other peoples, the Canaanites acknowledged a number of gods, and strictly the Master was simply

271

one of them, though he was one of the most prominent, but the Old Testament also uses the plural *Masters* (*Baals*) to refer to other gods in general.

Medes, Medo-Persia, Persia, Persians

Media lies between Mesopotamia and Persia. In the 550s BC Cyrus the Great gained control of Media and also of Persia, and turned Medo-Persia into the third Middle Eastern superpower. Cyrus took control of the **Babylonian** Empire in 539 BC, which opened up the possibility of **Judahites** returning from Babylon after the **exile**. Judah and surrounding peoples such as Samaria, Ammon, and Ashdod were then Persian provinces or colonies. The Persians stayed in power for two centuries until defeated by **Greece**.

Philistia, Philistines

The Philistines were people who came from across the Mediterranean to settle in Canaan at the same time as the **Israelites** were establishing themselves in Canaan, so that the two peoples formed an accidental pincer movement on the existent inhabitants of the country and became each other's rivals for control of the area.

remain, remainder, remains, remnant

The Prophets warn that **Yahweh**'s chastisement will mean **Israel** (and other peoples) being cut down so that only small remains or a remainder or remnant will survive. But at least some remains of Israel will survive—so the idea of "remains" can become a sign of hope. It can also become a challenge—the few that remain are challenged to become faithful remains, a faithful remnant.

Seleucids, Seleucus, see Greece

Sheol

The most frequent of the Hebrew names for the place where we go when we die (another is "the Pit"). In the New Testament it is called Hades. It isn't a place of punishment or suffering but simply a resting place for everyone, a kind of nonphysical analogue to the tomb as the resting place for our bodies.

Torah

This Hebrew word is traditionally translated "law," but this gives the wrong impression, as the word covers instruction in a broader sense. The framework of "the Torah" (the books from Genesis to Deuteronomy) is the story of Yahweh's relationship with the world and with Israel, though the Torah is dominated by instructions. "Teaching" is the nearest English word. The Hebrew word can thus apply to the teaching of people such as prophets as well as to the instructions in Genesis to Deuteronomy. It is sometimes not clear whether it refers to the Torah or to teaching in that wider sense.

well-being

The Hebrew word *shalom* can suggest peace after there has been conflict, but it often points to a richer notion of fullness of life. The KJV sometimes translates it "welfare" and modern translations use words such as "well-being" or "prosperity." It suggests that everything is going well for you.

Yahweh

In most English Bibles, the word "LORD" often comes in all capitals as does sometimes the word "GOD." These actually represent the name of God, Yahweh. In later Old Testament times, Israelites stopped using the name and started to refer to Yahweh as "the Lord." There may be two reasons. They wanted other people to recognize that Yahweh was the one true God, but this strange foreign-sounding name could give the impression that Yahweh was just Israel's tribal god. A term such as "the Lord" was one anyone could recognize. In addition, they didn't want to fall foul of the warning in the Ten Commandments about misusing Yahweh's name. Translations into other languages then followed suit and substituted an expression such as "the Lord" for the name Yahweh. The downsides are that often the text refers to Yahweh and not some other (so-called) god or lord and that the practice obscures the fact that God wanted to be known by name and instead gives the impression that God is much more "lordly" and patriarchal than actually God is. (The form "Jehovah" isn't a real word but a mixture of the consonants of

Yahweh and the vowels of that word for "Lord," to remind people in reading Scripture that they should say "the Lord" and not the actual name.)

Yahweh Armies

This title for God usually appears in English Bibles as "the LORD of Hosts," but it is a more puzzling expression than that implies. The word for *LORD* represents the name of God, **Yahweh**, and the word for *Hosts* is the regular Hebrew word for *armies*; it is the word that appears on the back of an Israeli military truck. More literally the expression thus means "Yahweh [of] Armies," which is just as odd in Hebrew as "Goldingay of Armies" would be. Yet in general terms its likely implication is clear; it suggests that Yahweh is the embodiment of or controller of all war-making power, in heaven or on earth. Sometimes the Old Testament uses the longer expression "Yahweh, God of Armies."

Yahweh's Day

The oldest occurrence of the expression "the Day of the Lord," "Yahweh's Day," comes in Amos 5, which indicates that people saw it as a time when **Yahweh** would bring great blessing on them. Amos declares that the opposite is the case. Henceforth the expression always has sinister connotations. Yahweh's Day is a day when Yahweh acts in decisive fashion. It doesn't happen just once; there are various occasions that the Old Testament describes as Yahweh's Day, such as Jerusalem's fall in 587 and Babylon's fall in 539. In Isaiah, Sennacherib's devastation of Judah was such an embodiment of Yahweh's Day (22:5).

Zion

The word is an alternative name for the city of Jerusalem. Jerusalem is more a political name; other peoples would refer to the city as "Jerusalem." Zion is more a religious name, a designation of the city that focuses on its being the place where **Yahweh** dwells and is worshiped.